Dawn or Dusk?

DAWN OR DUSK?

by

BERNARD HELLER

with a foreword by

GEORGE N. SHUSTER
President, Hunter College, N.Y.C.
U.S. State Commissioner for Bavaria, 1950-1951

Also by BERNARD HELLER

A HARVEST OF WEEDS
THE ODYSSEY OF A FAITH
EPISTLE TO AN APOSTATE

THE BOOKMAN'S, INC.
NEW YORK

"These last years have produced more evil than the most inveterate pessimists could ever have imagined. But what is so strange is that our sense of justice and fair dealing should have been so impaired that the knowledge we have acquired of the roots of evil should not have had an educational effect."—ALBERT EINSTEIN.

TABLE OF CONTENTS

Acknowledgments

Many years passed before the author mustered enough courage to present the manuscript of the book to a publisher. Various factors account for the deferment.

1. The musings and reflections in it could easily be misunderstood as antagonism to Christianity's mission and aim. Much care was therefore required to couch the opinions and views so that their purport would not be misconstrued.
2. Another explanation for the delay were the exhortations of friends to put off the publication of the book. For the advocacy of the graded and unequal responsibility of Germans for the diabolical acts of the Nazis would be considered as an attempt to water down, if not to extenuate, the villainy that had been committed by them. Some who were partially informed of the contents termed the effort an "apology" for the herrenvolk. Coming from a Rabbi they could be doubly resented particularly by those whose kin and kith had been exterminated in gas chambers. The wounds were still raw and the pain too intense for the consideration of such views.

Aside from the above facts the chapters were written without any forethought that they would constitute an integrated tome. It was Prof. O. J. Campbell who saw the potential unity in the series of descriptions and reflections. I render him heartfelt thanks for his encouragement. To Mordekhai Nurock, Eugene Hevesi, Mrs. Seymour Fox and Dr. Dumont Kenny I am indebted for good advice as well as a reading of the manuscript.

To Dr. Walter Feder I am singularly indebted. His scrutiny of the text and his judicious elimination of passages and rearrangement of the order of the chapters greatly improved the whole qualitatively and made it more readable.

"Some books," Emerson observed, "leave us free and some books make us free." It is my prayer that this volume will be accorded a place in the latter category.

Foreword

by
GEORGE N. SHUSTER

ONE reason Dr. Heller asked me to read his manuscript, is no doubt because it fell to my lot to see at first hand a good many of the tragic developments with which it is concerned. I am happy to respond, though I shall be brief because this book is manifestly an honest endeavor to help prepare a future in which some at least of the agony of recent years will find no place. This is being written on the day when the press reports Ben-Gurion's inability to proceed immediately to establish the relationships between Israel and Germany which many of us had thought would be considerably to the advantage of both countries. But time is required to heal deep wounds, and so once again the work which Dr. Heller has done seems to me not only desirable but necessary.

Having said these things, I must of course immediately add that I am not in agreement with everything in these pages. My emphasis would differ from Dr. Heller's, and my interpretation of this or that trend or tendency would by no means be the same as his. But in three things I heartily concur—that it is imperative to see Jewish faith and tradition as they are, and not as caricaturists have presented them, if one hopes to understand what the assault on Judaism implied; that Nazism must not be identified with Germany, and that indeed there will have to be a reconciliation between Jew and German; and that there are weaknesses in European culture, despite its superiority in many respects, which need to be faced squarely if the mistakes of the past are to be avoided.

Let me make a few comments. First, I think it helpful to distinguish carefully between the major forms of anti-Semitism (or anti-Catholicism, for that matter). To be sure, all are deplorable; but if we are ever to comprehend the

viciousness of Nazism we must finally see that this was not
due to a failure to know about the Jewish faith, or even to
the more normal sociological frictions which develop in a
pluralistic society. For example, many Germans thought
that because some Jewish intellectuals supported Bolshevism, Jewish support of this reprehensible movement was
very great. It is quite possible to combat this kind of misconception. But Hitler's anti-Semitism, based as it was on
a false blend of mysticism and racism the sources of which
can now be identified, was radically irrational and therefore
impervious to evidence or argument. At the outset many
Germans probably endorsed some of Hitler's anti-Semitic
utterances because they were in one manner or other prejudiced against Jews. But as Rauschning, for instance, demonstrates they had no idea of the monstrous forms which the
crusade against Jews had taken in the Fuehrer's mind.

I believe it is very important to stress the point if there
is ever to be a genuine understanding between Germans and
Jews. Some people are repulsed by certain aspects of Jewish
ritual just as they are by the popular Catholic practice of
kissing hierarchical rings. There are those who are hostile
to strict Methodists because these frown on dancing and
card playing, just as there are others who think Jewish
skullcaps are funny. No such person, however lacking in magnanimity he may be, should be deemed to have anything in
common with Hitler. I conclude by saying frankly that some
Jews seem to me to be making a great mistake about Germany because they consider every criticism of Jews a recru-
descence of Nazism. Of course such a mistake is a natural
one to make, in view of the fact that emotions have justifi-
ably run so high. Yet the man who says, yes, I did err in
thinking that because there were so many Jews among
Hungarian Communists, Communism was a Jewish movement, but that by no manner of means indicates that I
condone what Hitler did in Auschwitz, is being very fair and
if one wishes to deal with him one must concur.

The observation is especially important when one considers
the attitudes of the Christian Churches. It is quite true, and
one may honestly deplore it, that when Hitler came to

power the Churches were concerned primarily with their own problems and therefore were less vocal about the anti-Semitic program than they should have been. But by comparison with the rest of Europe their conduct was nevertheless exemplary, as I can testify. During 1933 I was in Germany on a study tour. When the anti-Aryan laws were passed, I used my own money to make a trip to England for the purpose of trying to get a campaign of organized protest under way. It may be added that the only person who urged me to do so was a German Catholic prelate. But though I tried my best, the only affirmative response I received in London was from the Jesuit editor of an influential publication. The climate of opinion in England at the time happened to be one of rather remarkable optimism about the Nazis.

The famous Concordat signed by the Vatican with Hitler is a case in point. This had a long and somewhat complicated history but the gist of it is that the major proponents of the Concordat were so pessimistic about Nazism that they wanted to use any means within reach to stay off disaster for the longest possible period. To say as some do that the Papacy was under illusions about Hitler is not to be realistic. I may add at this point that the reigning Holy Father, Pope Pius XII, made the unprecedented offer to me of giving permission to study the Vatican archives for the whole Nazi period. This I could not accept for financial reasons. But one result would certainly have been to clear up once and for all the questions of that Concordat.

I have indicated that in my judgment there are weaknesses in European culture which have to be recognized. The basic ones seem to be: the waning of the power of love as a social force, derivative in large measure from the Jewish and Christian faiths and the stratification of interests. Among truly religious people there was a good deal of mutual respect among Christians and Jews, as the popularity of Martin Buber, for example, indicates. But this solidarity was not from the sociological point of view very influential. By comparison Jews were held in high esteem among segments of the aristocracy and in portions of the labor movement. The first is testified to by considerable intermarriage;

the second, by the positions of leadership often held by Jews. But there was practically no liaison between Jews and the middle class, or between Jews and the military. It was to these groups that Nazism appealed. But I do not think that the situation in this respect is specifically German. It is, rather, European.

Notwithstanding the above difference of point of view, I consider Dr. Heller's work a very noble book and should like to commend him in particular for two things: first the ability to present the Jewish religion in terms of what is deepest and most constructive in it; secondly, for the remarkably human (and humane) way in which he has discussed the relationship between Jews and Germans. What I think he is saying in essence is that the Jew can approach the German problem rightly only if he does so in the light of his religious traditions *properly understood,* and the German can approach it also only if he does so again in the light of his cultural, historical tradition, properly understood too, with all its light and shadow.

GEORGE N. SHUSTER

Preface

PATHWAYS TO A GOAL

"Whatever thou takest in hand, remember the end, and thou shalt never do amiss."—APOCRYPHA, BEN SIRACH

THERE are wondrous events in the life of nations for which various explanations have been proposed and we remain ever intrigued, mystified and overawed by their occurrence. Speculation on the cause of such events and reflection on their implications are almost irrepressible. The Revelation at Sinai, the Sermon on the Mount, the American Declaration of Independence and Lincoln's Emancipation Proclamation are examples of such events.

Aberrations and crimes have also stained the pages of history. The continuous study of the circumstances and forces which have been responsible for the errors and defections may serve as a future warning and a deterrent and thus preclude their possible repetition.

The frightful havoc which the Nazis inflicted upon the world, the enormity of their crimes and the prolonged acquiescence, if not approval, by the German people to the pagan ideology and moral nihilism which were clearly enunciated in *Mein Kampf* (which during Hitler's regime outsold the Bible) make an examination and a scrutiny of the causes of this horrendous period ever timely. It becomes even more urgent when we consider the many questions involving these events to which no clear and satisfactory answers have yet been given.

Are the Germans innately warlike and destined by their very national character to be militaristic or were they conditioned to be bellicose by historic circumstances? If the latter be the case, may not these situations be controlled or counter-

acted and their effects altered? Was Nazism the cause of
the moral collapse of the Third Reich or was it the inevitable
climax of centuries of miseducation and spiritual astigmatism? Were the European powers totally blameless for the
emergence of the National Socialist movement? Was anti-
Semitism the product of a phobia, a sort of blind and brutal
force erupting from the dark regions of the Fuehrer's diseased soul, or was it a technique conceived and planned to
arrest the spread of unemployment, or a psychological trick
to divert the attention of the multitude from social evils and
the hazards of political ventures?

In seeking the cause of the Germans' capitulation to a
program devoid of moral principles, we must also probe the
tenets and the tendencies of the philosophies which enchanted them. Are we thorough in our search for the causes
of the recurrent spasms of moral depravity and barbaric
brutality on the part of the Teutons, if we persist in by-
passing their sanctuaries and ignore the altars at which
they worshipped?

Is the reversion to savagery to be charged against human
nature, or against the faulty educational technique of the
Church, or perhaps against the advocacy of unattainable
ideals which are identified with some transcendent beatitudes and utopian declarations?

Many Jews were and some still are prone to pin the blame
of Nazi crimes upon all Germans. A major objective of this
book is to plead for a fair, sane and realistic attitude towards
the people of Germany all of whom are not equally guilty for
the beastly acts of the Nazis. To reach this conclusion one
must ponder these questions:

Is a sweeping condemnation in accord with the teachings
of Judaism? Does it imply or foster a spirit of total revenge
against all Germans, even for such a heinous crime as the
cold-blooded extermination of six million of their kin? Was
Henry Morgenthau's alleged proposal to reduce Germany to
an exclusively agrarian community a personal conception,
or did he reflect the sentiments of American Jewry?

If the national soul of Germany is to become an arena of

a mighty conflict between the revived Bismarckian craving for power and domination and the new forces, the representatives of which are now at the helm of government, will we not jeopardize the chances of world peace as well as our own security if we let ourselves be drawn to a belief in the assured metamorphosis of the German people or to a prejudiced conviction of their incorrigibility?

The demurrer which is here entered against the total and indiscriminate condemnation of all Germans for the ghoulish acts of the "Herrenvolk" will undoubtedly puzzle the reader, for the author is a Jew who prizes his kinship with his fellow Jews. Their suffering and martyrdom during the Hitler regime occasioned him poignant pain, which was not unlike that experienced by Jeremiah when catastrophe had overwhelmed the Judean nation.

The author feels sure that his attitude and plea are not influenced by the American Government's present favorable disposition towards West Germany. He also disclaims any connection between his frame of mind and such super-idealistic moral dicta as the exhortation to "love one's enemy" and "to turn the other cheek"—dicta which are notoriously honored in their breach. The author feels impelled to lift his voice in protest against the prevailing tendency to blame all Germans by his sense of fairness and his regard for justice, and also by a regard for the teachings of Judaism, the religion which at times has been falsely characterized as vindictive.

On the other hand the author wishes to alert the democratic and internationally minded within and without the New Germany to the lurking peril of its restored sovereignty and (restricted) right to rearm since it was not preceded by an effective program of political reorientation. The book poses the question of the likelihood of Germany's readoption of old beliefs and aspirations since it will be shown the occupational governments failed to expose the errors and falsehoods on which Hitler erected the structure of his ideology. There prevailed a naive supposition that a decade of intensive totalitarian indoctrination could be blithely discarded by the consciousness of the defeat. The prodigal handouts of American chocolate bars, chewing gum and baseball bats to children were deemed capable of effectuating a change of disposition on the part of the German people.

Do these procedures rule out the possibility of a relapse into the old way? Konrad Adenauer, Germany's present truly great and moral leader, must soon give way to a successor. Will his successor be wise and strong enough to lead and direct the nation on the course outlined by Adenauer? In the face of the 'fait accompli,' what attitude will the United States and the Western Democracies assume towards the Germany of tomorrow?

This book aims also to plead with Nazi-uncontaminated and remorseful Germans (the number of whom the writer believes has been underestimated) to make Germany use its singularly fateful position to preserve and extend peace and freedom in the world. It repudiates the view that there is something in the blood corpuscles and chromosomes of the Germans which have made and will continue to make them warlike, a view which in itself suggests the fallacious and detestable Nazi dogma of racism.

In concluding the foreword, the author wishes to stress the fact that his intent is not to produce an abstruse treatise in political science or history. He offers personal reactions to and evaluations of what he conceived to be tendencies in the thinking and behavior of Germans over an extended period of time and which he feels contributed to the blunting and perversion of the ethical sensitivity of the Teutonic people.

The author is not unaware of the fact that subjective dispositions may have influenced and given form to his judgment. In answer to those who would discount his appraisals and conclusions on the ground that they are not free of such subjective elements he would reply with the observation that no reading or reporting of history is possible without its being colored by the perspective and purpose of the historian. Events of the past, like a landscape, are surveyed from a specific point of vantage. When the work is intended to be an artistic portrait and not a mere camera reproduction, what is in the mind and soul of the painter is as essential as is the vista which is indiscriminately observed by the multitude.

Part I

THE GERMANS ARE BOTH A LUCKY
AND LUCKLESS PEOPLE

Chapter 1

BRITTLE YET RESILIENT

"Behind a frowning Providence
He hides a smiling face." COWPER

ONE would have to search the annals of man from the very dawn of history to find a nation which was concomitantly subject to ill and good fortune as was and is the case with Germany. Twice vanquished in bloody world conflicts, veritable Armageddons which she courted, Germany nevertheless managed to evade the full measure of retribution for her transgressions. It seems as if Germany has a guardian angel which prevents Nemesis from wreaking vengeance upon that miscreant state.

Germany has been the object of undue consideration on the part of her erstwhile adversaries because they realize that she is the heartland of Europe. Her infirmities or soundness, depression or prosperity within her borders have a bearing upon the well-being of all the continental states. Germany's geographic position endows her with singular strategic advantages. Her borders are contiguous to lands with Slavic populations whose political and economic ideologies are diametrically opposed to those of the Western Nations. If Germany ever becomes disposed to link her political and economic policy with the programs of Russia and her satellites, such an association could become well-nigh invincible. The sun of freedom would sink and the shadow of the Kremlin would lengthen until it covered the face of the earth. If Germany could be relied upon to remain aloof she might serve as a buffer state *(provided no belligerent would violate her neutrality).* However if she could genuinely be converted to the democratic way of life and resolutely cast her fate with the Western Powers, then the possibility of a Third World War would diminish. The realization of the world's present need of a sound and strong, yet not unbridled and irresponsible Germany, impelled the United States, Great Britain and even France to impose upon her, not the severe peace conditions conceived while war was being waged against her, but magnanimous stipulations that were the product of considerate and circumspect deliberation.

Three incidents neatly illustrate the change of fortune which that country experienced within a brief period. They all took place on trains running between Paris and Frankfurt-am-Main.

The first incident occurred in February, 1949. The setting was a compartment in the second class section of a train which left Paris in the early part of the evening and was due to arrive in Frankfurt-am-Main a little after dawn the next morning. When the train left Paris, the compartment was occupied by three Frenchmen, a resident of the Saar, an American soldier and myself. At subsequent stations some occupants of the compartment left the train.

At the French-Saar and Saar-German borders, the train came to a halt for the change of conductors and the examination of passports and baggage by respective officials. At these stops one became keenly aware of the artificiality of these demarcations and sensed the dejected spirits of the men in charge of these posts. One felt the gloom that hung like a pall over the drab and dimly lit stations.

After the train crossed the Saar-German border, the soldier and I were the only occupants of the compartment. As the train proceeded, the soldier stretched himself out on the empty seats and fell asleep. I continued with my reading. About a half hour later there was a gentle knock on the door which was slowly opened by a youthful looking man. He was dressed in a shabby dark suit and a hat which resembled more the head-gear of a miner than that of a train conductor. I looked at his shoes and they were shabbier than those we in America are wont to consign to the ash can. I studied his face and saw unmistakable evidence of undernourishment. On his chest hung a kerosene lamp, by whose dim light he deciphered the passengers' tickets. He courteously asked me for my ticket, which he looked at and punched. When he came to ask the slumbering soldier to show him his travelling orders, he seemed hesitant and fearful. He finally proceeded to gently tap the soldier so that he would awaken. The latter slowly opened his eyes, and as he became aware of the individual who had disturbed him, his eyes glowered as he scowled at the silent and quivering railroad employee, "You dirty s.o.b. of a Kraut, what the h— do you mean by waking me?" "Es ist mein pflicht" was the apologetic reply. The soldier threw his orders at him and then stretched out again on the empty seats, still mumbling abuse. The conductor cast a quick glance at his orders and returned them to him, departing with a 'Danke schön."

The second incident occurred on the same (railroad) line about eight months later. It is to be remembered that in this interval the economic situation in Western Germany had visibly improved. The currency reform at the beginning of the year altered the farmers' reluctance to bring their produce to the city. The merchants were tempted to bring their wares out of hiding and offer them for sale. The Russian threat of isolation and starvation of the residents of West Berlin and the United States forces stationed there by the imposition of blockade, proved utterly ineffective. A German government and parliament was being set up in Bonn and it was envisaged that it would take over many of the functions and powers of the American Military Government. The German was beginning to discard the feeling that he was a member of a subjugated country and had to cower before Americans. He was beginning to sense that the victors needed his support.

The train this time was en route to Paris from Frankfurt-am-Main. I was in a second class compartment which was near the center of the train. The compartment at the end of the car was literally occupied by G.I.s. When the train made its wonted halt at the last station in Germany before it proceeded into the Saar, there was a commotion in the end compartment. Arguments and shouting in English and German resounded through the entire train car. The curious

passengers left their compartments and stood in the narrow
corridor to ascertain what the heated debate was all about
and to see who the contending parties were. Not content
with being a distant observer, I went close to the scene.
There I learned what engendered the controversy and who
the disputants were. A G.I. in the compartment, having had
a bit too much liquor, had vomited and soiled the floor. The
conductor reported the matter to a station official, who
ordered the mess cleaned up and now demanded from the
G.I. a specified number of marks as payment for the work.
The G.I. who vomited was too sick to indicate his disposition in the matter and his buddies stubbornly refused to
comply with the official's demand. "In the U.S.A." declared
one G.I., "no railroad North or South of the Mason and
Dixon Line, East or West of the Mississippi, prosperous or
in receivership would stoop to ask payment of a sick pas-
senger for something which is not of his volition but is an
act of God."

After this peroration, the two M.P.s who were called to
enforce the demands of the irate official seemed indisposed
to coerce the pallid and half conscious G.I. to part with the
designated sum. When the official realized that time was
passing and that his efforts were in vain, he waved his
hand and signaled the conductor to order the train to proceed. As the train was pulling out, with the heads of passengers protruding from the lowered windows, he cried out,
"And these American swine are our rulers."

The third incident was related to me in January, 1951 by
a friend who had just visited Germany. He was on his way
to Frankfurt-am-Main on the same line. The cars, he told
me, were now spotlessly clean and some were either new
or freshly painted. The stations in Germany were repaired,
well lighted and devoid of the drabness of the post-war
years. Streams of people were moving simultaneously in
opposite directions. There were individuals waiting to
board outgoing trains or to meet friends who were due to
arrive there. There were no loiterers.

He related to me that he was the sole civilian in his compartment, which was also of the second class section. All the

other occupants were United States Army men. One was a lieutenant, another a sergeant and the others were privates. They were seemingly returning from a holiday in the French capital. The train halted at the Saar-German border for the usual custom and passport inspection. After a little wait, two pairs of officials appeared at the door of their compartment. The first examined and stamped the passengers' passports; the other inquired what one had in the baggage and then asked that the latter be opened for inspection. These officials maintained a soldierly posture. They were smartly dressed in impressive uniforms and wore military hats with gleaming insignia and visors. They addressed the passengers civilly but in a commanding tone. The soldiers' papers were carefully scrutinized and their baggage was thoroughly examined; in fact it seemed to my friend that the officials were more courteous to visitors and tourists. In examining the baggage of a G.I., one of the officials came upon a bottle of perfume and some wearing apparel which the G.I. had purchased in France for his wife or fräulein and which he had failed to declare. The official, despite the G.I.'s pleas and protestations, took the undeclared items after giving the soldier a receipt. When the soldier gave vent to vehement indignation, the official retorted, "You fail to realize, Mr. American, that times have changed and that the pinching shoe is now on your foot."

Chapter 2

SEEDS AND ROOTS

"Hitler, in his doctrine of the glorious German people pre-destined to world domination, was bound to fight the Jews."
BASIL J. MATHEWS

WHEN the world was apprised of the staggering number of Jews who were fiendishly "liquidated" in the gas chambers and crematoriums of the Nazis, many wondered how a highly gifted and enlightened people like the Germans could have sunk to such a state of savagery. The mystification however fades away as we become cognizant of a quirk in the human psyche which is responsible for such impulsive and regressive behavior. These alternating orientations and modes of conduct are like the pendulum of a clock, the further they tend in a given direction the more kinetic energy they acquire in swinging back.

How can we account for this phenomenon? Ordinary individuals and people tend to live on an even keel. The burning desire to serve man or God, the passion to sway and dominate, the craving for fame and glory move not the average but the super-normal or abnormal. There is little likelihood that the average individual will reach out for the stars or descend to a bottomless pit. Messiahs true or false do not emerge from mediocrities.

Only those who aspire to attain unscaled peaks expose themselves to the danger of a headlong descent. The higher the summit, the loftier the aspiration, the greater the hazard becomes. Genuine saints are not less but rather more susceptible to the siren voice of the tempter. It is the awareness of this fact which prompted the plaint of Isaiah, "Who is blind as my servant or deaf as my messenger that I

send?" [1] Even in the wilderness, Jesus is conceived to have
had to wrestle with the Devil.[2]

It is also to be noted that no transgressor is to be deemed
irreclaimable and that spiritual heights attained by a penitent sinner may at times be the very product and consequence of his depravity. Sins "red as scarlet" may be made
"as white as snow," [3] Holy Writ assures us. Even those
who are allured by a life of sin are inclined to eulogize one
who is not prey to their failings. In Tin Pan Alley, the
writers of the popular ballads dealing most tenderly with
mother love, I am told, are frequently those who are notoriously derelict in filial duties.

The mysterious inception of man's disposition to esteem, yearn and strive for moral perfection was beyond the
purview of those who gave rise to the legend purporting to
account for Adam and Eve's expulsion from the Garden of
Eden. The passage in Genesis asserting that man was made
in God's image[4] evidences a keen awareness of the inadequacy of a material explanation for the presence of an
inner light in man which is not only unquenchable but
blazes forth when the wind is most strong.

The very nonchalant and bravado pose of those who find
themselves in the crushing grip of vicious habits attest to
this suppressed wish to become free of what seems to them
to be an irresistible pull to wrong-doing. If during sleep
the seamy side of human nature has free play, then in the
evanescent moments of the derelict's daydreams, the yearning for the good and what one could have been breaks
through the shell of moral callousness.

When Jesus insisted on ministering to admitted sinners
rather than to the self-righteous he was impelled not merely
by the hope of arresting their degradation but also by the
desire to inspire them to scale sky-soaring peaks. "From
the depths" the Psalmist cried unto God.[5] In Kabbalis-
tic lore this explanation is more than an opinion or an hypothesis. It is an immovable truth that assumes the form
of an adage.

Saints and sinners, virtue and vice are not unrelated to

each other. Saints and sinners are not incapable of revers-
ing their roles, and by a baffling procedure transmute the
very essence of virtue into vice, and vice into virtue. Shakespeare succinctly voiced this fact when he wrote "Some rise
by sin, and some by virtue fall." [6]

The Germans were never a stolid people, unaspiring and
uninspired. Preceding centuries and the very present testify
to their being an uncommonly-industrious, well-disciplined
and gifted folk. In music, literature, science and philosophy they attained an enviable position, the very pinnacle of
success.

Now what made this nation topple from the spiritual
zenith to the nadir of moral decadence? What aberration
made them replace a Goethe, a Lessing and a Beethoven
with a Hitler, a Goebbels and a Streicher?

The Germans, dazzled by their signal achievements in
the century preceding World War I, allowed themselves to
become intoxicated with their worth and importance. They
considered themselves to be the élite of mankind. Their
distinctive life and thought indicated the direction and
destination of the *Weltgeist*.

For the evidence of such a claim the reader must turn to
Fichte's "Addresses to the German Nation" (1807-1808)
which are termed the "Bible of German Patriotism." Here
is a sample of "revealed wisdom" contained in these addresses "Only the German really has a people and is entitled
to count as one, and he alone is capable of real and rational
love of his nation . . . To have character and to be a German undoubtedly means the same thing."

In terming themselves "The Chosen People" the Jews
are supposed to have entertained a like belief. This assumption however is totally erroneous. A comparison of the difference between the Jewish and German concept of the
chosen people will make salient the insolent conceit of the
latter.

The concept among the Jews was not associated with the
myth of racial superiority and the supposedly pure and
peerless bloodstream coursing in their veins. Moses, their
hero, who led Israel out of the thraldom of Egypt and laid

the foundation of Judaism, wedded the daughter of Jethro, a Midianite woman. Their most extolled King, David, to whom is credited the authorship of the soul-lifting Psalms is declared to be the descendant of the marriage of a Hebrew and a Moabite, Ruth.

The Jewish concept of the Chosen People is not the product of a belief in the superiority or the moral excellence of that people. A collection of the Scriptural denunciations of the sins and evil dispositions of the "Chosen People" would make the most vicious anti-Semitic brochure appear moderate and restrained. To what extent the biblical delineations of Israel's moral delinquencies were exact or magnified is a theme that needs separate discussion. The point that is made here is that the Jewish concept of the Chosen People was not prompted by national jingoism. The Jews did not claim that they alone are God's darlings. The prophet Amos spoke of God's equal solicitude for the Ethiopians, the Philistines and the Syrians.[7] Isaiah, Jeremiah and Jonah stress the same tenet.[8]

The Jewish concept of the Chosen People implies not that Jews are destined to be the master-race, but rather the servant of God. Their selection for the role does not promise favorite treatment and prerogatives but grief and calumny until the dawn of that day when men will realize that the victim suffered in behalf of his very tormentor.[9] Moral sensitivity, like the aptitude for music appreciation involves pain and suffering. In the former it ensues when vice and corruption abound, in the latter when the grating and the cacophonous offend the ear.

The self-appraisal of the Germans was bred by pride, that of the Jews by humility. The Jew found himself the possessor of a spiritual legacy, a body of sacred lore and literature, *a Torah*. He was not arrogant enough to credit himself with having originated it. It was deemed to have been given to him by God, as recompense for the devotion and goodness of his forbears, the Patriarchs.[10] Others conceived the gift as an act of pure Grace on the part of God. The corollary of both views involved the Jew's dedication to the Torah and Its Teachings.[11]

Scripture and Talmud often speak of the Divine Presence
(the Shechinah) dwelling with and in Israel. They emphasize, however, the idea that the Being worthy of adora-
tion is not so much the "Almächtiger Gott" as the "Algnä-
diger Gott." They reiterate in diverse ways the saying of
Rabbi Yochanan, "In each instance where thou findest
the greatness of God mentioned, there thou findest also His
humility." [12]

The Jewish sages provided an antiseptic against the possible abuse of the belief that the Divine Presence had established its abode in the midst of Israel. The intimate relationship, said they, was conditioned by the kind of life
which the Jews would lead. The bond could and would be
broken were they to default morally and spiritually. Between the connotation of the Jewish concept of the Chosen
People and that of the "Herrenvolk" there is a gaping chasm.
While the Jews harnessed their national wagon to the stars,
the Germans harnessed the stars to their national wagon.

The series of genuine achievements led the Germans to
think of themselves as a "master race" only to sink to a
shocking level of moral depravity. The Jews on the other
hand as they became aware of the intrinsic worth and import of their spiritual heritage developed the moral concept
of the Chosen People. "That doctrine," Basil J. Mathews
rightly maintains "has been the core of steel that has kept
the Jewish people alive through thousands of years of persecution."

Chapter 3

MALT IN THE DEVIL'S BREW

"Those who would treat politics and morality apart will never understand the one or the other." JOHN MORLEY

THE German's sense of right and wrong was blunted by theories and affirmations of Teutonic thinkers decades before Hitler and Nazism made their appearance. If the myth of Nordic superiority and puffed-up national pride were not enough to make the German leaders and people headstrong and heedless, their philosophers had already hammered into their minds notions to the effect that the validity of ethical principles and practices was contingent on their conforming to the national will and the intent of the state. It was Fichte who affirmed that the striving of the state and its interest are higher objectives than the securing of peace, property, personal freedom and well-being for all. As a result of such teaching Bethmann Hollweg did not recoil from proclaiming to the world that a solemn treaty was a "scrap of paper."

Such a course was not deemed to be restricted only to national policy but was made applicable to the actions of individuals, especially those who felt that they belonged to the coterie of supermen. For them a transvaluation of values was advocated.[1] "Thus spake Zarathrustra" was to Nietzsche what the manipulated dummy is to the ventriloquist.

In this scheme, representative government and the will of the people are deprecated and looked upon with contempt. To King Frederick William IV of Prussia, a constitution was nothing more than "an inscribed sheet of paper" which he declared could not be allowed "to come between this land and God Almighty in Heaven." He termed the Imperial

Crown proferred him by the German National Constituent Assembly a "crown of filth and mud." If he was to become the Emperor of Germany, he could be exalted to that august role only by his peers.

Bismarck had no higher regard for representative government which he dubbed a muddy wave of parliamentarianism. He berated the creed of the liberals of the 1848-9 revolution: "Not by majority decisions and resolutions will the great issues of our time be settled," he thundered, "but by blood and iron."

Friedrich von Holstein (1836-1909) followed Bismarck as the actual director of German foreign policy. At the beginning he was an admirer of the Chancellor but later he became critical of Bismarck's personality and policies. The Holstein papers (Vol. I), whose publication the American State Department recently sanctioned, disclose to us the man who provided the mold and pattern for modern Germany. In one of the memoirs Von Holstein asserts that one of the greatest difficulties in dealing with Bismarck was his complete contempt not only for mankind but for the truth as well. Future historians will be forced to recognize that the Bismarck regime was a constant orgy of scorn and abuse of mankind. "His intellect was the slave of his temperament and justified outbursts for which there was no genuine cause."

Hegel greatly swayed the thinking of Germans. He is classified in textbooks of philosophy as a rationalist and transcendentalist; he was a notable exponent of what is termed the deductive and dialectic method of investigation. He looked down on those who endeavored to envisage reality by piecemeal empiric examination of data. He insisted that the comprehension of the *whole* must be accorded priority over the knowledge and understanding of its fragments.

Plato, it will be recalled, thought along similar lines. The sublimated mental abstraction or universal idea of a thing, Plato maintained, enabled us to recognize and comprehend the perceptible and individual object. Likewise, it was the

universal etherealized ethical values that made us aware
of the goodness of specific acts and attitudes.

Now it may be asked what bearing did the monistic and
transcendental speculations of a Hegel have upon the moral
derelictions of the Germans? What relation can there be
between a metaphysics which denies the autonomy of the
world of sense and contends that it is the materialized shad-
owy projection of a world comprehensible only to the mind
and the German's addiction to militarism and veneration
for authority? What is the connection between the Hegelian assertion that a positive affirmation implies and carries
with it a negative declaration and the German facility in
rationalizing and justifying his aggression and chronic
disregard of the rights of others?

Plato's and Hegel's glorification of abstract and universal ideas and their imputation of great import to the understanding of the meaning which they attached to these ideas
have led to the disparagement and at times utter disregard
of pressing tasks and momentous issues. When reality is
to be found in a realm of the mind which is beyond and
above the flux of perceptible things and temporal events
why should one allow oneself to become engrossed in matters that are illusory and ephemeral? Plato extolled justice
in the abstract but was unmoved by the prevalent institution of slavery. Obsession with and sublimation of and
speculation about the essence and scope of a virtue or ideal
are often substitutes for the failure to apply remedial
action to a specific social malady. "There is no more fatal
cause of error and deception," asserts F. C. S. Schiller,
"than the trust in abstract dicta which by themselves mean
nothing, and whose real meaning lies in the applications
which are not supplied." [2]

The Hegelian notion that things below acquire a foundation and validity from transcendental essence of a supra-
mundane realm where absolute truth is not a figment but
a fact, engenders a receptiveness to authoritarianism
which does not halt at the boundaries marking the area of
philosophy or religion. This mood persists even when one

steps over into the realm of politics. Here again I quote F. C. S. Schiller: "The absolutistic view of truth logically demands that truth be fully unified. A plurality of authority implies a plurality of truth; and this is inadmissible. . . . If there is no single infallibility to cover the whole realm of thought, if there are a number of authorities all claiming to speak infallibly in the name of their respective sciences, it is impossible to avoid conflicts and collisions between them; and this must discredit, weaken, and perhaps destroy, the whole principle of authority as such." [3] As William James observed, "In the universe of Hegel, the absolute block whose parts have no loose play, the pure plethora of necessary being with the oxygen of possibility all suffocated out of its lungs, there can be neither good nor bad, but one dead level of mere fate." [4]

The postulate that the Universal Spirit is enshrined and can be discerned best in the history and culture of Germany, induced its exponents to believe that not Man but Germany is the measure of all things. No formal, moral rules must be allowed to deter its advancement. "That is just which is good for the state" was the pronouncement not of a general or a politician but of Germany's most eminent philosopher. And with the avowal of the principle of negation and contradiction the view that each affirmation involves a contrary implication and the German's endemic metaphysical disposition, it was not difficult for him to see black in white and white in black. It was not caprice or concert alone that made Mussolini, Hitler and Stalin speak with pontifical authority on all matters.

Morris Cohen sums up well the tenets of Hegel's philosophy. "The glorification of the national state naturally makes Hegel cold to the Kantian cosmopolitan ideal of perpetual peace founded on a world federation of republics. Each national state is absolute and war is not only necessary but a spiritual good. Since ethics is embodied in the state and there is no sovereign over all states, they are in relation to each other in a 'state of nature' not subject to genuine moral laws. They are not, for instance, obliged to keep their agreements. From this anarchic and amoralistic

view of international relations Hegel tries to escape by
regarding history as the court in which providence passes
judgment on the various nations. This makes history a the-
odicy; but it also makes mere survival the test of national
righteousness, a doctrine that misses the tragedy of history
and is equivalent to Napoleon's dictum that God is on the
side of the heaviest artillery. This phase of Hegel's doctrine, however, is covered by the use of logical instead of
theological terms, by an attempt to show that development in time follows the order of the categories of logic.
But, as the number of logical categories is finite, history
completes itself in the Prussia of his day. Moreover, to display this logical order one people and only one can at any
time represent the world spirit; the rest are negligible and
have no rights." [5]

The bitter and unrelenting anti-Semitism of the Nazis
too is traceable to former advocates who loom large in the
moulding of the national character of Germans. The rationalizations of the Nazis' hostility to Jews were linked with
recent events. The psychologic forces that brought it into
being and the economic advantages which were sought and
the political allurements which dazzled them have their
seeds in antecedent avowals.

The Nazis filled the air with the charge that the Jews
were a subversive and corrupting influence in German life.
The list of sins which they laid at their door would be com-
ical if the consequences of their libels had not been so
tragic. It was the Jews, they claimed, who in World War I
deprived the Germans of a deserved victory, by stabbing
them in the back. It was the Jews who conceived and supported the "Democratic" (which term was synonymous
with "decadent") Weimar Republic. "Die Juden sind unser
Umgluck," was their lament and the only remedy was to
restrict their freedom, deprive them of their rights and to
eliminate or liquidate their very persons. Even this prescription did not originate with Hitler. Fichte, in 1793,
wrote, "There is spread throughout nearly every country of
Europe a powerful inimical state which wars continually
against all others and often succeeds in bitterly oppressing

their peoples; this State is Jewry . . . The only way I can see to give the (Jews) civil rights is to cut off their heads in a single night and equip them with new ones devoid of every Jewish idea . . . To protect ourselves against them, again I see no means except to conquer their Promised Land and pack them all off to it." [6]

The Nazis, it will be noticed, went a bit further than Fichte in their diagnosis and cure. They traced the bacilli not to ideas in Jewish heads, but to the blood corpuscles which coursed in Jewish veins. The Promised Land was too near the Western World. Hitler, therefore, proposed to dump the Jews on the distant, disease-breeding and torrid isle of Madagascar. He envisaged that the sequestered Jews of Europe and later of the world would rot away there until they would all die off and in due course of time Jews could disappear from the face of the earth. His villainous project would have been actualized had not the Lord remembered His promise concerning Israel's ultimate fate.

"I will not make a full end of thee. For I will correct thee in measure, and will not utterly destroy thee." [7]

Part II

TOBOGGANING TO INFAMY

Chapter 1

DECEIT AND TREACHERY SKULK WITH HATRED

"Beware of false prophets which come to you in sheep's clothing, but inwardly they are ravening wolves."
MATT. VII:15

To ASCERTAIN the degree of blame which is to be attributed to the German people for Hitler's reign of evil it is important that we comprehend how his party came to obtain unchallenged control of all phases of life in the Reich. Having come into power, the Nazis were able to proscribe freedom of action and thought and thus stifle overt opposition. Opponents were either silenced, forced to go underground or become exposed to attacks by mobs, or were subjected to protective custody which meant being dispatched to a concentration camp. The rest of the population were in various degrees mesmerized by glowing promises of restored national glory, the spurious elimination of unemployment, the scrapping of political divisions and antagonisms and their replacement by a compulsory (meretricious) unity of will and aim. The frequent staging of Nazi parades and conclaves with dazzling displays of the latest military equipment and corps of goose-stepping soldiers, followed by the blood stirring harangues of an over-extolled, well-nigh deified Fuehrer played their parts in the engendering of a collective hypnoidal state. Hitler's apparently uncanny ability to obtain bloodless victories from the timid and appeasing representatives of European states served as the "coup de grâce."

The questions, however, that press for a clear and exact analysis are: Had Hitler been truly summoned to assume the reins of government by the will of the majority of German people or was his call to leadership the product of machinations and intrigues? Was the atmosphere poisoned

with false and vicious charges against the factions opposing Hitler and his ideology in order to produce alarm and
panic amongst the uninformed and unsuspecting multitudes?

On January 30, 1933, Paul von Hindenburg, President
of the German Republic, summoned Adolf Hitler and authorized him to form a coalition government without ample
protection against its transformation into a dictatorship.
This event evoked diverse reactions.

Some looked upon the phenomenon of the rise of Nazism
as if it were a rash which, with time, would heal and pass
away. The Nazis, they felt, are adept in exploiting the current economic and political ills. The unthinking masses
are entranced by the oratory of their spellbinding leader,
and the spectacular parades of his followers. The Nazis,
however, have no sound workable program, they reasoned.
Their proposals to deprive the 600,000 German Jews of
their citizenship despite the fact that some of their forbears had resided in the land since Roman days, and that
these German Jews had contributed immeasurably to the
commercial, industrial and cultural development of Germany was as fantastic as it was vicious. A few months in
power and the German electorate would realize the non-
sense in exalting an erstwhile paperhanger as a chancellor
even if he was a master in delivering screeching harangues.
Or, said they, it is not unlikely that he may sober up with
the acquisition of power and responsibility, and modify if
not discard his preelection promises. "The soup is never as
hot when it is served as when it is cooked" was the adage
which they were wont to quote. Others were seized with
fear and consternation at Hindenburg's invitation to Hitler. The Nazis were a band of brigands driven by lust for
political power and a craving for the posts and possessions
of the defenceless Jewish minority. They appraised their
leader for what he was, a psychopath obsessed with delusions of grandeur, a megalomaniac who believed himself to
be the redeemer of Germany and the savior of mankind.

They had read Hitler's *Mein Kampf* and they were horrified by the brazen admission of contempt for objective

truth and moral principles. They shuddered at the brutal and inhuman anti-Jewish regulations which the party espoused. The steps he proposed to take to recover Germany's lost territory and to restore to her the power and glory which once had been hers conjured up fears of the possibility of a new war. They rightly perceived that *Mein Kampf* was looked upon by the populace not as the broodings of an imprisoned political agitator, but as a considered pronouncement, on a par with, or even above Holy Writ.

That this party should have obtained 6,400,000 votes and won 107 seats in the Reichstag in the election of 1930 was ominous but not incomprehensible. It was accounted for by the havoc which the fantastic depreciation of the mark wrought in the life-savings of countless Germans and the misleading, if not utterly false, propaganda of the Nazis, which contended that the Jews were the major beneficiaries of the downward plunges of the German currency. To this must be added the growing ranks of unemployed which were the consequence of the impact of the worldwide depression. These conditions made the jobless German worker, idle doctor and lawyer, and insolvent merchant covet the posts, clientele and trade of the Jews, which the Nazis promised they would make available to the German. That the stalwart, morally-minded and pietistic von Hindenburg should consent to entrust the safety of the Reich and the fate of 600,000 German Jews, (96,000 of whom had served in the army, and 35,000 of whom had been awarded military decorations and 12,000 of whom had died in battle in the last war) to this God-defying, Church-spurning Lucifer and his swastika-waving pagan hordes, indicated the degree of the present weakness and corruptibility of the German character.

The fright of the democratically minded individual was intensified by the realization that the proponents of totalitarianism resorted to ballots *only to worm their way to positions of political dominance.* Once they came into power they never relinquished it, even if there should be a reversal of disposition on the part of the populace. Their staged elections were fraudulent and farcical. In democratic countries, popular suffrage, they realized, was comparable to a revolving door which enabled one to make an exit as well as an entrance. In a dictatorship, the door opened but to admit the party and persons to power. The door then was slammed shut.

With Hitler's assumption of the Chancellorship and von Hindenburg's consent to the dissolution of the Reichstag, a new election was set for March 5, 1933. On the eve of that election (February 27,) it will be recalled, the Reichstag fire broke out. The Nazis claimed that it had been set off by a Dutch communist. They used the incident to engender hysteria in the hearts of the voters. This gave the government an excuse to issue a sweeping decree "to prevent communist acts of violence."

On March 5, 1933, thirty-nine million, six hundred and fifty-five thousand Germans [88.7 per cent of all qualified voters] cast their ballots. The results are significant in determining to what extent the German people may be held accountable for the subsequent actions of Hitler and the Nazis.

The Nazis *obtained 43.9* per cent of the vote. The Communists, despite stringent police regulation polled 12.3 per cent of the vote. The balance or 43.8 per cent of the electorate was divided among the various parties (Social Democratic Party 18.3 per cent, Center Party 11.2 per cent, Nationalist Front 8.0 per cent, Bavarian Peoples Party 2.7 per cent, others 3.6 per cent).

The Nazis, it will be observed, although they polled a large vote did not have a clear majority. Hitler, however, was determined to terminate the Weimar regime. So on March 23 he addressed the new Reichstag. The communists were prevented from showing themselves on that occasion and only ninety-four of the one hundred and twenty five Social Democrats were permitted to be present. Hitler delivered a prepared speech asking for the passage of an *Enabling Bill,* which would grant him additional powers to be used only, he said, in emergencies. He promised to respect the existing political set-up and religious institutions. He concluded his address with an overt threat and

challenge. His exact words are illuminating in revealing a persistent pattern of chicanery culminating in an ulti-
matum.

"The Government will only make use of these powers in
so far as they are essential for carrying out the vitally-
necessary measures. Neither the existence of the Reichstag
nor that of the Reichsrat is menaced. The position and
rights of the President of the Reich remain unaffected. It
will always be the foremost task of the Government to act
in harmony with his aims. The separate existence of the
federal states will not be done away with. The rights of the
churches will not be diminished and their relationship to
the state will not be modified. The number of cases in which
an internal necessity exists for having recourse to such a
law is a limited one. All the more, however, the Government insists upon the passing of the law. They prefer a
clear decision in any case. They offer the parties of the
Reichstag the possibility of a peaceful settlement and, consequently, of an understanding to be arrived at in the future. But the *Government is equally resolved and ready to
meet the announcement of refusal and thus of resistance.*
It is for you, Gentlemen, now to decide for peace or
war." [1]

Attention should be called to the fact that the Social
Democrats present at that session did not cringe in the face
of the threat. However, the Enabling Act was passed by
a vote of 444 to 94, thus precipitating the foulest episode
in the annals of human cruelty.

Here is an evaluation of the event by a noted American
historian, penned before Hitler engulfed the world in the
bloodiest of wars.

"The Weimar republic succumbed to the Third Reich of
Hitler for many reasons. Above all, it broke down under
the crushing tasks imposed upon it by the war and the
Treaty of Versailles. It was forced to liquidate the mistakes
and calamities of the old regime and deal with foreign powers which mistrusted it and which only belatedly gave it
their confidence. In the second place it was undermined by
intrigues and treachery which surrounded the presidential

office, Hindenburg was in truth the agent of the German people who led them along the paths of dictatorship and away from democracy. Furthermore, the republicans lacked courage and determination. Their forces crumbled without a fight, and the force acts of the Nazis and their immediate predecessors were accepted without a struggle. The German people themselves must also carry the responsibility for Hitler's accession to power. They did not stir themselves against the intrigues and arbitrary acts of the governments which succeeded Dr. Bruening, and they allowed themselves to be frightened by the alleged communist menace. They could have eliminated Hitler in the March election of 1933 or earlier, but they rallied to his standard in sufficient numbers to enable him to complete his plan. Their political inexperience, the economic distress, the foreign pressure, and the intrigues and force acts were too much for the regime; and in the face of a determined, fanatical force sweeping the country with surprising power, the Weimar system collapsed." [2]

Chapter 2

THE CRAVEN'S CLOAK

"How many cowards, whose hearts are all as false as stairs of sand, wear yet upon their chins the beards of Hercules and frowning Mars, Who inward search'd, have livers white as milk." SHAKESPEARE, Merchant of Venice

WHEN Hitler was given the sweeping dictatorial powers that he had demanded of the Reichstag, Germany was enmeshed in a series of complex domestic and international problems. Why did Hitler make the actualization of his anti-Semitic program the first order of business? What was there so urgent about the Nazi determination to debase, disenfranchise and despoil (and during the war utterly to exterminate) the defenceless Jews of Germany?

The postwar character studies of the Fuehrer and of the Duce disclose the cowardly streak that was part of their psychic make-up. Their heroic poses and their disposition to display themselves caparisoned in military regalia of the highest rank, and their jingoistic speeches are to the psycho-analyst but ways of concealing from themselves as well as from their adorers the pusillanimity of their natures when they personally had to face danger. Hitler was wont, in the early days of the party, to fling himself to the ground and hug it when the meetings were stormed by opponents. His face, we are informed, was pale and his body quivered until the brawl was over. After becoming the idol of the Germans, he nonetheless insisted on having all possible protection and safeguards against personal injury. His eagle's nest at Berchtesgaden, the Festung of his underground Bunker in Berlin, his preference of suicide to capture and trial, are all evidence of a terror-ridden soul.

His attack on the helpless Jews in Germany afforded Hitler the opportunity of obtaining a sure and hazardless victory. Such an easy victory was not within the grasp had he tackled economic or international issues. His magnification of the powers and influence of world Jewry served his end psychologically and politically. He could make his selected adversary appear as a monster who subsists on sucking the blood and devouring the flesh of unsuspecting, peace-loving and noble Nordics; then in the face of such mortal dangers he would be able to unify the splintered political parties in the Reich. The discredited forgeries known as "The Protocols of the Elders of Zion," purporting to be the minutes recording the aims and plans of World Jewry to dominate and to enslave the Christian world, were fully utilized by Nazi propaganda. Goebbels and Streicher used the fabricated documents to poison the minds and souls of gullible and unsuspecting Germans and inflame them against Jews.

In anti-Semitism, Hitler also perceived a palliative if not an enduring remedy for the economic ills of Germany. The issuing of fantastic quantities of German marks by the government printing presses deprived the thrifty and the conservative of their life-savings. The property-less and income-less swelled the ranks of the now uprooted middle class. What a swift and simple solution to the problem of unemployment and economic recession was at hand if Jews were deprived of the rights of German citizenship and of pursuing professional careers and of conducting business! All their posts and vocations and mercantile and manufacturing establishments could be taken over by the Nordics. Being disenfranchised and stigmatized as sub-human, they would not have to be taken into account in any census. No attention need be paid to their welfare and condition.

To make the proposed Nazi procedure of pirating and purloining the possessions and positions of Jews appear warranted, a propaganda of justification had to be initiated. One had to reckon with the few decent and defiant Germans who were not taken in by the pronouncements of Herr Goebbels.

The charge that the Jews were responsible for and were the major beneficiaries of the ruinous currency inflation of the early twenties was taken up and dinned into the minds of the German masses. Before Hitler was swept into power, German Jews refused to condescend to reply to such rigged up imputations. With Goebbels as guide and boss of all organs of information refutation of the charge was impossible. As a result, the libel persists in Germany to this day amongst the uncritical and unenlightened.

The persistence of this belief amongst the German masses that the Jews had engineered and profited from the currency inflation makes advisable and pertinent a disclosure of its planners and major profiteers.

The situation in Germany after World War I bore *some* resemblance to what prevailed in that unhappy land after the termination of the last war. Bolshevism, then too, was a menace. German communists exploited the havoc of the inflationary rise of the cost of living. They wooed the army of unemployed. The victors of World War I did not stand in terror of Russia. She was then not as powerful as she is now nor was her army anywhere near Germany, not to mention on the very soil and in the city that formerly was the capital of Germany. Germans then, therefore, were wise enough not to bank on the threat-implying plea to the allies, "Help us or the multitude may turn to communism!"

They then approached the Allies with the following proposal. "You imposed huge reparations upon us. We want to honor our promises. This we can only do if we can get our industries to be productive. Make available to us loans so that we can rebuild and improve our destroyed factories and power plants. To do this we must install in them new and efficient machinery." The United States responded by granting Germany huge sums. The Dawes Plan and the Young Loan had been to Germany what the Marshall Plan now is to the nations of Europe.

There followed the floating of a series of German municipal loans which American bankers sponsored and sold to private citizens. Germany's reputation for skill, ingenuity and efficiency and the soundness of her pre-war currency lured many individuals, particularly in the United States, to purchase marks in the hope that with the rebuilding and modernization of her industry, the value of the mark would be greatly enhanced.

When Germany obtained from the outside world all possible loans and aid, the government then set its printing press going at full speed turning out marks until astronomical figures were necessary to compute the daily increase. This currency depreciation, in addition to the Germans' acquisition of foreign exchange through the sale of marks, enabled the government to wipe out its internal debt. This was not the result of an accident. The German politicians planned it that way. The depreciation of the mark immeasurably aided the giant trusts like Krupps, A. G. Farben and Hugo Stinnes vastly to extend their industrial empires, which were essential if Germany was ever again to undertake a military venture.

It should be noted that these corporations not only did not have a single Jew on their board of directors but that they encouraged, fed and helped to finance the Nazi party into its position of dominance.

As to the Jews of foreign lands and the part they were

alleged to have had in defrauding the German people of their savings and substance, the joke circulated that it was rare to find one Jew who did not succumb to the lure of buying enough, now worthless, marks to paper his house.

Chapter 3

CURS OF LOW DEGREE

"The heart is deceitful above all things and desperately wicked—." JER. XVII:9

HAVING shown the baselessness of the libel, we can now expose the baseness of the libellers. With each additinal political success the moral depravity of the Nazi regime hit a new low. Property and human rights of the Jew were disregarded and then utterly repudiated by the enactment of discriminatory legislation. Respected and fervently patriotic German Jewish citizens were made outcasts, and terrorized by Nazi hoodlums and swaggering storm-troopers. They were attacked on the streets, their homes were invaded in the middle of the night and the occupants hauled to unknown destinations for what was called "protective custody."

Martin Niemoeller was at first well disposed to Hitler and the New Order which he was to institute. Later, having become cognizant of the wickedness and lawlessness of the Nazis, he became critical of the movement. As a result he was made an inmate of the Sachenhausen Concentration Camp. His reflections and reactions to what he witnessed there impelled him to declare,

"No power on earth can force me not to see in the Jew my fellow man.

"You see, Germany had lost the war. We had an alarming crisis, inflation, an enormous unemployment problem. Certain Polish and Russian Jews had taken refuge in Germany; the great mass of the poor and unemployed believed them to be well-to-do. Envy developed into hatred. Instead of feeling sorry for these miserable refugees, some people begrudged them the little they had. Hitler quickly stimulated these low passions, which finally brought him to power. Today, Hitler persecutes both Jews and Christians alike.

"I have seen with my own eyes and heard with my own ears how Jews have been maltreated. I had a chance to 'study' this prison, which is built underground like a cave. When they whipped the Jews and I heard these poor creatures cry out like wounded animals, I knelt down and prayed to God. I never prayed so fervently before in all my life. I almost collapsed. Without my prayers, I could not have lived through the next day. But the Lord gave me new confidence and faith." [1]

The Herrenvolk were devoid of magnanimity, sense of honor, respect for men of learning and science, and veneration for the creations of the human spirit. For a price the Nazis permitted Sigmund Freud to leave Germany and only without his possessions, of course. Einstein had to depart leaving his life savings and property in Hitler's Reich.

On the eve of May 10, 1933 the Nazis staged in Berlin a spectacular and solemn ceremony on the immense Franz Joseph Platz between the University of Berlin and the State Opera on Unter den Linden. Books written by Jews, (and they included even those of Helen Keller), and those of non Jews whose contents were disapproved of by Goebbels, Rosenberg and Company were to be publicly burnt.

Here is a description of this event by the wife of Edgar A. Mowrer, who like her husband is a noted journalist and author.

"Germans are among the most likable people in Europe and surely average no greater number of bullies and sadists than any other nation; the difference was that Hitler's regime was built on sadists and bullies, from the top down. . . .

"The evening of the bonfire, the Soviet Embassy gave a big party . . .

"About eleven o'clock we crowded to the front-room windows as the torchlight procession swept into sight. Thirty thousand university students and school boys marched down Unter den Linden brandishing fire and singing patriotic songs. At regular intervals in the parade were huge trucks loaded with books.

" 'There go the tumbrels,' I said, and with most of the guests, we left the Bolsheviks and walked towards the great square between the opera house and the new University auditorium. Many people had assembled to watch the ceremony, but not nearly as many as I had expected. Shame kept them indoors.

"We cut through the crowd and stood by the great unlighted pyre erected in the middle of the square. Dr. Goebbels limped to the microphone and addressed the spectators. This was his particular show; he had organized it with his customary showman's eye and was the only important member of the Government taking part in it. How triumphant he must have felt, burning Werfel, Schnitzler, Sternheim—he, the neglected author whose puerile play, *The Wanderer,* had been refused by every theatre in Germany between 1925 and 1930; who had not been able to obtain even a reporter's job on a Berlin daily under the Republic. He talked sarcastically about the 'blight of internationally minded authors' and urged his hearers to foster 'national culture.' I held my breath while he hurled the first volume into the flames: it was like burning something alive. Then students followed with whole armfuls of books, while school boys screamed into the microphone their condemnation of this and that author, and as each name was mentioned the crowd booed and hissed. You felt Goebbels' venom behind their denunciations. Children of fourteen mouthing abuse at Heine! Erich Remarque's *All Quiet on the Western Front* received the greatest condemnation. It would never do for such an unheroic description of war to dishearten soldiers of the Third Reich." [2]

Here is a part of Goebbels' address on this occasion.

"Fellow students, German men and women!" he said as he stepped before a microphone for all Germany to hear him. "The age of extreme Jewish intellectualism has now ended, and the success of the German revolution has again given the right of way to the German spirit . . .

"You are doing the right thing in committing the evil spirit of the past to the flames at this late hour of the night. It is a strong, great, and symbolic act, an act that is to bear witness before all the world to the fact that the spiritual foundation of the November Republic has disappeared. From these ashes there will rise the phoenix of a new spirit . . .

"The past is lying in flames. The future will rise from the flames within our own hearts . . . Brightened by these flames our vow shall be: The Reich and the Nation of our Fuehrer Adolf Hitler: Heil! Heil!" [3]

On November 9, 1938, a minor Nazi official in the German embassy in Paris was shot to death by a distraught Jewish lad Herschel Grynzpan of Poland. Hitler was apprised of the incident when he and his Old Guard were in Munich celebrating the 1925 beer-cellar putsch. In a fit of rage he gave orders for a general pogrom on Jews, and this was followed by a confiscation of $800,000,000 worth of property belonging to German Jews and the imposition of an additional fine of $400,000,000 on a selected list of wealthy Jews.

On November 10, 1938, Nazi mobs were mustered in large cities. They proceeded to attack Jews and to loot and pillage Jewish shops. They invaded hallowed and historic synagogues and desecrated their contents. They smashed the Arks containing Holy Scrolls. They then set fire to the edifices.

Louis Lochner has an interesting observation in connection with this event and Nazi veracity.

"A striking example of Goebbels' capacity for unabashed prevarication was given to foreign correspondents accredited at Berlin on November 10, 1938, the day after Hitler had given the 'go' sign to his hordes to loot Jewish shops, demolish Jewish property, set fire to synagogues, and arrest innocent Jews. We were asked to come to the Propaganda Ministry late that forenoon, as Dr. Goebbels wished to make a statement.

"Ordinarily at our daily press conference, which was usually conducted by the section chief in charge of foreign press matters of the Propaganda Ministry, we sat in armchairs on which one could easily write. Also, there was always ample opportunity for asking questions. This time we were led into the so-called 'Throne Room' a large, ceremonial Hall of the Leopold Palace, housing the Propaganda Ministry. There were no seats. We stood around until it was time for the Minister to appear.

"Suddenly he entered with quick, nervous steps, invited us to stand in a semi-circle about him, and then delivered a declaration to the effect that 'all the accounts that have come to your ears about alleged looting and destruction of Jewish property are a stinking lie (*sind erstunken und erlogen*). Not a hair of a Jew was disturbed (*den Juden ist kein haar gekruemmt worden*).'

"We looked at one another in amazement. In all our journalistic careers no one among us had experienced anything like it.

"Only three minutes from the Wilhelmplatz, on which the Propaganda Ministry was located, was Berlin's famous shopping street, the Leipziger Strasse, at the head of which was Wertheim's internationally known department store, its great show windows broken, its celebrated displays a pile of rubble. Yet Goebbels dared tell us that what we had seen with our own eyes was a 'stinking lie.' " [4]

And Hitler's organ *Schwarze Korps* that month had this to say:

"The Jews must be relegated to special streets; they must be distinguished by special signs and deprived of the right to possess land or a house.

"The organ then advocated their exclusion from all remunerative occupations, so that they would be forced to sustain themselves in devious illegal ways.

"When they have reached this point," the article continued, "we shall find ourselves in the necessity of exter-

minating the Jewish world with the methods that we always use in the struggle against criminals, that is, with the
sword and with fire. The result will be the complete end of
the Jews in Germany, their total destruction." [5]

All this is but a prelude to what took place when England
and France and later the United States declared war on
the Axis. Hitler charged that the war was brought about
by World Jewry, who used Britain and America as the
manipulator of a puppet show used marionettes. He was
resolved to see that no Jew should escape paying the extreme penalty, when victory came to the Nazis.

So much has been written about the victims of the concentration camps and the crematoriums and the martyrs
of the Warsaw Ghetto Uprising that a recital and description of these events would be repetitious and needlessly harrowing to the reader. All that will be said is that foul and
fiendish deeds testify to the unimaginable depravity of the
"Herrenvolk." The medieval Jewish poet's rhapsodic parable intending to make vivid the infinite sublimity of God,
may well be used in the reverse in conveying the magnitude
and egregiousness of the Nazi crimes. "If all the heavens
were parchment, and the trees of the world's forest were
made into pens and the oceans of water turned into ink,"
they would prove inadequate to describe the brutality and
sadism of the Nazis towards the Jews.

The nations of the world were too tired and weary to
take any military action to counter Hitler's aggressions.
He always proclaimed, it will be recalled, that his latest
would be his last action in which an international agreement was unilaterally abrogated. With it, he asserted, Germany's wants had been satisfied and its honor restored. The
foreign ministers of European countries and the State Department of the United States were inclined to take him at
his word. As for the Nazis mistreatment of the Jews within
the Reich, any step, other than a diplomatic hint of disapproval, it was feared, would be considered as an attempt
by foreign governments to meddle in the domestic affairs
of a sovereign state. And so the Jews of Germany and the
world had to resign themselves to be the butt and the target

of vicious attacks of the enemies of mankind, civilization and religion.

Nazism may be likened to a fire that started in Germany and ravaged the continent of Europe and wrought injury in diverse ways to lands that were separated from the scene of the blaze by oceans.

The Jew was the first to detect the fire; he was the first to be scorched by it and he warned the whole world of the danger of its spreading. His cries, however, remained unheeded. For a time he fought the blaze single-handed. England justly glories in the fact that she stood alone at Dunkirk. The Jews experienced a protracted Dunkirk from the day of Hitler's ascendancy to the helm of the German government until his invasion of Poland stirred the nations to take up arms against him.

What value is to be derived from citing again the fiendish misdeeds of the brown-shirted hordes of Hitler?

What took place in Germany during the years of the Nazi terror needs to be told and retold. In indicating the depths of depravity to which human beings can sink, the disclosure may become a warning to us to be on guard against the slumbering beast that lurks within the nature of each of us. Furthermore in an age when the craving for power, material possessions and lustful pleasure are addictions of nearly every one, at a time when success in business or politics evokes the homage of the multitude even though it often demands the repudiation of principle, in a land where despite the right of each individual to "life, liberty and the pursuit of happiness" mobs could nevertheless gather about a high school and jeer and threaten dark skinned youths because they wished to obtain an education like that given to white children [a right which the constitution and the Supreme Court of the United States declared to be inviolable] can we assert that we are completely immune to the potential dangers of the beast within us?

"The worst crime you can commit today against yourself and society," Odd Nansen, the intrepid Norwegian opponent of Nazism writes in his diary *From Day to Day* (penned while he was in a concentration camp) "is to forget what happened and sink back into indifference. What happened was worse than you have any idea of, and it was the indifference of mankind that let it take place."

Chapter 4

WHEN ROGUES RULE

"Ye have plowed wickedness.
Ye have reaped iniquity:
Ye have eaten the fruit of lies:
Because thou didst trust in thy way,
In the multitude of thy mighty men." Hos. X:13

THE Nazis contended that the Jews had been Germany's misfortune. It was they who corrupted and polluted the national life and spirit of the heroic Germans. With the internment of Jews in concentration camps and their degradation and decimation, it would be logical to expect that the behavior of Germans would then be above reproach. The conduct of Nazi leaders should now be exemplary, particularly during the war years when the nation was locked in battle with enemies who were bent on preventing the Reich from assuming the role which destiny had set for it.

To show that this was not the case we shall not invoke the testimony of critics of the new order which the Nazis initiated, or the views and judgments of impartial observers, but the penned opinions and reactions of its most zealous devotee. We shall let the diaries of the arch-evangelist of Hitler, Joseph Goebbels, act as the prosecuting attorney.

These diaries give us a close-up picture of the mind and souls of the frustrated yet vain, self-extolling, morally-insensitive, boundlessly-ambitious Balaam of Nazidom. The sinister Goebbels directed the domestic affairs of Ger-

many while the adored Fuehrer made his headquarters on
the Eastern Front, believing that his presence and exhortations could rally his battered and retreating armies to
make a stand against the Russians.

The diaries also disclose the deep jealousies and rivalries
among the Nazi bigwigs. They reveal to us their suspicions
of and antagonism to the military leaders. They also bring
to light the presence of not a few opponents and skeptics of
the regime, who found it extremely hazardous to give vent
to the slightest criticism. In considering the degree of
blame that is to be assigned to the German people this fact
must not be ignored.

*The lifting of the veil is urgent because to this day the
myth goes uncorrected that Nazism was a good idea but
that it was badly carried out.* (It will be shown later that
the victors of the Nazis have failed in a most vital task, the
re-education of the German masses.)

In the diaries we see the Nazis to be a group of common
thugs and thieves. They did not have to be lawless, because they enacted the law and made it so that it sided
with their arbitrary actions and despotic wills. Anyone
who dared to deviate from the course which the Fuehrer or
his deputy ordained was branded a criminal.

"The Fuehrer once more explained his standpoint with
regard to the administration of justice in wartime. He said
a people always consists of three parts: a small negative
part, made up of criminal elements, a small positive part
consisting of idealists, and then the broad masses that are
in constant doubt whether they should swing to the left or
to the right. . . . I now proposed to the Fuehrer that bicy-
cles be requisitioned in France as a punishment for attempts at assassination and that they be placed at the
disposal of German soldiers. The Fuehrer regarded this
proposal as wonderful and immediately ordered Jodl to see
to its practical execution.

"The question has been put to me whether the radio sets
in the Netherlands should be seized. Undoubtedly British
propaganda in the Netherlands was a decisive factor in
the recent strike. I therefore favor taking the radio sets

away from the Dutch as quickly as possible. Anyway, we can make good use of them in our air-raid areas."

That fraud and corruption tainted and vitiated not merely minor officials at the periphery, but the very core and the élite of Nazidom, are proved by the many notations bemoaning the financial malpractices and black-marketeering in foreign exchange by Nazi leaders.

"We are living in a leadership crisis and it is high time that the Fuehrer sweep with an iron broom. Funk told me a number of incidents about men around Goering that simply make one shudder . . . The events in question are connected with the Reichsbank, and Funk naturally knows the exact details."

Here is another notation with the editor's (Louis P. Lochner) revealing comment:

"My campaign against blackmarketeering is also very favorably received by the people. Here, too, the people demand that the proclamation of principles be brought into agreement with the behavior of the politically prominent."

"(This is a jibe at such men as Goering, Frick, many of the Gauleiters, Raeder, Brauchitsch, and others who were living or at least reported to be living, a life of luxury (chiefly due to black marketeering) while the whole nation was constantly pulling its belt tighter.)"

With the prevalence of such practices is it to be wondered that the German Etape (non-combat rear-guard battalions) in the Eastern Front were intent more on plunder in retreating than on saving the equipment?

"The conditions prevailing during the German retreat make your hair stand on end. The Etape abandoned tremendous quantities of food, weapons, and munitions without destroying them; on the other hand the Etape organizations on retreating took with them carpets, desks, pictures, furniture, even Russian stenographers, claiming these were important as booty. One can imagine what an impression this made upon the Waffen-SS when they met these caravans on their forward march against the Bolsheviks."

The diaries also shed light on the malpractices of the High Priests of Italian Fascism. "Ciano," writes Goebbels, "came to Germany with millions of lire which he wanted to convert into South American currency. He helped the Duce to transfer large sums to Switzerland.

"Edda Mussolini has something on her father that is either of a criminal nature or compromises him socially and politically. It is either a question of love affairs or of money. I have heard on a previous occasion that Ciano helped the Duce to transfer large sums of money from Italy to Switzerland. Such a revelation would naturally be an almost mortal blow to the Duce . . . The whole affair is certainly pretty strange and it is desirable that we hold on to the personalities involved so that no disaster may result."

The extravagance and indulgence of many of the leaders of the Nazi party were shocking and revolting. Before Hitler came to power the bigwigs of the movement were not renowned for their inherited wealth or prosperous businesses. They were wage-earners, army officers, teachers and second rate journalists. After Hitler's rise to power and their appointment to political office we find them, in due course of time, maintaining elegant city homes and summer places, and throwing parties with regal splendor.

"Costly parties were the order of the day in Hitler's Third Reich," wrote Louis P. Lochner in his Introduction to the Diaries. "The beer-hall fighters who had won their way to power and position by brute force considered themselves entitled to the spoils of war and Hitler approved. One high-water mark of such festivities had been the Goering Opera Ball." This ball took place on January 12, 1936, and to it the bemedalled Minister of Aviation had invited royalty, dukes and princes and leaders of giant industries and eminent generals and admirals. The prodigality and pomp and glitter of the Goering ball can be imagined from the item to the effect that when the American troops entered the Goering summer alpine home they found 25,000 bottles of champagne stored in his big wine cellar.

In July, 1937, Joseph Goebbels gave a party entertaining

the delegates to the convention of the International Chamber of Commerce. Louis P. Lochner was one of the guests and here is his description of the event.

"Peacock Island, charmingly located in idyllic Wannsee, some fifteen miles outside of Berlin on the way to Potsdam, with its romantic castle erected in 1794 for Frederick Wilhelm III, had been converted into a scene from the Arabian Nights. As we crossed over from the mainland on a pontoon bridge, the path leading to where Dr. and Mrs. Goebbels waited to receive their guests was lined on both sides with hundreds of the prettiest girls from Berlin's numerous higher schools. All of them were dressed in white silk breeches and blouses, white silk stockings, and white leather slippers. Each held a white wand. They bowed as the guests slowly walked several hundred yards to the reception line.

"On a beautiful greensward tables had been set for groups of twelve, ten, eight, and smaller parties. We were some three thousand guests. A sumptuous dinner was served the like of which we had not eaten in Berlin for years, for Rudolf Hess had already delivered himself of the slogan, guns instead of butter. Fringing the greensward on one side was the longest bar I have ever seen, with eighty attendants at our service to concoct any drink that might be wanted, or to serve champagne without limit. Every lady guest was presented with an artistic figurine from the Prussian State Porcelain Factory.

"In another part of the island a gigantic rotunda had been constructed in which the guests could dance, and on which, later in the evening the ensemble of the Civic Opera performed a charming ballet and other members of Berlin's artist colony put on a floor show.

"All for the glory of the Third Reich! But the official communiqué for the German press was stilted and drab. The common people were not to know that the days of Augustus the Strong of Saxony and Poland had returned to Germany under the auspices of the tribune of the people, Joseph Goebbels."

The Nazis were devoid of compassion. Cruelty they identified with manliness and pity with sentimentality. This disposition was particularly evident in the Nazis resolve to exterminate the 11,000,000 Jews in Europe. They were averse to spare even half-Jews and those who professed adherence to Christianity.

One would have imagined that the herrenvolk would be regardful at least of the suffering of their own wounded soldiers. The Goebbels Diaries contradict such a supposition.

"From Upper Silesia I received information to the effect that wounded soldiers are still being transported in unheated boxcars, and that the soldiers are lying some with frozen limbs, in these trains, without blankets, neglected and unfed for seventy or eighty hours. I am raising Cain with the hospital echelons of the Army and am arranging for the Party to take over in order that at least this extremely difficult and embarrassing problem may be solved.

"We are informed that people of means would gobble up sleepers and first class seats whereas German servicemen had to put up with all sorts of inconveniences."

S. Ansky's "The Dybbuk" is a Yiddish play which has been translated into many languages and made into a stirring film. This play has been acclaimed as one of the great literary works of our period. Unique in plot and story, it is superb in its delineation of character and psychology of various personalities. It also depicts realistically Jewish life in a Ukrainian village, the poverty of the multitude, the pride and snobbery of those blessed with possessions, the gentleness and saintliness of their other-worldly chassidic Rabbi and the followers' responsiveness to his mystical ideas and noble ethical teachings.

Joseph Goebbels in the Diary informs us that he had the film shown to him and then proceeds with this commentary:

"In the evening I had a look at the Polish-Yiddish motion picture, *The Dybbuk.* . . .looking at this film I realized once again that the Jewish race is the most dangerous one that inhabits the globe, and that we must show them no mercy and no indulgence. This riffraff must be eliminated and destroyed. Otherwise it won't be possible to bring peace to the world."

That this play should call forth a base and biased estimate of the "dramatis personae" was to be expected. Insensitive as the Nazis were to and unappreciative of moods and tenets of religion, and particularly its overtones, any other reaction on their part would have been surprising.

One, however, does expect even from a Nazi a more gallant appraisal of the death defying uprising of the Jews of the Warsaw Ghetto. This very denigration of their exploit, however, eloquently attests to the Jews' bravery and heroism.

"Reports from the occupied areas contain no sensational news. The only noteworthy item is the exceedingly serious fights in Warsaw between the police and even a part of our Wehrmacht on the one hand and the rebellious Jews on the other. The Jews have actually succeeded in making a defensive position of the Ghetto. Heavy engagements are being fought there which led even to the Jewish Supreme Command's issuing daily communiques. Of course, this fun won't last very long. But it shows what is to be expected of the Jews when they are in possession of arms. Unfortunately some of their weapons are good German ones, especially machine guns. Heaven only knows how they got them. Attempts at assassination and acts of sabotage are occurring in the General Government at far beyond the normal rate.

"There will never be any rebellion within the Reich against our leadership. The people would never think of such a thing. There isn't any Jewish leadership here for it. Criminals in such a serious crisis would not be turned loose on the people but stood up against the wall."

Chapter 5

MILITARY DEFEAT AND MORAL TURPITUDE

"Could he with reason murmur at his case,
Himself sole author of his own disgrace." COWPER

THE depravity of the Nazi leaders percolated the strata of German society until it tainted the moral disposition and demeanor of the common people, *Der Kleiner Mann.* Goebbels' diary teems with notations to that effect.

When the Nazis were in the habit of staging spectacular parades and mammoth mass gatherings at which Hitler screamed the Reich's grievances against the supposed injustices of the peace treaties of World War I, when Germany proceeded unilaterally to alter the stipulations of the Treaty of Versailles and without opposition annex Austria and the Sudetenland, when victory of the Wehrmacht appeared unpreventable and the Luftwaffe dominated the skies of England as well as Europe, the youth of Germany flocked to the colors. To wear a uniform with the emblem of the Swastika was a distinction and a privilege. The heroic mood, the willingness and readiness to offer one's life for the Vaterland was deemed to be the earmark of the German character.

The mettle of a people is shown not by its deportment when success crowns its efforts, but by how it carries itself when it is under fire and when it finds itself in the grip of adversity and faces defeat.

How did the herrenvolk comport itself when bombs rained upon its cities and when its Panzer divisions on the Eastern Front retreated without being able to make any creditable stand against Russians?

When things were not going their way the ardor for military service on the part of the brave and valiant youth of

Germany cooled off. They were then in quest of professions which exempted them from military service. Herr Goebbels fumed at the alarming decrease of students in technical schools and those stressing the study of natural sciences. Exemption from military service was not accorded to students engaged in these studies as was the case with students of medicine whose numbers as a result multiplied.

What a contrast there is between the behavior of the English when the Luftwaffe pulverized Coventry, and made its devastating nightly raids on London, or when heartrending reports came of the necessary withdrawal of the remnants of their armies at Dunkirk!

Here are some notations in Goebbels' diaries illustrating the difference in moods:

"During the night we had an air alert of pretty long duration. Many provinces throughout the Reich were affected. In reality, however, only ten nuisance planes flew over these provinces. We must therefore record the absurd fact that ten nuisance planes could drive fifteen to eighteen million people out of their beds.

"It is a curious thing that every individual soldier returning from the Eastern Front considers himself personally quite superior to the Bolshevik soldier, yet we are retreating and retreating.

"The neutral countries are asking themselves whether our retreat is really based on military consideration. They cannot imagine that our fighting spirit should have sunk so low in the course of one summer as to compel us thus to withdraw our front. Many regard it as a tactical move to enable us to arrive at a separate peace with the Soviets. Personally, I cannot imagine how that could be arranged . . .

"Speer claims that the production deficit in the armament industry is not too great after an enemy air raid. The fact that bombed cities undergo pretty bad dislocations of public life, as a result of which the workers often stay away from their workbenches for weeks, is far more aggravating. Thus, for instance, the Lanz works at Mannheim have been completely ready for production for a fortnight, yet only 60 per cent of the workers have thus far returned.

"On Stalin's orders the Free German Officers' Committee in

Moscow has gone in for propaganda in a large way. General Seydlitz has even made a broadcast. Certainly no general of old Prussian stock can sink lower.

"I intend awarding a badge to all who have been totally bombed out. Practice has shown that many doubtful elements are using bomb warfare to secure unauthorized advantages for themselves . . ."

Chastity and continence were labelled by Nazis as aspects of bourgeois morality which could be disregarded especially when the ideological objectives of the new order demanded such a course. The race theories of the Nazis and the desire to breed future Germans who would exemplify the superior biological characteristics of the Nordics were invoked as sanctions. Free and uninhibited sex-relations and child bearing for the State between German maedchen and Nordic males, especially if the latter were soldiers and army officers, were extolled as acts of patriotism. This indoctrination, to which the opposition by parents spelled internment in a concentration camp, produced and fostered a moral gangrene on the social body of Hitler's Germany. Here is a sketch of its result by Judy Barden, a noted American foreign correspondent:

"All over Germany at this time, the most beautiful hospitals flew a white flag with a red spot in the center. These flags denoted maternity hospitals for unmarried mothers. They were filled with girls of seventeen to twenty-five. I visited one of these institutions in May 1945. It was an exquisite place built on the lines of an exotic Swiss chalet. Young mothers nursed their babies in the sunshine on the veranda. Other mothers wandered around chatting happily with the nurses and with each other. I was unwelcome.

"The things I thought these mothers would fall for, like glugging over their babies, admiring their hospital, showing sympathy for them, fell as flat as a Russian promise. In fact my attitude of sympathy was obviously resented.

"A few candy bars and liberal handing around of cigarettes eased the tension somewhat, and as it slowly penetrated that my skin was like that of an elephant and I intended staying no matter what their attitude they thawed out.

"Their stories were stark and shattering.

"I remember wanting to write them for *The Sun* and then decided against it. They were just too much in the raw. *The Sun* would have been horrified and even its most broadminded readers could not have understood the attitude of these girls.

"Their aim in life was to propagate the species. They were hand-picked specimens who had originally volunteered for the job. Once they had passed the tests of health, beauty and curves, they were dispatched to various officers' leave centers where they stayed until they were pregnant. It was as simple as that.

"Once they became pregnant they were treated with every luxury left in Germany. The care they received was far better than that of the average mothers having a legitimate child. They were helping to build a strong Germany. They were proud of their 'career,' indifferent to the fact that they didn't know the fathers' names." [1]

Geobbels, in his diaries, wrote the following on this very same subject:

"Prostitution in Berlin is causing us many a headache these days. During a raid we found that 15 per cent of all women arrested had VD, most of them even syphilis. We must certainly do something now about it. In the long run we cannot possibly avoid setting up a 'red-light district' in the Reich capital similar to those in Hamburg, Nuremberg, and other large cities. You simply cannot organize and administer a city of four millions in accordance with conceptions of bourgeois morals."

In the Midrash an ancient Rabbi asserted that a wanton disregard of moral principles by the populace which is not inspired by its leaders is not unrectifiable. From this statement we may infer the converse, that when the relapse from or rebellion against moral values is initiated and sponsored by the supposedly élite, then the trend is to be looked upon with alarm.[2]

The Rabbi's statement is the result of keen observation and sound reasoning. Human beings are mortals with frail natures and conflicting or ambivalent dispositions. Good and evil vie for their allegiance and devotion. At one moment they may be enchanted by the soft and gentle voice of the good and at another moment they may find the lure and the glitter of the temptress, the rival of the good, irresistible. As long as the leaders, to whom the average man looks for the pattern of moral behavior, espouse what is noble and exemplify what is good, then faith in the ultimate soundness of the average man's ultimate choice is unshakeable. If his leaders are venal and debased then the moral standards of the multitude are bound to fall to lower and lower levels. The moral fate of that society is then in grave peril.

Chapter 6

THE PLAGUE WAS NOT STAYED

"Rabbi Phineas ben Jair says: 'When the Temple was destroyed the Associates and the freemen were put to shame and walked with covered head, and the men of good works waxed feeble; and the men of violence and men of loud tongue prevailed. And (now) there is none that expoundeth (to Israel) and none that seeketh (compassion for them), and none that inquireth (after his fellow's welfare). On whom can we stay ourselves? On Our Father in Heaven'— —."
MISHNAH SOTA[1]

THE moral decadence of the Herrenvolk did not come to an end with the ignominious defeat of the Nazis.

With the collapse and surrender of the Reich's fighting forces and the fall of the Hitler regime the cancer that afflicted the social fabric of Germany became glaringly exposed. Up to then, Goebbels' propaganda either covered the infected sections of German life with a silky veil or daubed its sickly and pallid features with pinkish paint and powder. Now the Germans saw and poignantly felt the lamentable consequences of their embracement of the Nazi ideology, with its chauvinistic avowals and disregard of hallowed beliefs and time-tested moral principles. They now realized the terrible price which a nation must pay when

it surrenders its God-endowed reason and prefers instead
to follow blindly the supposedly-unerring intuitions of
an obsessed megalomaniac.

What was the reaction of the populace at that moment?
In 1918 the Germans explained away their defeat with the
charge that they were lured by a false promise to capitu-
late.

In the first period after World War II every German one
encountered was wont to disclaim that he ever had been a
Nazi adherent. This prevailed to such an extent that a popular story was then current amongst Americans to the
effect that "Hitler was found dead. His body was lying in
a Munich street. His fist was tightly clenched. His fingers
were pried open and a piece of paper was found in it. On that
piece of paper was written, 'I was never a Nazi!' "

When the Wehrmacht crumbled and the victorious battalions of the Russians, English, French and American
armies spread over the land and assumed control of the
cities and districts, the Germans were gripped by terror
over the retribution which they assumed the conquerors
would exact from the populace. Especially did they dread
the Americans whose fighting force Goebbels described
as consisting of illiterate whites and sex-starved Negro
soldiers. After they came in contact with the G.I.s and found
them to be humane, and extra generous with children, they
heaved a sigh of relief. The problems of the Military Government then began. Countless Germans, desiring to in-
gratiate themselves with the occupation authorities, turned
informers and proffered charges to the authorities that
these and those of their townsmen and friends had been
Nazis.

"Then it began," writes Ralph Harwood, "Counter Intelligence Corps agents fanned out over the *Landkreis* with
lists drawn from the records of the former *Kreisleiter*.
Thousands of Nazi party members were picked up in arrest
sweeps and bundled off to hastily erected internment camps
in the area. In the strongly Catholic town of Buchen
proper there were 260 names on the list.

"Stunned and frightened by this seeming about-face on

the part of the Occupation Authorities, the good citizens scrambled to extricate themselves from the suspect groups. As the demand for questionnaires followed each other in quick succession—a thriving business in sworn statements was struck up among the people. Affidavits were exchanged in a system of mutual protection and were sold for a few cigarettes. And, conversely, bitter denunciations and false accusations flew thick and fast. Signed and anonymous, they flooded the Military Government headquarters daily as people sought to whitewash themselves by blackening others, or simply to wreak vengeance on old enemies." [2]

When the Occupation Forces took over vanquished Germany and attempted to institute stable and orderly government for its districts, cities, towns and hamlets, they encountered the herculean task of solving the problem of a shortage of food.

The scarcity was so great in towns and especially in the large cities, that hungry and undernourished Germans were disposed to pay fantastic sums for edible things. When fear became wide-spread that the depreciated reichmark was doomed to the fate of its predecessor after World War I, not only food but other necessities became unavailable. Business transactions increasingly assumed the form of barter.

What happened to the food and produce which the German farmers raised? Farms were not a target for the British and American bombings. Furthermore the great bulk of the German army were now prisoners and the task of feeding them was a responsibility of the victor.

The explanation is to be found in the fact that farmers were averse to part with their produce for the number of reichmarks which the authorities set as the legal price. Owing to the diminished number of livestock, a restriction was placed on the slaughtering of cattle and swine until the depletion could be rectified. The breeders would take some livestock into the forest or into a remote field in the night and there slaughter them and cart off the carcasses before dawn to the teeming cities where they fetched fantastic sums on the black market. The officers of the Military Government whose task it was to see that the available food in the countryside was channeled into outlets which would result in equitable distribution were no match for the recalcitrant and hoarding farmfolk.

It was astounding to see how, after the currency reforms of December 1948, there was an ever increasing inflow of produce coming into the cities from the farms and how quickly the shelves of storekeepers became filled with goods and how their shop-windows displayed supposedly unprocurable articles for sale.

The craving of the iron-willed herrenvolk for coffee and American cigarettes seemed insatiable. The number of marks that a German was willing to pay for cartons of cigarettes or the valuable objects (such as Leica cameras, meissen figurines, jewelry and in some cases even autocars) which he exchanged for these luxuries are fantastic but true.

In Berlin's palmiest days a carton of Camels brought 2000 marks, then translatable into 200 good American dollars at the army post office. Four years later a carton yielded only 20 marks, officially six dollars and definitely not convertible. Coffee tobogganed from ten dollars a pound to one-sixth of that in the same period.

West Germany had at the beginning of the decade a refugee population of over eleven million. These did not constitute an intrusion of an alien folk but were Germans who lived in Silesia and the territory which had been incorporated into the New Poland, now a Soviet Satellite. The plight of these refugees in the early postwar years was pitiful. Their condition in the economically-restored West Germany was disturbing, even as late as 1950. Many were still without possessions, without homesteads and without reliable employment. They still had to be maintained in barracks of the erstwhile concentration camps, and were fed and clothed by the Red Cross and other charitable agencies. Their numbers waxed with the return of war prisoners, and illegal entrants from East Germany. The standards of mere subsistence in the camps were demoralizing. The inmates had gotten to feel apathetic towards the

future. There was a tendency towards crime and vagrancy
amongst the adolescent groups of the refugees.

The residents of Western Germany did not display any
particularly brotherly feeling towards these refugees. Their
sympathy was measured and their generosity was grudg-
ingly given. One not infrequently would hear a West German give vent to his anger at and impatience with these
expellees, in the verbal outburst, "They should have stayed
and fought instead of fleeing." The kindliness and the
warmth with which the Israelis received and shared the
little they had with the survivors of the Nazis and continue
to share with destitute co-religionists exiled from Iraq, Ye-
men and Egypt who keep coming to them for shelter and
haven and who outnumber the hosts, stands in marked
contrast with the attitude of the Hitler and Goebbel-led
Germans.

As to the moral ideals of the Nazi-indoctrinated youth,
I shall let the reader derive his own conclusions from the
scenes which I personally witnessed.

Paraphrasing the words of Jeremiah in the Book of
Lamentations I can say, "I am the man who hath twice seen
the affliction of Germany by the rod of God's wrath." I was
in that unhappy land in 1924 and in 1949. I witnessed the
paralysis of her industrial establishments and the consequent unemployment of her masses and the hunger and
poverty which followed the Kaiser's wanton and unsuccess-
ful military venture. I saw the seething hate and the smoldering anger that was engendered in the hearts of the Germans when Clemenceau insisted that the stipulations of the
Versailles Treaty be carried out without modification. I,
with other passengers, was besieged by ragged and bare-
footed urchins as we walked off the planks that bridged
our ship with the wharf at Hamburg. Their outstretched
hands and imploring eyes begging for coins saddened and
depressed us.

Such scenes one expected in the slums of the Far East
and of the Near East but not in Germany. I saw the tragic
effects of an uncontrolled and ruinous monetary inflation.
I saw in Frankfurt-am-Main respectable men and women

with haggard faces and emaciated bodies standing in long queues to purchase a bit of food with sums that represented the earnings and savings of years. I saw merchants living most luxuriously in the midst of such want because they were eager to spend their daily profits lest by tomorrow the currency might shrink to a fraction of what it was then. In Berlin's Friedrichstrasse I saw girls in their teens offering themselves to any bypasser for the price of a meager meal or a cheap garment.

All this degradation and misery paled into insignificance beside what I encountered in Germany *four* years after the defeat and surrender of Hitler's armies.

In February of 1949, I arrived in Frankfurt-am-Main early in the morning. The mammoth station was bleak and cold and dirty. The translucent roof was damaged and the gray sky was visible through the large broken panes. A shabbily dressed porter carried my baggage and received the standard number of cigarettes for his services. It was against the law for Americans to have unauthorized German marks or to give United States currency, even military script, to Germans.

After I obtained room in one of the hotels taken over by the American Military Government, I took a stroll in the vicinity of the Bahnhof and along the main avenues of that old and historic city. The strewn rubble, consisting of broken bricks, twisted steel and splintered wooden rafts, the result of continuous bombardings of American and British fliers, were gathered into heaps, placed near the curb of the pavement. The city with its numerous roofless buildings and their jagged walls presented a grim and stark appearance. At night when one walked through the dimly lit streets these skeleton structures assumed the form of petrified giant-like phantoms and gave one, unaccustomed to such surroundings, weird and eerie feelings.

In the centre of the city, especially in the vicinity of the Bahnhof, one saw countless loiterers, old and young were seen picking up butts of cigarettes as soon as they were discarded by American soldiers and civilians.

Opposite the Bahnhof was a building on the second floor

of which there was the Snack Bar Cafeteria catering to
army personnel, American civilian workers, and non-German
business men who were in the United States Zone
with military approval.

The Snack Bar was one of the favorite spots where soldiers brought their fräuleins. On the week-ends the place
was a beehive. The music coming from the loudspeaker of
a juke box was always going. The women with the soldiers
ranged from American women who came to Germany to be
with their husbands to the most repulsive of German prosti-
tutes.

The Nazi doctrines of the Germans' sacred obligation to
preserve the racial purity of the Herrenvolk was ignored
and forgotten by the fräuleins. Negro soldiers seemed to
have been popular with these German maedchen. Various
reasons were given, not the least of them being the generosity of these dark-skinned soldiers. As a result many fräuleins found themselves to be mothers of Negro babies. These
mothers discovered that it was profitable to wheel the
baby carriage with their dark-skinned infant in front of
the barracks of Negro solders. The latter, when encountering a fräulein with a colored baby were wont to drop
coins, chocolate bars, cigarettes or whatever they had into
these carriages. The intake became so munificent and
the knowledge of this disposition so widespread that these
mothers would hire their dark-skinned babies to other fräuleins who would wheel them before other barracks or in
the streets where Negro soldiers were known to pass. The
fräuleins would then divide the loot.

The Diaries of Goebbels and the eye-witness account by
able reporters of the Germans' obscene behavior during and
after the war reveal the baselessness of the Herrenvolk's
claim to singular and superior moral attributes. On the
contrary they show how susceptible they were to moral
corrosion and decay, which literally dehumanized them.

Part III

INFLUENCES OF WHICH WE ARE UNAWARE

To ACCOUNT for the behavior of the German people in the preceding four decades we must reckon, not merely with the forces and factors which had a direct impact upon the life and thought of that people but also those influences of which the people were unaware. *The distant, indirect and subtle influences can not be disregarded or discounted.* Psychoanalytic studies establish the importance of reckoning with distant subliminal factors. An inland body of water is fed by surface streams which channel to it the downpour of rain and the flow of melted snow from nearby mountains. These streams are observable and their supply is ascertainable. If this body of water is also being replenished by hidden subterranean springs then the determination of the combination of these springs to the reservoir is vital knowledge.

Chapter 1

DUBIOUS CRITERIA OF GOODNESS

"The success of any great moral enterprise does not depend upon numbers." GARRISON

IN THE spring of 1949 I had an experience which indelibly impressed itself on my mind. It was an encounter with a young man whose father had been a Jew and whose mother was of German stock and a Christian. This young man was baptized and was brought up oblivious of any connection with the people from which his father hailed. Hitler came, and a series of situations provoked reactions on his part which made the Nazis fume and which landed him in a concentration camp.

The fearless protests and exploits of this young man which brought upon him the hatred and sadistic whippings by former friends and now fanatical Nazis make up a tale of courage worthy to be televised or dramatized on the stage. I shall not describe or even list the incidents which caused him to be dispatched to the concentration camp and to be marked for the fate of the gas chamber. These incidents, though intriguing, are not relevant to the theme of this chapter.

I met this young man in Frescati, a suburb of Rome. I went there to visit a temporary and migratory *Yeshiva*. It was a place where erstwhile inmates of a concentration camp lived, prayed and studied Torah, under the aegis of a venerable Rabbi, who had also been an inmate of the camp. The house in which they resided, prayed and studied was a large rundown manor which the now-impoverished owner was unable to keep up. He therefore leased it to the Joint Distribution Committee to house the escapees until they would be able to obtain visas for their intended final destination.

What brought me to the Yeshiva in Frescati?

In 1949 Professor Salo Baron, Chairman of the Committee in charge of the recovery of the cultural objects which the Nazis had looted from liquidated Jewish individuals and institutions, asked me to go to Europe and assume directorship of the work of the committee. One of my tasks was to provide former inmates of the concentration camps with those books and religious objects which we had recovered and which they needed for the resumption of spiritual life.

When I completed my survey of the cultural needs of the Frescati Yeshiva, I took leave of the men and their gentle and sagacious Rabbi. Coming out of the building which was situated on the hilltop I felt stimulated by the brisk and clear atmosphere. Beneath, one could scan the entire panorama of Rome with all its ineffable beauty and splendor. One could spot the various notable buildings in the distance. A farsighted person could even espy individuals, who like tiny Lilliputians, were moving across St. Peter's Square.

As I was proceeding toward the pathway which led to the street my attention was attracted to a young man who was lost in meditation. His face was delicate, his complexion fair. The hair on his head was sandy-colored and the tuft of blondish beard on his chin seemed to have sprouted only recently. When I came close to him I saw the light blue color of his eyes. I deliberately walked by him twice but he seemed to be in a trance. His seeming unawareness of my presence intensified my desire to meet and speak with this strange-looking "yeshiva bochur" [1] of Frescati. I walked past him a third time, and when I was within talking range I pointed to St. Peter's and then to the shabby building which housed the students of the Torah and commented in Yiddish on the ironic contrast.

Then came the big surprise. The young man was aroused from his reverie. He turned his frowned face to me. His eyes glowered. And then with prophetic seriousness he replied in German, "The dilapidated building in which Torah is studied and the God of Israel is invoked and his devotees are taught to live a holy life will outlast the mighty and majestic buildings that you see yonder."

For a few minutes, I remained speechless. I then decided to play the part of a skeptic who accepted only the testimony of undisputed facts. I demanded of him a warrant for his "declarations."

"About 2000 years ago," he informed me, "Rome dispatched her legions to the Holy Land where the Jewish inhabitants dared defy her imperial rule. The object of the expedition was to put an end to the rebellious Judean State. When one of the eminent Rabbis of that day perceived that the Commonwealth was nearing its end he managed to obtain an audience with the supreme commander. The Rabbi obtained from him permission to establish an academy in a small hamlet where Jewish savants could gather to study their sacred lore. This village school was more impregnable than military ramparts and bastions. It survived the mammoth pagan temples of Rome.

"The validity and vitality of religion are not to be gauged by the size and elegance of its cathedrals but by the heartfelt convictions and abiding conduct of the ordinary run of its devotees."

"What in nature validates your prognosis that the weak will vanquish the strong? The triumph of a David over Goliath was a singular feat, unrepeatable. Is not God, however, as Voltaire put it 'always on the side of the heaviest battalions'?"

There was an interval of silence, and the Yeshiva student of Frescati retorted in a slow tempo, and seemingly more attentive to the phrasing of his thoughts. "When one affirms the existence of God and the values which are identified with religion he maintains that the divine is not perceived in or through power. To attribute supreme value and meaning to things because they are big and strong is equivalent to the worship of idolatry. Neither are we to deem that there is a necessary connection between success and goodness. To the prophet Elijah there was revealed a timeless and transcendent truth. The Bible relates that in his quest for God he discovered that the source of what is divine was not to be found in mountain-moving and rock-rending winds, or in surface-shaking earthquakes or in flashing flames of fire, but rather in the still small voice. The lowly and the weak and those burdened with grief are nearer to God than are the great and eminent who are prone to be obsessed with their achievements. 'The Lord is nigh unto them that are of a broken heart.' [2] 'The sacrifices of God are a broken spirit: A broken and contrite heart O God, thou wilt not despise.' [3] The first Christians were not unaware of this fact when they pictured Jesus, the paragon of spirituality, to have been born not in a regal palace but in a lowly manger."

At this point I followed with the question, "Aren't you depreciating the Church and predicting its decline and decay just because it is widespread and strong, and aren't you exalting the Synagogue because it is puny and pallid? Is it a vice to be large and a virtue to be midget-like? If size and power indicate spiritual emptiness, why make Roman Catholicism and Judaism the antipodal extremes? There are Faiths whose devotees exceed the former in numbers and there are sects that are smaller and weaker than the latter."

"I did not predict," he replied, "the inexorable disappearance of the Church and the unconditional survival of the Synagogue. I was not considering their persistence and continuance but their effectiveness and the fulfillment of the aim for which they came into being. I do not look to the emergence of a Universal Church to which men of all climes and environments and cultural antecedents will belong and to their adoption of a set of unvarying dogmas and to their conformance to the stipulations of *One Code* of religious practices. There is no single gateway leading to the All-Merciful One. I believe this teaching is implicit in, if not explicitly taught by, Judaism. It is inherent in the saying of the prophet Micah, "For let all the people walk each one in the name of its God, and we will walk in the name of the Lord, our God, for ever and ever." [4]

This statement is doubly significant when we consider that it follows the vision of the coming of a day when all mankind will stream into Mount Zion and render homage to God, whose Moral Law was there revealed to the world and the fulfillment of which would result in the beating of swords into ploughshares and spears into pruninghooks. Religious unity devoid of uniformity was also espoused by the Talmudic Sages of Blessed Memory when they taught, "The pious of all nations will inherit heaven." [5]

When he finished I thought that I noted a desire on the part of the young man to bring the interview to an end. "I shall ask you one final question," I said. "What are the specific sins of which you seem to think the Church is guilty, and what are the virtues which you attribute to the Synagogue?"

A suppressed smile settled on his now soft countenance as he retorted, "Your question can't be answered swiftly and succintly in the vanishing interlude that 'one stands on one foot,'—as the Talmud proverbially phrased it. It requires an enumeration of commissions and omissions of specific acts and an examination of the moral mood that accompanied each act. This will consume much time and now I want to join my confrères in the devotions which is followed by the discourse (Shiur) of our Rabbi. If you will be here tomorrow we may resume the discussion." "It is agreed," was my quick response. We bid each other "Shalom"—

I did not move an inch from the spot but gazed with astonishment as the young man wended his way to the dilapidated house and disappeared after crossing the threshold.

I proceeded to my hotel oblivious of the noise of speeding vehicles and the throngs that were rushing past me or moving me along with them. My mind was totally absorbed with the conversation and the declarations of what I felt was a singular individual.

Chapter 2

PERCEIVING EVIL, THE GREAT AND THE NOBLE
MUST SPEAK UP

"Silence is tantamount to admission." TALMUD
"Silence gives consent." POPE BONIFACE VIII

THE dawn of the next morning found me awake, alert
and keenly eager to resume the terminated colloquy.
In my mind the incident of the day before was reenacted. I
brooded over the views and declarations of the young man,
whose appearance and inattention to my presence piqued
me to engage him in conversation.

"What made the experience so extraordinary?" I asked
myself. "Was it due to the setting, the beggarly state of the
old crumbling villa overlooking the Vatican City with its
historic and majestic buildings and well-kept approaches?
Was the impression to be explained by the unexpected appearance of the "Torah"-proponent? A blue-eyed, sandy-
haired, fair-complexioned 'yeshiva bochur' couching his
impassioned replies in impeccable German, tinged here and
there with an English expression or phrase, was a strange
phenomenon, if not a character, out of cast. His references
to the manger, the locale of Christ's birth, as proof of the
universality of the belief that the validity and effectiveness
of religious teachings were not to be gauged by material
tokens and results added to my bafflement."

When I arrived at the yeshiva the morning service was
already finished. Many still had their phylacteries (tefillin)
on arm and forehead, and the prayer-shawl (talesim) over
their shoulders. All were engaged in informal perusal of
rabbin c lore which was dominantly ethical in content and
edifyi g in intent. This exercise constituted a prescribed

postlude to the morning prayers, and the prelude to the day's routine. The Rabbi and the students of the Frescati yeshiva looked to the fervently moral and saintly teacher, Israel Lipkin, as their guide and model.[1]

I slowly and unobtrusively walked about the study hall glancing here and there at the books from which individuals were reading with melodious intonations. I strained my ear to catch the words which would indicate to me the theme and the tractate that engrossed them and moved them to the meditations and sing-song recitations. I overheard an elderly man expound to his younger colleague the wisdom of the Rabbinic admonition "Flee from lordship," which they had just read; "Power intoxicates and has a tendency to blunt moral sensitivity" he declared. The Talmud Yerushalmi commenting on Ex. XXXII:17 makes Moses say, "A man (Joshua) designated to exercise rulership over six hundred thousand men, gets so that he does not know how to distinguish between one voice and another voice (moral overtones)." [2] To the query of the younger colleague, "What shall the man do upon whom the mantle of authority falls?", the older associate offered the view of the Rabbi to the effect that whatever authority is given to a man is given conditionally and made authentic only by the law.[3] The elderly man then took a Pentateuch and thumbed the pages until he came to the passage in Deuteronomy which he read aloud. "When thou art come into the land which the Lord thy God giveth thee—and shalt say: I will set a king over me; like the nations that are round about me; thou shalt in any wise set him king over thee—and it shall be when he sitteth upon the throne of his kingdom, that he shall write him a copy of this law in a book—and it shall be with him and he shall read therein all the days of his life; that he may learn to fear the Lord his God, to keep all the words of this law and these statutes, to do them." [4]

From another side of the room came a soft subdued recitative chant the words of which however could be discerned " 'Be not over righteous and also do not consider yourself hopelessly wicked.' Both attitudes are detrimental

to moral betterment. Life according to the Rabbis is likened
to a journey along a road, on one side of which there is the
heat of scorching fires and on the other blasts of frigid
winds. 'How shall one proceed?' it is asked. And the answer
is, 'Pursue a course midway between the two extremes.' "
At this point I heard the voice of my friend offering supplement to the reply, "and such moderation is not to be con-
fused with oscillation between the extremes."

It took quite a bit of time for the breakfast to be completed. This was not due to the multiplicity of the dishes
which were available, but rather to the length of time which
was consumed in moving the chairs and tables from the
study hall and synagogue to the dining room and also the
time taken up by the ritual of the washing of the hands before the meal and the recitation of grace at the conclusion of the meal. The repast was prolonged by continuous
discussion and expounding of Rabbinic sayings and decisions.

At last came the moment for the resumption of the conversation. We decided to talk as we wandered about the
grounds of the former manor.

"In the concluding minutes of our discussion yesterday
you referred to sins of which Christendom was guilty. I
would like to ask you for a bill of particulars. This, in legal
parlance, means a listing of what you consider the specific
transgressions of the Church."

After a moment of reflection he proceeded to answer.

"When the followers of the Galilean formed themselves
into a Church and decided to link its weal and fate with the
ruling regime they succumbed to the evils which ensnared
emperor, king and princeling. The Church capitulated to
the craving for power and domination. It frowned upon
any set limitations and bounds. It was to be a Church that
was to encircle the globe. All men were to be made subject
to it. If the Church had been content to achieve the goal
by moral suasion an extenuation of its aspirations could
be imagined. But to attain its ambition it did not shrink
from the use of force, even if it involved waging of wars
and the brutal slaying of unarmed men, women and chil-

dren. The Inquisition, the Crusades, the massacre of St. Bartholemew's Day are ineradicable stains that mar the record of Christendom. He who had been hailed by angelic hosts as 'The Prince of Peace' had been made by supposed devotees a signal for war and a call to arms.

"The ecclesiastic defenders of the Church had no difficulty in propounding rationalizations to conceal from themselves and others the real forces that drove them to their course of action. They were bent, they told themselves, either on bestowing salvation on otherwise doomed souls or on extirpating evil influences in society. They also were not at a loss in supporting their aggressiveness with dicta from the Gospel. Their sin consisted in the fact that they based their conduct not on the authentic saying of Jesus that "All who take the sword shall perish by the sword" [5] but on words that may very likely have been attributed to him at a later date, "Think not that I am come to send peace on earth; I came not to send peace but a sword." [6] "He that hath no sword, let him sell his garment, and buy one." [7]

At this point I interposed these questions. "Assuming your imputations of guilt to the Church to be irrefutable, has not its attitude and procedure radically changed since medieval times? Is it fair to adjudge the recent and present demeanor of the Church by standards which were deemed proper in days gone by? Would you not protest if the Synagogue's attitude towards war was determined by the injunction that the Israelites slay all the inhabitants of Canaan after their entrance into the Promised Land and thus remove all enticement to Baal worship instead of basing the Synagogue's attitude on Micah's and Isaiah's prophecy of the coming of days when "men would beat their swords into ploughshares and their spears into pruning hooks"— and on the prayer, "Grant us peace," which is recited thrice daily by the devout?"

"I commend the spirit which prompts you to ask the question. The assumptions on which they are based, however, are flimsy. I have cited the Church's sins of commission. They have taken place in the past, in medieval times. The Church is not free of sins of omission also. This delinquency has marked the demeanor of the Church ever since the emergence of nationalism and the rise of modern States. These States declared might and conquest by arms a valid arbiter of Right. Statesmen and political leaders professing to be Christian glorified and apotheosized warfare and the hierarchy expediently remained silent."

I asked him to cite instances and examples. He then excused himself for a moment and went into the house. After a few minutes he returned with a German book. He then read to me the following passages:

"Perpetual peace is a dream," writes Field Marshal von Moltke, "and it is not even a beautiful dream. War is an element in the order of the world ordained by God. Without war the world would stagnate and lose itself in materialism." [8] He then cited Nietzsche's declaration: "It is mere illusion and pretty sentiment to expect much (even anything at all) of mankind if it forgets how to make war. As yet no means are known which call so much into action as a great war, that rough energy born of the camp, that deep impersonality born of hatred, that conscience born of murder and cold bloodedness, that fervor born of effort in the annihilation of the enemy, that proud indifference to loss, to one's own existence, to that of one's fellows, that earthquake-like soul-shaking which a people needs when it is not losing its vitality." [9] "A thousand touching traits testify to the sacred power of the love which a righteous war awakes in noble nations," asserted Heinrich von Treitschke. "War is elevating, because the individual disappears before the great conception of the State— What a perversion of morality to wish to abolish heroism among men! . . . God will see to it that war always recurs as a drastic medicine for the human race.[10] Like views were affirmed by Bernhard von Bülow and a host of notable figures in modern Germany," he added.

As he read the above passages I thought of Israel Zangwill's acid but warranted comment after he observed the attitude of the English, the exemplars par excellence of enlightenment and humanitarianism, during the first World War. "In the foggy mentality of Britain, it did not prove impossible to reconcile poison gas with the Holy Ghost and a host of war pulpiteers arose, more noxious than war-profiteers, to explain this heavenly harmony." [11]

Continued the yeshiva bochur, "If Von Moltke and Von Treitschke also are personages too far receded in the past then I would cite the bestowal of a blessing by the Church on Mussolini's attack on Ethiopia and the failure to provoke any ecclesiastical disapproval of the rapture of the Duce's son as he watched the bursting of bombs drop from his plane on defenseless villages. 'Onward Christian Soldiers marching as to war' to this very day is an esteemed hymn that is lustily sung in all Christian churches."

"Had the Synagogue been in the place of the Church do you think her policy and procedure would have been different?" I asked.

"I don't know," was his frank reply, "if the Synagogue would or would not have committed the same transgressions. If she had I don't think she would be liable to a like criticism and censure."

"Why not?" was my astonished query.

"The Synagogue never claimed to be other than a human institution manned by fallible and peccable mortals. To the Synagogue was never given the promise that "the gates of hell shall not prevail against it." [12]

"Judaism, in its incipient state," he continued, "was not immune to the virus of militarism. When Moses and the Israelites behind the hosts of Pharaoh and their chariots engulfed by the waves of the Red Sea they lifted up their voices in song and extolled God as a 'man of war.' [13] In one Psalm David acclaims God with the words, 'Blessed be the Lord my rock who traineth my hands for war and my fingers for battle.' " [14]

Note however that this praise of military skill was uttered millennia before the glorifications of war which I cited. And even then these opinions were not without exceptions. A pacific disposition is not totally absent in Mosaic writing[15] and the derogation of reliance on military power is found in the Psalter[16] as well as in the utterances of the Prophets.[17]

What an advance there is to be recorded in the interval
between Moses' and the Israelites' bestowal upon God the
epithet "The Lord is a man of War" and the Rabbis' imagined scene in heaven at that moment! God is conceived by
the Rabbis to have enjoined the angels against offering
their wonted hosannas to Him, because, as He sadly observed, "My children (the Egyptians) are drowning in the
sea and you propose to regale Me with song!" [18]

"At a time when soldiery and the bearing of arms was an
extolled vocation the Rabbis proscribed the carrying of a
sword on the Sabbath day because a sword, said they, was
not an ornament but a token of ignominy.[19]

"The reason which they give for the Biblical injunction
against the erection of an altar of hewn stones manifests
their disparagement of anything that is even remotely connected with warfare. To fashion an altar of stone, implements of iron are required to hew the stones to required
size and shape. Out of iron, spears and swords are made.
These implements of war, say the Rabbis, tear assunder the
bonds that unite Man to his Father in Heaven. The purpose of the altar, however, is to bring about the reconciliation of Man with God. Therefore commanded the All Merciful One, 'Let not the altars which are to unite Man and God
be fashioned by iron, which is the metal war-waging instruments are made of and the functions of which are antipodal to that of the altar.' "[20]

Believing that the above cited default of the Church was
pretty well covered I asked my friend to proceed to what he
considered the second failing.

"To support my second charge I will need a New Testament," he informed me. The request astonished me. A Talmudic Sage of Babylonia was reputed to be so conversant
with astronomy that the galaxies of the skies were said to
have been known to him as the streets of the city in which
he lived. However, a 'yeshiva bocher' at home in the lore of
the Church was something that I did not expect.

When the request for the New Testament was made I
feared that it may have been a ruse to terminate the colloquy. "I know that there is no New Testament in the

yeshiva. If I obtain one could we resume the discussion in the afternoon? I am due to leave Rome tomorrow."

"Yes," was his reply.

"Bring if you can a New Testament in German; if that is not available an English one will do."

I welcomed the recess. It enabled me to return to my hotel and record in my diary my questions and his replies while they were fresh in my mind.

Chapter 3

THE BANEFUL USE OF CREEDS

"(Churchmen) Prove their doctrine orthodox
By apostolic blows and knocks." BUTLER

WE MET again that afternoon and without loss of time we got set for what I supposed would be the final interview.

"What would you say was the second transgression of the Church?" I asked.

"Intolerance and suppression of divergent beliefs," was his quick answer. "The followers of Jesus, as soon as they broke away from Judaism and declared themselves a severed sect and a separate Church began to plant in the Vineyard of the Lord seeds of dogmatic illiberality which, in due course of time, were bound to grow up into noxious weeds.

"Consider the mood and spirit which prompted some sayings in the New Testament and then contrast the promulgations and actions of subsequent Church Councils." He then with ease turned the pages to these passages.

"Judge not, that ye be not judged." [1]

"And if any man hear my words, and believe not, I judge him not: for I came not to judge the world, but to save the world." [2]

"When the woman taken in adultery was brought before Jesus for judgement what was Jesus' response? 'He that is without sin among you, let him first cast a stone at her.' " [3]

"In my Father's house are many mansions." [4]

"The followers of Jesus who founded the new ecclesia and claimed to base its professions on his teachings ironically manifested an attitude and pursued a policy which was utterly contrary to the spirit of Jesus as it may be inferred from the passages which I have just read.

"The builders of the New Church failed to provide the fledgling Faith with the integument which would protect it from the infections of Caesarism which were cupidity for dominion and lust for power. The Church aped the Empire in its desire to extend its realm and to multiply its subjects. This became strikingly evident when the Church courted and won the patronage of Emperor Constantine. Just as the directors of the destiny of the Empire deemed it essential to consolidate and unify the divergent ethnic groups which it subdued by regimenting their thinking and stipulating for them mores and standards, so the heads of the Church considered it imperative to restrict the reflections and limit the freedom of speculation of its communicants. By prescribing and defining their beliefs, the Church maintained a hold on their minds as well as on their souls and bodies."

"Aren't you," I asked, "unfair in your conception and interpretation of the aims of the promulgators of creeds? Was not their intent primarily to elucidate and make distinct the ideas and ideals which the group in question espoused or was supposed to espouse? Would you impute the same intent to Moses Maimonides who propounded the Thirteen Articles of Belief?"

My question evoked this reply.

"Answering the first part of your query I would say that you would be justified in offering an objection to my version if the formulators and sponsors of the Creed had not resorted to threats and punishment to bludgeon dissidents to disavow their heterodox beliefs. The convocation of

Councils and the promulgations of Official Creeds were not so much aimed to illuminate as to dominate independently-minded and adventuresome churchmen. Anathemas, expulsions and the actual infliction of bodily harm were invoked to get the blind to see the transcendent truths which became apparent to the theologians at these assemblies.

"I don't know whether you are conversant with Church history. I had an occasion before the war to make a study of these theological gatherings.[5]

"The Council of Nicaea in 325 heaped maledictions on Arius, the leader of the left wing party. The Council of Ephesus was used by Bishop Cyril to depose and banish Nestorius with a farewell token of a dozen anathemas. The Bishop did not recoil from resorting to trickery currently practiced by unscrupulous politicians and labor leaders to obtain what they are determined to get. He did not wait for all the Churchmen to arrive to introduce his motion and have it then considered. He suspected that many would not support his proposal, so he railroaded through his motion before the probable opponents appeared on the scene. When the late comers arrived and learned what had taken place they turned the tables and deposed, excommunicated and anathematized Cyril and his confrères. The Bishop was undaunted. He retaliated with a third session which reenacted the proceedings of the first session.

"At a second Council of Ephesus, about two decades later, the burning question was whether Jesus possessed two natures, human and divine, or only one. The proponent of the diverse views who bitterly fought with Pope Leo over the issue was the intrepid Bishop of Alexandria, Dioscurus. The Pontiff apparently failed to vanquish his rival. For he convoked a new council at Chalcedon two years later. The previous gathering Pope Leo termed a synod of robbers. Its actions were repudiated and the Bishop of Alexandria was deposed and excommunicated.

At the Council at Constantinople the Churchman Chrysostom was banished from his Episcopal See for having opposed the imperial court and for having criticized the growing worldly disposition of the Christians of his time. Chrysostom had to end his days in exile.

"These were but a few of the arenas in which churchmen were locked in battle that they believed were for the glory of God but which some historians and many social psychoanalysts would consider manifestations of a will to power.

"Answering the second part of your query I admit that Judaism is not a creedless religion. It has dogmas, that is articles of belief and tenets which do not lend themselves to syllogistic proof. Their validity or tenability, however, also can not be conclusively disproved by logic. Examples of such doctrines are the sense of assurance of the existence and reality of God, the unconditioned imperativeness of the Moral Law, the inescapability of retribution resulting from wilful defiance of the Divine Commandments, their Revelation from God, the Selection of Israel, etc. These do not belong in the same category, however, as do belief in Immaculate Conception, the Incarnation of God in One Man and the Ascension of a specified mortal corpse to heaven.

"A second distinction to be noted is that Judaism's tenets are not congealed particularly about their borderline. They may be compared to pencil sketches, in the viewing and impressions of which the observer's apperceptive background and imagination play no small role. The dogmas of Christianity on the other hand are to be likened to close-up photographs where the outlines are in bold relief and are unshiftable.

"Lastly, creeds in Judaism represent avowals of individuals and not formal definitions and stipulations of an ecclesiastical Consistory. That's why one may detect in the theological speculations of the Sages two tendencies heading in opposite directions. In one there is evident a progressive economy in creedal avowals; in the other, each single commandment (mitzva) is deemed to embody and exemplify a fundamental religious doctrine.[6]

"If Jews and Judaism were so liberal and nonchalant in regard to religious professions and practices, how do you square," I asked, "that conception with the Biblical injunction to the Israelites that, upon occupation of the Promised Land, they should exterminate all the devotees of Baal and extirpate every vestige of foreign worship? How account for the multitudinous regulations in the Mishnah and Talmud (Abodah Zara) which were intended not only to widen the chasm between Jews and non-Jews but also stigmatized mores and forms remotely connected with the religious life of Gentiles as defiling tokens of heathenism?"

To these queries the young savant replied: "The evidence which forms the basis of your imputing severe bigotry to the ancient Israelites is questionable. When we read the books Judges, Samuel, Kings and the Prophets, wherein the demeanor of the Israelites is described after their conquest and settlement of Canaan, we find that they neglected to carry out the above Deuteronomic injunction. We find them living side by side with the natives, adopting their everyday way of life, marrying their women folk, and imitating their cult practices. Baal is even identified with the true God."

Now how could that have been the case if the command to slay all the votaries of Baal and to extirpate all semblance of alien worship had taken place? The conclusion of Biblical scholars and students of ancient history is that the injunction does not signify what *had been done* but the later rumination or post facto conception of the Deuteronomic writer what *should have been done* which would have prevented the abominable consequences.

The laws in the Mishna and Gemara to which you refer to prove that Jews then were addicted to irreconcilable hostility to foreign faiths are inconclusive. The contents of the tractate "Abodah Zara" attest to the fact that the Sages of that time were worried about the baneful influence of paganism which was powerful and glamorous. They were eager to protect Jewish thought and life against the spiritual corrosion which would result from unhindered imitation of heathen practices. They decided against the frequenting of Roman circuses and theatres by Jews. For vestiges of paganism were still ingrained in those places and tinged the performances which were produced there. By means of such legislation the Rabbis had also hoped to immunize Jews against current superstitions, and immoral practices.

"Despite all the Rabbinic prohibitions, association with non-Jews was not eliminated. The bridge between Jews and Gentiles was not sundered. Rabbinic literature records the friendly exchanges of ideas and mental skirmishes or disputations that took place between Jewish Sages and pagan philosophers.

"The writings of Philo, Josephus and the Church Fathers reveal that a give-and-take process did mark the cultural relationship between Jews and Gentiles. Instances can be found in Rabbinic writings of Jews and Gentiles being in business together and even carousing together. We are given an instance in Sidon where the Rabbis permitted the use in the services of sacred books which were written by a gentile scribe. We are told that in the Synagogue of Nehardea there stood a statue even though the making of such an object was in defiance of a commandment of the Decalogue. So you see that despite the proscription of fraternization with heathens and the adoption of their mores, the peaceful coexistence of Judaism and other faiths and a reciprocal influence was the prevailing order."

"Was not Judaism also imperialistic?" I asked. "Did it not also hope for the coming of the day when it would supplant other Creeds and Communions and wield universal sway? Is not the refrain of the daily prayers, 'On that day the Lord will be One and His Name one?' If Jews did not resort to coercion in imposing their beliefs on others was it not due to the fact that they happened to lack power and might? When they were strong didn't they compel the Idumeans to adopt Judaism?"

For the first time I noted that my friend seemed to be hard put for a quick answer. After a minute of silence during which he was stroking the tufts of hair of his reddish blond beard, he slowly proceeded to reply. He commenced by calling my attention to the fact that my query dealt with a hypothetic or assumptive situation. He rightly observed that there was no certainty or assurance in answers to such "iffy" questions.

After stating this qualification he continued, "A survey of the trend and direction of Jewish history and an analytic examination of the ideals and aspirations of Judaism, as they are articulated in its classic literature, would justify the inference that had that Faith enjoyed the privileged status of Christianity and played the role that the latter did, Judaism may have shied clear of being aggressively expansionistic. The Idumean adventure was an isolated incident."

The inner desires of a people, he argued, are mirrored in the delineations of its progenitors, and in the depiction of its millennial visions.

"The pacific 'live and let-live' disposition of Judaism is discernible in Abraham's proposal to Lot when the attendants of their herds were in bitter conflict over grazing lands. 'And Abraham said unto Lot: Let there be no strife, I pray thee, between me and thee, and between my herdsmen and thy herdsmen: for we are human and brethren. Is not the whole land before thee? Separate thyself, I pray thee, from me: If thou wilt take the left hand then I will go to the right; or if thou take the right hand, then I will go to the left.' " [7]

It is also evident in the blessing which Isaac bestowed upon Jacob and is in marked contrast to that which was immediately thereafter given to Esau, the prototype of Gentile nations. "And by the sword shalt thou live" was the high point of Esau's benediction. [8]

"In the millennial vision of Micah and Isaiah the nations are not compelled or driven to acknowledge the sovereignty of Israel's God. It is the result of an inner and voluntary urge.

> *"And it shall come to pass in the end of days*
> *That the mountain of the Lord's House*
> *Shall be established as the top of the mountain,*
> *And shall be exalted above the hills*
> *And all nations shall flow unto it.*
> *And many people shall go and say*

Come ye and let us go up to the mountain of the Lord,
To the House of God of Jacob."

"It is only when people have a sense of freedom and are assured that their right and freedom to think, believe and live according to the dictates of their conscience are not jeopardized that they will decide to 'beat their swords into ploughshares and resolve not to learn war any more.' [9]

"The distinction between God 'as He is,' the transcendent autonomous *I am That I am,* and God *'as He is dimly and relatively conceived'* by the limited mind of mortal man, fostered in Judaism the tendency to be magnanimous to and tolerant of sincere seekers of religious truth even when they avow their beliefs in unorthodox expressions and formulations. An affirmation that the absolute and ultimate nature of God is beyond our ken is implicit in the Commandment, 'Thou shalt not make unto thee a graven image nor any manner of likeness of anything that is in the heaven above or that is in the earth or that is in the water under the earth.' [10] It forms also the basis of God's refusal to grant Moses his wish to behold God's countenance. Said the Lord: 'Thou canst not see My face, for man shall not see Me and live." [11]

To Moses God declares that His actions may be discernible in the imprints of His presence. "Thou shalt see my back, but My Face shall not be seen!" [12]

I could not resist putting to him the question, "If the ultimate essence of the Godhead cannot be gauged and grasped by human mind and yet the craving of the heart of man for communion with Him is insuppressible how does Judaism resolve the enigma? What was done to cut the Gordian knot?"

"The reality of God," he replied, "was considered a fact, an a priori truth, an experience which could be as little negated as the reality of sunlight or the sense of self or the mystery and wonder that every phase and movement of nature evokes. Our conceptions and envisagement of God are therefore deemed to be but pragmatic tokens and symbols which indicate His reality, and intensify our sense of

His Presence and aid our awareness of the profound significance of that consciousness.

"In the above exposition you have an explanation for Judaism's non-insistence on inflexible dogmatic avowals and formulations. Only concepts and beliefs which tend to debase man and engender unethical and immoral behavior have been eschewed and denounced. Views and opinions that vary from the conventional declarations but do not have deleterious effects on man's actions and aspirations are recognized as legitimate and even accorded respect. The test and criteria of true belief is sincerity and noble living."

At this point a welcome break ensued. The aid of the yeshiva student was sought by confreres in the exposition of a Talmudic passage many words of which were of Greek origin.

Chapter 4

SELF-SCRUTINY AND MORAL IMPROVEMENT

"To regret deeply is to live afresh." THOREAU

WE RESUMED the interview after a lapse of more than an hour. I began the discussion.

"You spoke about Judaism being broadminded and unjaundiced in its attitude to and appraisal of other Faiths. Does not your version and evaluation of the momentous events in the history of Christianity evidence a contrary attitude? Does not your derogation of the affirmations and actions of the Church and your accolades to the Synagogue and exaltations of its tenets betoken an astigmatism and bias?"

"To be analytic and critical in the evaluation of a movement or an institution," he replied, "is not equivalent

to being intolerant and inimical. The Bible emphatically
enjoins us to rebuke a neighbor for avoidable failings. Silence prompted by expediency or timidity is counted as a
sin.[1]

"The world has gone through the convulsions of a cata-
strophic war. Cities and regions, the product of the toil and
sweat of generations have been turned into heaps of ruins.
Millions have been slain on battlefields and countless numbers of human beings have had their lives snuffed out by the
orders of a frenzied and fiendish megalomaniac and his
mesmerized henchmen who were under the illusion that
they were ushering into the world a New Order with radically different standards and values.

"The dominant religion in Europe was impotent to forestall the cataclysm. Moreover its disposition and demeanor
in the past provided the tactics and strategies by which the
promoters of the vaunted New Order were to attain their
goal."

Noticing the astonishment that was registered on my
countenance, he continued;

"You gape at me for making the statement, so let me
justify it by pointing out the similarities between the Gas
Chambers and Crematoriums and the Auto de Fé, the
Gestapo and the Inquisition, the Concentration Camps and
the Pale of Settlement, the Ghetto, the Star of David as
an insignia of a pariah and leprous alien and the Yellow
Badge the Jews were forced to wear in the Middle Ages, the
proscription of Nazi unapproved views and reporting of news
by Goebbels' Propaganda Ministry and the close scrutiny of
non-Christian lore and literature by the Church-appointed
Censors, the flames of the Nazi bonfires which were fed by
books penned by Jews and the burning of the Talmud at
the conclusion of the staged Disputations between Christian Ecclesiastics and their coerced opponents, the Rabbis.
Where did the Nazis get the suggestion to ascribe infallibility to the Fuehrer's decisions and deem him to be the incarnation and personification of the divine? Was there no connection between the charge that the Jews were guilty of
deicide and the accusation of the Nazis that Jews entertain

a secret devilish design to weaken the brave Ayrians, enslave mankind and destroy civilization? Is there no connection between the supposition of the Church Fathers that the Jews were now the cursed instead of the chosen of God (because they refused to hail Jesus as the Son of God and repudiate the Torah) and the contention of the swastika-bearers that the Jews were sub-humans?"

"Do you impute," I asked, "base motives to the Church in resorting to the above tactics and procedures, and do you believe that it knowingly set up patterns for vicious groups like the Nazis to copy?"

"Please do not put extra meanings into my words," he heatedly replied. "Whether the Nazis adopted their procedure with or without the knowledge of what the Church did to retain the loyalty or induce conformity of its followers is a matter of opinion. That the theoreticians and strategists of Nazidom ignored the above historic facts is most unlikely.

"As to your concrete questions, no man will admit even to himself that he is propelled or lured to do certain things by base motives. He resorts, as I have already pointed out, to a form of rationalization to conceal such motives from his conscious thinking. Incidentally, that disposition to rationalize and extenuate one's misdeeds is not without implication regarding the view that man has an innate streak of goodness with which he must reckon. This notion is inherent in the saying of the Talmudic Sage, 'No man sinneth until he is overcome by a spirit of folly.' That Rabbi accented the belief in 'original virtue' rather than 'original sin.' [2]

"Not being aware of the baneful character of its procedure the Church cannot be charged with the act of intentionally providing the Nazis with an ideological design and a course of action which spelt incalculable grief and injury to many, including the devotees of the Church."

"Do you feel," I then asked, "that the Church can lay claim to any significant attainments? What in your opinion ought to be its present aims and goals? Does it seem to you a mammoth organization, the legacy of an Age of Faith,

and now kept up by fear and the enchantment of the color-
ful rituals and processionals? Does it contribute to the spiritual stimulation and development of its devotees, or are
its proffered rewards only bliss in the hereafter?"

"One must be hopelessly petty-minded and prejudiced or
utterly blind not to see the impressive achievements of the
Church ever since it came into existence," he replied.

"It did succeed in weaning many millions from the worship of the grossest form of idolatry. The Church strove to
purge the vestigial remains of paganism with which the
converts would not part. Even the dogma of the triune nature of God is now being given a metaphorical explanation,
so that it will not violently clash with the monotheistic conception.

"Christianity dotted Europe with shrines. Its abbeys and
chapels were conducive to meditation and private devotion.
Its cathedrals provided the setting for elaborate rites and
ceremonies which evoked the awe of the worshipping spectators. The arms-bearing aggressive suppliant when he entered the vast edifice became conscious of his microscopic
smallness and was prompted to feel humble, at least while
in God's House. (The persecuted Jew, on the other hand,
who in the rialto and on the streets was vilified and made
to feel subservient and inferior to the gentile, needed a synagogue which would mollify his wounded ego and where he
would recover his sense of self-respect and even importance. As a result his places of worship were small and
cozy.)

"The notable art of the Middle-Ages is admitted to have
been inspired by the religious saga of the personages who
nurtured and guided the Church.

"The Church has to its credit the founding of schools and
universities which promoted learning. It is a calumny to
term that period a Dark Age. While independent speculation and untethered investigation were discouraged, erudi-
tion and the firm grounding of the pillars of the Faith became vocations and dedicated assignments of such servants
of the Church as Albertus Magnus, Duns Scotus, Thomas
Aquinas. In the galaxy of savants which it produced one

will find mathematicians, grammarians, astronomers, historians as well as theologians and philosophers.

"The charge that the Church is or was averse to the private reading of Scripture is also untrue. The Church forbade its communicants to read the unauthorized translations of the Bible for fear that the differing renditions may lead the readers astray or weaken their faith in the validity of the Church's dogma and pronouncements. The daily reading and study of the approved translations, however, were not only countenanced but encouraged." He referred me to the statements of Pope Pius VI and Pope Benedict XV.

Later I looked up the reference. Pope Pius VI wrote April (1778) to the Archbishop of Florence:

"At a time when a great many books which grossly attack the Catholic religion are being circulated—you judge exceedingly well that the faithful should be urged to read the Holy Scriptures."

Another Pope Benedict (XV) in his Encyclical on St. Jerome quotes his admonition, "Love the Bible and wisdom will love you: love it and it will preserve you, honor it and it will embrace you." This is followed by another of St. Jerome's quotations wherein he exhorted his pupils to "read the Bible assiduously" adding; "No one can fail to see what profit and sweet tranquility must result in well disposed souls from a devout reading of the Bible."

He resumed, "As to man's need of the Church, that is conditioned on what the Church deems is her major objective. If she will conceive her *primary* role to function as an agency through which an impalpable bliss in a hereafter can be obtained then her scope and appeal, I believe, are bound to shrink. Man has become dominantly concerned with his weal and security *here on earth*. Fear of what will happen to his soul after it leaves its mortal abode, the body, is becoming less and less a factor in the quest of the good and abundant life. And this disposition may be a felicitous sign. For the increased emphasis on the ethical and social aspects of religion, instead of on its creedal assumptions and dogmatic promulgations, will make the modern aware of the pertinence and value of a commitment to the

Church and what it advocates in order to develop our better
natures and exalt our inter-personal (man to fellowman)
relationships. He then proceeded to list the specific interests and concerns of the Church, the Synagogue and the
Mosque. They were,

1. The cultivation of a sense of the abiding Presence of
   God with whom Man can directly commune.
2. The realization by Man of his unique relationship and
   kinship with the Divine.
3. A perception of the wondrous aspects of natural phenomena whose mystery scientific explanations are impotent to penetrate and decipher.
4. An awareness of the sacredness of life.
5. The exemplification by Man of the sovereignty of
   moral principles by which alone man attests to God's
   Reality. For in striving after what is right and just
   and good and noble we mirror the Divine within us."

"In proposing such a program for the Church, are you
not," I asked, "depriving it of an exclusive prerogative and
a claim to finality?"

"Yes, that seems to be so. Religions will have diminish-
ingly valid grounds to contend that they have a monopoly
on religious truths and moral virtues. They will all have
like roles or no role at all. They will all have to stand as
equals before God and pose as equals before Man."

"Do you maintain," I continued, "that the theological
avowals of each Faith are to be identical? In your scheme
will not the distinctive features of each religion evaporate
and leave a residue of sameness?"

"That need not be so," he reflected. "Religions may have
a common conceptual basis, yet some may stress certain
ideals and aspects while others may place the emphasis on
different ones. Take for example, the alleged accent which
Judaism gives to the attribute of Justice and Christianity
gives to Love. If the claim is warranted then each comple-
ments the other and each suffers without the opposite.

"Religion is not solely a cognitive endeavor, the attempt

of the mind to comprehend God. It is also a psychologic phenomenon, an emotional drive in man for spiritual security in a vast and indifferent and at times unfriendly universe. In the emotional expression of religion ethnic differences, cultural diversities and variations of environmental conditions (which cover climate, the kind and sufficiency of food available, impact of historic happenings) will not be downed."

"Do you mean that an individual may consider one religion as good as the other and feel free to don or doff them as he would pieces of clothing?"

"That also doesn't follow. In a democratic society, it must be admitted, no religion can maintain an unyielding grip on its members if and when they feel indisposed to follow the footsteps of their forbears. The relationship of a communicant to his denomination and faith is to an extent comparable to the relationship of a wedded couple. In sects and communions where divorce is forbidden, separation is not proscribed to an incompatible couple. And where divorce is not outlawed the groundless and wilfull sundering of marital ties is not tolerated in civilized communities. The truly faithful despite the legitimacy of separation and divorce deem the union binding until death doth them part. The prayer in our 'grace after meals' where we offer thanks to God 'for the covenant which Thou hast sealed in our flesh' is meant to convey that connotation. In fact, those who are happily wedded consider their mate the best or most adorable creature in the world. They would, however, expose themselves to censure and social ostracism if they went further and declared that beside their sweetheart all others are hags."

"How do the views you have just voiced dovetail with your previously stated views?"

"As I already mentioned my derogation of some of the assumptions and ambitions of the Church was not prompted by hostility. On the contrary I am moved by a friendly disposition to point out what seems to me to have been the Church's failings. I believe that the Church can serve Man and God better when it will cease to emulate Caesarism and what it implies. It will also serve God and Man better when it will not consider itself an Impeccable Institution. It will then be disposed to assess its acts and pronouncements more critically and frequently. On the Day of Atonement the High Priest in the ancient Temple implored God's forgiveness for his people only after he importuned the Almighty to wipe away his own sins and those of his household, the sons of Aaron. 'Confession is good for the soul' is an accepted dictum. That applies to an institution no less than to an individual. Confession, however, requires an awareness of sin. And a bona fide awareness of sin is the product of introspection and self-criticism. One who is inured or brave enough to scrutinize his own actions will not be prone to lay the blame for the evil that has befallen him at the door of others, even the malefactors. He will discover causes for the misfortune within himself. This should be especially the case with religiously-minded persons who believe that a Judge weighs the actions of men and nations, and that events do not happen by chance and have no moral aim. Justice, the religionist affirms, is due to catch up with those who are guilty of misdeeds.

"In the last four decades the Church has suffered staggering defections. I shall not mention a waning of regard and homage on the part of a multitude who are but lukewarm or nominal adherents. I have in mind rather the repudiation and the withdrawal of support from the Church by the governments of Poland, Czechoslovakia, Hungary, and to a lesser extent by the regimes of other countries.[3]

"In the face of such ordeals and calamities, it is not enough to brand the political cliques that are responsible for the upheaval as godless revolutionists, veritable agents of Satan, or to be content with calling the pious to pray for the penitence and change of heart of the evil doers. One must place the mirror before one's soul and microscopically examine all one's past deeds and disposition, and endeavor to uncover the mistakes and errors which henceforth are to be avoided."

"How about the Jews?" I interjected. "They too have incurred frightful losses. Six million have been wiped out. Do they direct their gaze within and endeavor to ferret out their covert and overt transgressions which could have been partly responsible for the unspeakable tragedies?"

A painful expression settled on the countenance of the Yeshiva Student as he haltingly replied to my question in a tone which gave unmistakable evidence that his soul was heavy and sad.

"When Rome put an end to the Judean State, and torches kindled flames which enveloped and destroyed the Sanctuary in Jerusalem and tens of thousands of men, women and children were mercilessly slain by maddened soldiers and the rest of the population were sent into exile or taken captive, the Sages were not disposed to account for the catastrophe by referring to the malevolence and brutality of Rome. They looked within their souls and reappraised their acts and attitudes. And they arrived at the conclusion that their tribulation and suffering were heaven-sent punishment for their moral callousness and spiritual deficiencies.

" 'On account of our sins were we exiled from our land' was their penitent admission. And not only did they re-examine the course the nation had followed but each individual was made to feel that his personal misconduct adversely affected the fate of his people. The Rabbis asked the question, 'Why was the land destroyed?' and they gave a series of answers nearly all involving misdeeds of individuals.[4] Perceiving the purging effects of wholesome self-criticism the Rabbis devised a formula which they believed could stave off an impending calamity.

"If a man sees trouble coming upon him let him examine closely his conduct (whether he is guilty of sins of commission). If he discovers nothing that was wrong, then let him consider whether he has neglected the study of the Torah (whether he is guilty of sins of omission). If he does not find himself derelict in this respect then may he consider that his sufferings are chastisements of love.[5]

"It was such spiritual inventories following national disasters that enabled Jews to transform the tragedies into moral triumphs.

"The grievous calamities and colossal casualties which Jewry suffered in recent decades makes all the previous ordeals seem puny by comparison. And no voice ringingly cries out exhorting Jewry to turn their gaze inward and endeavor to reassess their former hopes and goals. Not a whisper of penitential lament emanates from the synagogues. The absence of that appeal in the cacophonous shouts that are heard in the camp of modern Israel—alarm me.

"On the Day of Atonement Jews in the synagogues vociferously chant the sentence in the liturgy.

"*'And repentance, prayer, and charity avert the evil decree.'*

"I understand that the passage is retained even in the prayer books of Liberal Jews and that it is recited in unison with the Rabbi leading.

"Jews, it seems to me, are prodigious with charity (*tsedaka*), parsimonious with prayers (*tefilla*) and petrous in their response to even feeble calls to repentance—(*teshuvah*)."

Part IV

GERMANY IN COURT

Chapter 1

THE SUMMONS

"He that judges without informing himself to the utmost that he is capable, cannot acquit himself of judging amiss."
JOHN LOCKE

BEFORE the suspected and indicted are convicted or acquitted an enlightened public demands that as much data as can be mustered pertaining to the background and mental make-up of the culprit shall be made available to the judge and jury. In such a court of justice the aid of social workers and psychiatrists is sought. They uncover the early character-marring incidents of the defendant, the factors which engendered his ambitions, the temptations with which he had to wrestle, the frustrations which embittered his soul and the deceptions which blunted and blighted his perspectives.

Such knowledge is essential in determining the degree of guilt or non-guilt of the accused. With such data we are enabled to answer the pertinent queries:

1. Did the guilty know what they were doing?
2. Were they aware that their deeds were iniquitous?
3. To what extent are they to be credited with an ability to pursue an alternate course?

Justice is personified by the figure of a tall graceful blindfolded woman holding aloft balanced scales. The deprivation of sight is to indicate that Justice is not a respecter of persons. Equal justice is to be rendered to rich and poor, to the eminent and to the lowly, to friend and to foe, to native and to stranger.[1] As to the discernment of the facts which brought about the act, Justice must not only be open-eyed but must microscopically examine all evidence which accounts for or may extenuate the misdeed. True

Justice is tempered with mercy. The Rabbis assert that the names (YHWH and Elohim) given to God each connote one of the above attributes.

Chapter 2

A NATION'S CHARACTER IS NOT PREDETERMINED

> *"As some divinely gifted man,*
> *Whose life in low estate began,*
> *And on a simple village green;*
> *Who breaks his birth's invidious bar."* TENNYSON

AMONG the important discoveries in the story of the evolution of science were primitive man's observation that sparks ensue when two hard substances are rubbed against one another which can start a fire, and the invention of the wheel coupled with the conclusion that the attachment of wheels to a vehicle would facilitate and accelerate transportation.

The discoveries of fire and the wheel seem obvious and trivial when compared with modern inventions. Yet without the discoveries of fire and the wheel subsequent inventions would have been impossible.

The ethical advance which the 'lex talionis' signified has been obscured by the unwarranted low appraisal which has been attributed to the Scriptural command "a life for a life, an eye for an eye, a tooth for a tooth."

First it should be noted that the 'lex talionis' is admittedly a horrible form of punishment when taken literally. Where capital punishment is practiced, one may say that the lex talionis has not been abolished. Many contend it has not been effective in deterring the commission of crime. Instead of cultivating a more wholesome disposition on the part of the guilty, the taking of an "eye for an eye" cannot but poison the mind of the punished against society and its agencies of justice.

All these defects, however, must not blind us to the fact that the practice is the outgrowth of man's yearning for justice, crude as the procedure may be. It is the product of a realization of man's right to live unmolested. Without such disposition and intuitive realization civilized society, reared on concepts of divine justice and divine law, would vanish.

The *lex talionis* in the Bible is not so much a prescription of *what to do* in a specific situation as a prescription of *what not to do*. It is intended to rule out the infliction of excessive retribution upon the wrong-doer and to check the disposition on the part of kin to indulge in continuing family feuds and tribal vendettas.[1]

Israel Zangwill's observation merits quotation here. "Compare 'a tooth for a tooth,' with 'a life for a sheep' which was British law little more than a century ago, at which period indeed no fewer than 200 misdemeanors were punishable with death." [2]

The Scriptural law (eye for an eye) makes the *amplification* and *extension* of the penalty a violation of Divine Justice. *It thus affirms the principle, fundamental in the procedure of justice, that punishment must fit the crime and that the infliction of punishment should be confined as far as possible, to the criminal.*

During the war with Germany and for some years after the war, Germans, all Germans, were daubed as being an innately cruel and warlike people. The German, it was said, looks upon the world as an arena and life as a contest. There is something in the blood of the German, it is maintained, which makes him thrill at the sight of men arrayed in uniforms marching with precision to the strains of martial music. His proclivity to militarism and his complacency with the cruelties which war entails are not something which he acquired but are endemic to his nature and psychic make-up. How else is one to explain the apotheosis of war not merely by German generals but also by their eminent philosophers and historians?

The supposition that militarism is ingrained and congenital in the German character is responsible for the widespread fear that Germany is bound to make another try to dominate the continent of Europe, if not the world, when she again feels herself strong enough for the exploit. To prevent her from going berserk a third time, men with political experience and students of international affairs (like Lord Vansittart) deem it prudent that Germany be kept disarmed and that her industrial potential, which could easily be converted to the making of guns and tanks, should be restricted.

To contend that a people is biologically and prenatally conditioned to a particular mode of behavior or belief is to affirm the vile and discredited racial myth which Chamberlain and Hitler espoused. No microscopic examination, however, has revealed any difference between the protoplasmic cells or blood corpuscles of an African Hottentot and a member of any elite circle of Europe or America. Anthropologists and sociologists all agree (and their agreement is based on vast research and cogent reasoning) that individuals and groups are not born mean or magnanimous, militant or pacific, defiant or obedient. Heredity may dispose one to act in a certain way, but the decisive factor is the physical environment and cultural milieu in which the individual or group moves. This involves creeds and ideals with which one was imbued, the social patterns which one found or adopted, and the economic interests which one identified with one's welfare. If the Germans are to be branded as a singularly arrogant and aggressive people, they were not born but bred that way. (It is interesting to note that after the dazzling mammoth but abortive military exploits of Napoleon, the very same charge had been levelled against the French.) *Given proper and wholesome surroundings and cultural stimuli and sufficient time, may not the German be reoriented and induced to slough off his alleged inborn disposition to be militaristic?*

A historic survey of the vicissitudes which the dwellers of the section of Europe now called Germany had to face may help to account for their amenability to military indoctrination. Vanquished by the legions of Caesar, who extended the rule of Rome as far north as Britain, overwhelmed by the invasion of the ferocious Huns of Asia, pillaged and plundered by the hordes of Attila, broken and fragmented into districts and petty states and made vassals to feudal lords and barons, reduced to a dependency and made the corridor to Russia by the advancing armies of Napoleon, and then suddenly to find themselves under Bismarck welded into a strong nation capable not only of warding off attacks but even of engaging in wars of conquest and creating for themselves an era of enviable prosperity—such a gamut of experience and swift acquisition of so much power and prestige is enough to dazzle and to intoxicate any but the most spiritually-minded people with its own worth and importance and imagined universal destiny.

The accolades of Bernhardi, Von Moltke, Nietzsche and Treitschke irk us even though their evaluations are not without some grain of truth. There are individuals, we must admit, for whom the encountering of hazards and the waging of battles bring out the latent heroic element in their make-up. Even if this were to apply to every participant in a war [and it doesn't, for war converts many into brutes and beasts], we still should despise war because the moral as well as the material cost far outweighs the supposed beneficent results.

Before we make the statements of some German jingoists the basis of a conclusion that the Germans are endemically a bellicose people we should counterbalance the statements with the universalistic and humanistic pronouncements of Germans of the stature of Goethe, Kant, and Thomas Mann. We should also ask ourselves whether exaltations of war are restricted to Germans. Were Nicolo Machiavelli and Thomas Hobbes Germans? Far from uncomplimentary appraisals of the latter's views were penned by Edmund Burke and Jonathan Swift. Both were born in Ireland and were of Irish stock. In *Vindication of Natural Society*, Burke wrote, 'War,' says Machiavelli, 'ought to be the only study of a prince' and by a prince he means every sort of state, however constituted. "He ought to consider peace only as a breathing-time, which gives him leisure to contrive, and furnishes ability to execute military plans." [3]

In the poem titled "A Rhapsody," Swift wrote, "Hobbes clearly proves that every creature was in a state of war by nature." [4]

I also cannot refrain from wondering whether something akin to the above estimates of war is not implicit in Sigmund Freud's reply to the letter of Albert Einstein on the subject, "Why War?"

"No single all embracing judgement can be passed on these wars of aggrandisement. Some, like the war between the Mongols and the Turks, have led to unmitigated misery; others, however, have furthered the transition from violence to law, since they brought larger units into being, within whose limits a recourse to violence was banned and a new regime determined all disputes. Thus the Roman conquests brought that boon, the *pax romana* to the Mediterranean lands. The French Kings' lust for aggrandisement created a new France, flourishing in peace and unity. Paradoxical as it sounds, we must admit that warfare well might serve to pave the way to that unbroken peace we so desire, for it is war that brings vast empires into being within whose frontiers all warfare is proscribed by a strong central power.

"Thus it would seem that any effort to replace brute force by the might of an ideal is, under present conditions, doomed to fail. Our logic is at fault if we ignore the fact that right is founded on brute force and even today needs violence to maintain it."

"You are amazed," continued Freud's letter to Einstein, "that it is so easy to infect men with war fever and you surmise that man has in him an active instinct for hatred and destruction, amenable to such stimulations. I entirely agree with you. I believe in the existence of this instinct and have been recently at pains to study its manifestations. In this connection may I set out a fragment of that knowledge of the instincts, which we psychoanalysts, after so many tentative essays and gropings in the dark, have compassed? We assume that human instincts are of two kinds, those that conserve and unify—and—the instincts to destroy and kill, which we assimilate as the aggressive or destructive instincts. Each of these instincts is every whit as indispensable as its opposite and all the phenomena of life derive from their activity, whether they work in concert or in opposition.

"That men are divided into leaders and the led is but another manifestation of their inborn and irremediable inequality. The second class constitutes the vast majority, they need a high command to make decisions for them, to which decisions they usually bow without demur." [5]

There are substantial differences between the quoted views of Von Moltke, Nietzsche, Treitschke, and Freud, besides the fact that the former are rhapsodic and glorify war and the latter is but analytic and avowedly objective. All the differences, whether they be explicit or implicit, must not be ignored or minimized. However both evaluations seem to me to tend in one direction and their pragmatic results, I fear, may be identical.

Freud would have recoiled from considering Hitler's way of carrying on warfare as fit to be classified with those which prevailed between the nations of Europe. Some of Freud's disciples, notably Eric Fromm, would offer an etiology of war and an evaluation of its results which would totally disagree with those propounded by Freud.

Whether my perception of some similarity between the appraisals of war by the designated Germans and Freud are justified or not, one would be laughed at if one would venture to assert with certitude or even to suggest that Freud's views and those of the author of Psalm 144 and the Song of the Israelites at the Red Sea have been determined not by reflections influenced by environment and vicissitudes, but by the tissues of their bodies and the blood that courses in their veins, both of which are a racial heritage which, it would be contended, cannot be shaken off.

Chapter 3

FAITH AND OBEDIENCE MAY ALSO TURN SOUR

"It is always right that a man be made to render a reason for the faith that is within him." SIDNEY SMITH

"One so small and knowing nothing knows but to obey." TENNYSON

A CONCEALED factor which may be termed a secondary cause of the moral blackout that debased the regimes of Hitler and Mussolini, was (and still is) the disposition of totalitarian governments to over-extol *faith* and *obedience* and to make them paramount virtues. (Lest I be misunderstood I wish to underscore the fact that I do not maintain that this tendency provoked or brought into being the nefarious regimes of Nazism and Fascism. It only conditioned the minds of the Germans and Italians to be receptive to the promise of the Nazis and Fascists when the situation seemed propitious for the presentation and implementation of their ideologies.)

An examination of the genesis and varied connotations which the terms *faith* and *obedience* acquired in the course of time will reveal the modification of and degree of distortion from the original to which the terms were subjected.

In the apotheosis of *faith* and *obedience* the followers of Jesus, I contend, drastically altered the meaning which those words had with the preacher of Galilee, to whom the terms had no different connotation from that which they had in the writings of the Old Testament. This transformation of the original meaning and over exaltation of their new significance proved to be alluring to those who sought domination of and absolute rule.

To support this contention I propose (1) to examine the

meaning attached to the words by Paul and his like-minded confreres, which meaning persisted and still persists in current (Christian theological) thinking, (2) to examine the contrasting meaning which these words have in the Old Testament and in the *authentic* utterances of Jesus.

When the divergence in meanings of the above terms in the early and in the later writings of the New Testament is exposed its implications for human behavior (e.g., the imperative to heed the dictates of reason and conscience and the duty to oppose tyranny and political malfeasance) will become apparent.

The term "faith" (or belief) may be used to designate *an emotional disposition* or *an intellectual avowal*. As *an emotional disposition* it aims to convey a sense of reliability or assuredness which a person has with regard to something or someone. This quality of feeling is not imposed from without but is engendered in and proceeds from the inner recesses of the believer's soul. As *an intellectual affirmation* it represents an assent of the mind induced by an authority external to it to which the mind deems it must submit.[1] (Those who maintain that faith involves a cerebral process may justify the endorsement of the specified dogma or dogmas as a reasonable act. They will, however, admit that without the mandate or warrant of the authority the likelihood of the mind's confirmation or ratification of the article of belief would be slim.)

The words "faith" and "belief" connote in the Jewish Scriptures almost exclusively trust, fidelity and constancy. They signify an attitude of relationship and a disposition of confidence, either of the being in whom trust is reposed or of the person who maintains and exemplifies the disposition.

B. B. Warfield, a noted Protestant theologian, describes the believer ('*Maamin*') in the Old Testament as "one whose state of mind is free from faint-heartedness (Isa. 7a and anxious haste (Isa. 28:16) and who stays himself upon the object of his contemplation with confidence and trust. The implication seems to be, not so much that of a passive dependence, as of a vigorous active commitment. He who, in the Hebrew sense, exercised faith is secure, assured, confident (Deut. 28:66, Job. 24:22, Ps. 27:15) and lays hold of the object of his confidence with firm trust." [2]

To believe in God in the Old Testament sense is not so much an intellectual avowal of the existence of God (which only a fool would deny, Ps. XIV:1, and Ps. LIII:2) as it implies to rest in the security and trustfulness upon God, with firm and unwavering confidence.

When we turn to the New Testament and study the meaning of the words "faith" and "belief" in their contextual setting we discern, as we proceed from the early writings (Matthew, Mark and Luke) to the later compositions (John, the Letters of Paul and the Johannine Epistles) that these words are endowed with new and extended connotations.[3]

The terms "faith" and "belief" preponderatingly continue to convey, in the early writings, the meaning of trust, constancy, unfailing solicitude and goodness of God or the sense of assurance in His promise of ultimate deliverance from oppressors or from the inner anguish of a guilt-stricken conscience. We also find, sporadically in earlier and more prevalently in later books, connotations which are other than indices of emotional intensity or a sense of identification or close relationship. The words "faith" and "belief," in these passages, have a cognitive signification. They imply intellectual assent, the mental attestation to the occurrence of an event or subscription to the affirmed nature of a being or thing which is universally known to be contrary to experience or the norms of rational thought.[4]

The added or extended meaning is more than implicit in passages such as:

"Faith is the substance of things hoped for, the evidence of things not seen" [5]
"Your faith should not stand in the wisdom of men, but in the power of God" [6]
"We walk by faith not by sight" [7]

"—that is the word of faith which we preach, that if thou shalt confess with thy mouth the Lord Jesus and shalt be-

lieve in thine heart that God hath raised him from the dead,
thou shalt be saved" [8]

> "Whom God hath set forth to be a propitiation through faith
> in his blood" [9]
> "To him give all the prophets witness that through his name,
> whosoever believeth in him shall receive remission of
> sins" [10]
> "One Lord, one faith, one baptism" [11]

The unequal frequency of the terms "faith" and "belief"
between the two Testaments is also noteworthy. The noun
and the verb occur in the New Testament about 480 times
(each about 240 times). This is in marked contrast to the
Jewish Scriptures where the terms are found only about
18 times. In the latter they are found in but 13 books while
in the New Testament they appear in nearly all the 27 divisions.

We see in the New Testament stages of extended meanings that are given to the term "faith" (also "belief").
Faith, as a feeling of trust in God's unremitting solicitude
for each human being (an attitude that can be fostered by
observing the lilies of the field and the sparrows in
the sky) [12] acquires a meaning of unwavering confidence in
the fulfillment of alleged promises made by the Old Testament Prophets relative to the advent and mission of Jesus,
the Messiah. Faith also spells the acceptance of the current
belief in the power of the Galilean to heal the sick and perform miraculous deeds. Faith came to connote also a con-
currence in the supposition, grown to a conviction, that
Jesus' death was an atonement for sin. In later writing it
was identified with belief in the divine nature of Jesus and
his singular and unmatched kinship with God of whose being Jesus was an indivisible part or aspect. Capping all these
connotations "faith" was equated with the belief that Christ
promulgated the Creed and founded the Church which was
the sole and only door to salvation and eternal bliss in the
hereafter. Jesus saith unto him (Thomas), "I am the Way,
the Truth and the Life; no man cometh unto the Father but
by me." [13]

When we examine the meaning attributed to the terms "faith" and "belief" by the foremost expositors of Christianity following the authors and compilers of the New Testament we see that they, even to a greater extent, accented the cognitive and mental connotation over the emotional and affectional. They spelt out and made clear the definition of faith as "the substance of things to be hoped for, the evidence of things that appear not." [14]

"Quod est enim fides nisi credere quod non vides?" "What is faith but belief in that which thou seest not?", was St. Augustine's rhetorical query and answer. "Faith," he continues, "has its eyes by which it in some sort sees that to be true which it does not yet see; and by which too, it most surely sees that it does not see what it believes."

"Faith has the character of a virtue," writes Thomas Aquinas, "not because of the things it believes, for faith is of things that appear not, but because it adheres to the testimony of one in whom truth is infallibly found." In another place he says "the arguments which induce us to believe, e.g., miracles, do not prove the faith itself, but only the truthfulness of him who declares it to us, and consequently they do not beget knowledge of faith's mysteries, but only faith.

"If anyone says that the assent of Christian faith is not free, but that it necessarily follows from the arguments which human reason can furnish in its favor, or if anyone says that God's grace is only necessary for that living faith which worketh through charity, let him be anathema," was the pronouncement of a Vatican Council (Sess. IV).

The incentive of faith is the reward of eternal life and the propelling force of faith is a will steeled and habituated to believe.

"The disposition of a believer is that of one who accepts another's word for some statement, because it seems fitting or useful to do so. In the same way we believe Divine revelation because the reward of eternal life is promised us for so doing. It is the will which is moved by the prospect of this reward to assent to what is said, even *though the intellect is not moved by something which it understands.*

Hence St. Augustine says: 'other things a man can do against his will, but to believe he must will.' "

Thomas' definition of "faith" as a religious and Christian doctrine is therefore "the act of the intellect assenting to a Divine truth owing to the movement of the will, which is itself moved by the Grace of God."

In man's striving for goodness, moral perfection or redemption the Fathers of the Church and the Medieval Christian theologians maintain that the doctrine of the essentiality of Divine Grace is inherent in the admonition of Jesus, "ask and you shall receive." This is in marked contrast to the Rabbinic dictum, "Everything is in the hands of heaven except the fear of Heaven." [15]

This conception of the essence of Faith and the dogmatic nature of the New Creed as well as the hierarchical organization of its representatives necessitated that subordination to men in authority be also extolled and deemed a superlative virtue. "Obedience" becomes a corollary to faith."

In the early writings of the New Testament exhortation to be obedient to external authority, in fact the very word obedience, is notably rare.[16]

When we come to the Epistles and Discourses of Paul we find him admonishing the wives to be obedient to their husbands[17] and servants to their masters.[18] In his Epistle to the Hebrews he urges his followers "to obey them that have the rule over you and submit yourself." [19]

As Christianity became the official State-Sponsored Faith with the multiplication, organization and self-government of its priesthood and as religious orders sprang into being which attracted vast numbers of men and women who sought the seclusion, shelter and self-surrender of a life in a convent or monastery, submission and obedience to those in authority, temporal as well as ecclesiastical, were deemed not only desirable but also the highest attestation of devotion and piety. Theoretically, limitation of allegiance due to temporal rulers was recognized. Actually, it was difficult to determine when the policy of watchful waiting and praying for correction of an abuse of power should give way to outright opposition and rebellion. The doctrine of

non-resistance to evil [20] the exhortation to pray "for kings
and for all that are in authority," [21] as well as Paul's clear
injunction "Obey them that have rule over you and submit
yourselves" [22] could always be invoked to make dubious the
obvious.

What obedience in a religious sense implied during the
Middle Ages and what it implies to the devotees of the
Roman Church may be seen from the statements of Prof.
Arthur Vermeersch, S.J., LL.D.

"The vow of obedience in the institutes approved by the
Holy See is held more and more to be made equally to the
Pope, who communicated his authority to the Roman con-
gregations entrusted with the direction of religious orders.
The superiors of the different orders, when they are clerics
and exempt from episcopal jurisdiction, similarly receive
a part of this authority and everyone who is placed at the
head of a community is invested with the domestic authority
necessary for the good government; the vow by which the
religious offers to God the obedience which he promises to
his superiors confirms and defines this authority.

"By reason of the vow of obedience and of the religious
profession a deliberate act of obedience and submission adds
merit of an act of the virtue of religion to the other merits
of the act." [23]

This is how Prof. Arthur Vermeersch justifies the disposition.

"*Philosophically* religious obedience is justified: (a) by
the experience of the mistakes and illusions to which a man
relying on his own unaided opinions is liable. The religious
proposes to rule his whole life by devotion to God and his
neighbor; how shall he best realize this ideal? By regulating
all his actions by his own judgment, or by choosing a prudent and enlightened guide who will give his advice without any consideration of himself? Is it not clear that the latter alternative shows a resolution more sincere, more generous, and at the same time more likely to lead to a successful
issue? The obedience is justified also (b) by the help of example and counsel afforded by community life and the acceptance of a rule of conduct the holiness of which is

vouched for by the Church; (c) lastly, since the object of
religious orders is not only the perfection of their members
but also the performance of spiritual and corporal works
of mercy, they need a union of effort which can only be
assured by religious obedience, just as military obedience is
indispensable for success in the operations of war.

"The expression 'blind obedience' signified not an un-
reasoning or unreasonable submission to authority, but a
keen appreciation of the right of authority, the reasonableness of submission, and blindness only to such selfish or
worldly considerations as would lessen regard for authority." [24]

*As a result of our study of the meanings of the words
"faith" and "obedience" in the New Testament we behold
Jesus, the individualist, the non-conformist and anti-au-
thoritarian transformed and made the foundation of an
Ideology and a Discipline which tended to subordinate, if
not totally to suppress the sincere, spontaneous thoughts,
feelings and actions of his devotees. From those who aspire
to emulate his life there was demanded a regimentation of
belief and an undeviating compliance with a promulgated
set of rules.*

*With a reverence for such a disposition and mood a politi-
cal spellbinder had few formidable obstacles to overcome to
induce the masses to goosestep physically as well as men-
tally, or to have them shout the Fascist motto: "Credere,
obedire, combatire," with the fervour of the Doxology.*

Judaism unfailingly emphasized that genuine Faith must
conform to and be confirmed by Reason and the Laws of
Nature. Miracles may not be invoked to warrant the acceptance of doctrines. Their reasonableness, their beneficence
and compatibility with time-tested hallowed values were to
be the criteria of their validity. "Lying lips," asserted the
author of Proverbs, "are an abomination to the Lord. But
they that deal truly are his delights." [25] A pious fraud
was deemed utterly incongruous with God's character and
the Divine Commandments,[26] Israel's God was an *"el emes"*
a God of Truth.[27] He desireth truth even in the inward
parts.[28]

The invocation of the Psalmist was that he walk in the paths of God's Truth and Mercy. The ideal priest was he in whose mouth was the law of truth.[29] Even the King of Judah deemed it his duty to enjoin the prophet (Micaiah) "Tell me nothing in the name of the Lord but that which is true." [30]

The Rabbis of the Talmud asserted that "the seal of the Holy One Blessed be He was truth." [31] Rational deductions in the ascertainment of the Law or Divine will were not to be relinquished even if a heavenly voice (Bath Kol) admonished that a contrary view be followed.[32]

What a difference there is between Maimonides rationale for subscribing to Scriptural doctrine and that of St. Thomas! To the latter there were two realms, the one of religion and the one of philosophy. Each had its distinctive and separate criterion for truth. What was deemed true in religion stood in no need of substantiation by the insights or tenets of philosophy.

To Maimonides this position was untenable, and this was most clearly evident in the reasons he gave for rejecting the Aristotelian notion of the eternity of matter, in preference to the Scriptural doctrine of "creatio ex nihilo." The former posed more difficulties. Had the reverse been the case Maimonides asserts that he would have been prone to adopt the view of the Stagirite philosopher. As to "creatio ex nihilo" of Scripture, that lent itself easily to a reinterpretation.

As for obedience it is significant that the Old Testament avoids enjoining upon the son to be obedient and submissive even to his parents. "*Honor* thy father and mother," the Decalogue stipulates. *There is not even a word in the vocabulary of Judaism which can exclusively and specifically mean obedience. The word that is used to connote obedience is "Shema" which means (1) to hear, (2) to heed and also (3) to understand, but never to submit to an external power for whatever reason.*[33]

Job is a hero in Jewish tradition. The Rabbis of the Talmud included his words in the Canon, even though his Promethean challenge of and charges against God have a blasphemous ring about them. The reason for their inclusion was that they were prompted by a sense of integrity and a genuine seeking for an understanding of the way of the Almighty. His submission came not before but after his bold intellectual venture.

When Jesus cried out on the Cross—"God, My God, why hast thou forsaken me?"—and only afterwards resignedly gave vent to "Father into thy hands I commit my spirit," he was in consonance with the disposition and demeanor evidenced at times by Abraham, Moses, Jeremiah, Job and the Psalmist.

A recently released film purported to reproduce the moods and behavior of Hitler and his trusted henchmen during the last ten days of his evil regime. We see in the fortified mammoth bunkers beneath the Reich Chancellery generals and lieutenants caparisoned in their military garb studying war maps and plotting retreats and shifts of the waning Nazi reinforcements. The brooding and raving Hitler is now patently demented. He is deaf to any hint that the hour of total defeat is nearing. He refuses to relinquish his faith in his intuition, bolstered by the predictions of his astrologer, that destiny was bound to turn the wheel of fortune to his advantage.

Everyone is aware of the inevitability of the approaching doom. Nevertheless they all undeviatingly carry out the Fuehrer's cruel and senseless orders. When an evanescent sense of compunction manages to reach their moribund conscience they drown the moral stirrings with swallows of cognac. Those of lower rank seek forgetfulness in dancing and sexual excitation with so-called patriotic women who have been quartered in the bunkers for just such purposes.

One newly arrived young officer, surveying the utter disregard for life on the part of Hitler and the moral bluntness and weakness of his confidants and misnamed advisers, dares to voice his criticism of their procedure. As a result he is fatally wounded and as he dies he proffers a last admonition to those who are attending to his wounds. "Never, never," he mumbles, "say 'yes, sir!' again."

The last testament of this erstwhile devotee of Hitler was a warning of a disillusioned and perhaps repentant man against the disposition of his countrymen to repose limitless faith in the unerring goodness and wisdom of any mortal man and to render unquestioning obedience to any human being.

Chapter 4

THE SANCTUARY BECOMES THE CITADEL

"For, behold, I have made thee this day a fortified city, and an iron pillar, and brazen walls, against the whole land— And they shall war against thee: but they shall not prevail against thee; For I am with thee, saith the Lord, to deliver thee" JER. I:18-19

"And I say unto thee, that thou art Peter, and upon this rock I will build my church; and the gates of hell shall not prevail against it" MATT. XVI:18

ABRAHAM'S intercession in behalf of the few righteous individuals who, he supposed, could be found in Sodom and Gomorrah and his argumentative colloquy with the Almighty on the unfairness of a mode of retribution which spelt the indiscriminate destruction of the righteous with the wicked, which colloquy he climaxed with his thundering query, "Shall not the Judge of all the earth do justly?" [1] —is one of the most sublime and stirring passages in all literature.

The prophet Ezekiel, many centuries later, espoused a like concept of justice. The context varied, but the theme remained the same. Ezekiel was not bent on staving off an imminent catastrophe which threatened to engulf the innocent with the guilty. He pleaded for the recognition of conditions and principles and criteria which would shield innocent children from the stigma and suffering which they had to bear because of the transgressions of their parents. He argued not with the Deity but with the people, who entertained contrary views. He supported his plea with the avowal of belief that his doctrine had the sanction of the Almighty. The concept of Justice implied to him the careful meting out of due retribution but to the transgressors. In the period between Abraham and Ezekiel, the concept of Justice had significantly advanced.[2]

The attribution of Nazi wickedness to every German and the consequent justification of identical culpability and retribution to each German is not only unfair but also un-Jewish. Despite the insidious poison that was eating its way into every phase of German life, some spots remained unassailable. In pronouncing judgment on the Germans we must not ignore the contrary and redeemable aspects. When the weight of the sins of that people plummeted one side of the scales downward as far as it could go, we must not assume that the other scale was bare and totally empty.

We have seen that in the last bonafide election of March 5, 1933, which came on the heels of President Hindenberg's calamitous invitation to Hitler to become the Chancellor, the Nazis failed to obtain a majority of the votes cast. They obtained the necessary majority (444 to 94), it should be noted, only after Nazi hooligans had prevented 112 of the opposition (81 Communists and 31 Social Democrats) from attending the Reichstag sessions. The 94 who voted solidly against the request were Social Democrats who were allowed or managed to be present at the sessions. To obtain the 444 votes Hitler had to resort to deceit and false promises to lure the 74 constituents of the Center Party, the 52 members of the Nationalist Front, the 18 votes of the Bavarian Peoples Party and the 9 votes of the other units.[3]

'You are what you eat' we are told by dietitians. The same may be said to be true with regard to the food which the mind craves. Subject one to an unvaried and monotonous diet and he will become debilitated and flabby. In a totalitarian state the information that is made available to the populace is restricted and doctored, if not utterly distorted and falsified. The result of subsisting on such pablum is a dulled and deadened mental state. The individual acquires a mood of resignation and fatalism or he may become a victim of hypnosis and uncritically and unresistingly do whatever is suggested to him.

Even if an individual can withstand the bombardment of propaganda and the impact of one-sided versions and maintain his mental autonomy, he would imperil his life and limb if he would express open disagreement with the ruling clique which is armed with power and has no scruples about using it to crush any incipient opposition. Some individuals may be defiant and heroic to the point of martyrdom. It is however unrealistic to expect the ordinary run of men to rise to such heights.

I had a taste of what it was to sojourn, even in time of peace, in a country which was on the verge of becoming a totalitarian state. It was my lot to have spent part of the summer of 1936 in Roumania. Goga, who aspired to be in Roumania what Hitler had been in Germany, had not yet become the country's Premier. The Iron Guard, a band of young Fascists, were not yet accorded the recognition and privileged status which the Storm Troopers had in the Reich. They were not even a uniformed unit indoctrinated with the tenet that unqualified obedience was due to the leader of their party which one day would rule the State. Force and lawlessness were not openly accepted as indispensable political weapons. There was as yet no iron-clad censorship and proscription of anti-Fascistic newspapers and journals. And yet fear and dread were so infectious that for practical purposes a program of repression had already set in and the thinking and feeling of the multitude unconsciously and unintentionally became vehemently, and one could say even ferociously, one-sided.

We have seen American prisoners of war released from the jails and stockades of North Korea who had been unable to shake off the effects of systematic and incessant propaganda of the Communists. We do not condemn them; we are disposed to pity these spongy, feeble and unresilient souls who succumbed to the pressure and the wiles of the enemy. We term them victims of brain washing. Now brain washing is not like an internal operation or a face-lifting of which procedure the patient is aware and to which he knowingly submits. It is like a sun-tan which is the result of painless exposure to the sun's rays. One doesn't in the process experience any poignant sensation at any time. However, after a prolonged period, one discovers that the pale or fair complexion has become dark and swarthy.

Loathsome and odious as the misdeeds of the promoters and executors of Nazism appear to us, so must the hazardous actions of the decent Germans be regarded by us to be grand and glorious. That there were not a few such Germans, despite the incessant pounding of propaganda, and the pain and peril to which they were subjected, has been indicated by the excellent study which was made by Paul Friedman, the results of which appeared in the Yivo Annual of Jewish Social Science (Vol. X 1955) under the title "Was There an 'Other Germany' during the Nazi Period?" This well-documented monograph, the prelude to a larger work, renders an affirmative reply to the question explicit and irresistible. That such a quest should have been pursued by a Jew and that the publication of the conclusion and supporting data should have been accorded space in a journal many supporters of which had lost all or some of their kin and kith in gas chambers and furnaces of the Nazis testifies to the Jew's passionate devotion to justice and fairness.

I shall venture to answer the question which Paul Friedman posed from inferences which are logically derived from many of the notations in the "Diaries of Goebbels."

Goebbels' entry under the date of February 17, 1942, wherein he voices his elation at the diminution of suicides is illuminating because it reveals what did take place as well as the hollow hypothesis which he proffered to account for the phenomenon. "Statistics on suicides show a decreasing curve. It looks indeed as though nobody wants voluntarily to depart this life. Everybody wants to live to see the end of the war, and rightly so, for it will surely be a joyful occasion for the entire people."

At that date the fortunes of war still smiled on Germany. The despair and disillusionment which drove many to com-

mit suicide very likely were the product of a realization of
the direction in which Germany was headed and their unwillingness to be identified with that shameful venture.

Goebbels states and repeats the view that the war presents
a matchlessly propitious time for the liquidation of the
Jews. It is to him now or never. Killing humans on a large
scale was an acceptable procedure at this moment. The
wholesale murder of Jews was made to appear as a just retribution for the initiation of the war which Hitler for
propaganda purposes imputed to World Jewry. Accessi-
bility to facts and a sensitized conscience may later multiply
the opponents to such a brutal programme.

Despite the Nazis' systematic and efficient endeavors to
confound the mind and harden the heart of Germans
against Jews there were not a few individuals who refused
to be cowed and browbeaten. In maintaining friendship
with Jews and displaying solicitude for their safety, they
(literally) placed themselves in jeopardy. Their goodness
is to be judged not by their accomplishment but by the risks
they took and the bravery which was involved.

"I, too, believe that our propaganda on the Jewish question
must continue undiminished," stated Goebbels. "How much is
still to be done about this can be seen from the following: in
connection with the evacuation of a prominent Berlin Jew, an
examination of his personal papers and effects revealed that as
late as the middle of 1941 the German Crown Prince wrote
this Jew very cordial letters and presented him with photographs with exceedingly friendly inscriptions. The House of
Hohenzollern of today isn't worth a tinker's dam."

"World Jewry will suffer a great catastrophe at the same
time as Bolshevism. The Fuehrer once more expressed his
determination to clean up the Jews in Europe pitilessly.
There must be no squeamish sentimentalism about it. We
must hasten this process with cold ruthlessness. This un-
compromising anti-Semitic attitude must prevail among
our own people *despite all objectors*. (Italics are the author's.)

"We are now definitely pushing the Jews out of Berlin. They were suddenly rounded up last Saturday, and are to be carted off to the East as quickly as possible. *Unfortunately our better circles, especially the intellectuals, once again have failed to understand our policy about Jews and in some cases have even taken their part. As a result our plans were tipped off prematurely, so that a lot of Jews slipped through our hands.* But we will catch them yet. I certainly won't rest until the capital of the Reich, at least, has become free of Jews."

To this entry Louis P. Lochner adds the following explanatory note:

"To the casual reader this 'premature tipping off' may not seem very surprising. It must be remembered, however, that every German who was caught giving shelter to a Jew or notifying him of pending measures was either executed or sent to a concentration camp."

The clergy, especially those of the Roman Catholic Church, resisted dictation by Nazi bigwigs. Their defiance grew out of a hoary tradition which affirms the sovereignty of the Church in spiritual matters. Here and there and now and then, the Church attempted, it is contended, to extend its realm so that it embraced part of the domain of Caesar. The Church, it can be said, was not impelled to such a course solely by love of power but because it wanted to make social and political life to comply with the tenets of Holy Writ as the Church or the specified denomination conceived and expounded Holy Writ. When the amplitude of the Church's domain was extended, a conflict between secular and religious interests was inevitable.

In Nazi Germany the antagonism was a different kind. There the Nazis were aggressive and presumptuous. They wanted all supreme power to reside in the will and judgment of the Fuehrer. The Church was to serve as a handmaid to the State. To many Nazis, Hitler was the incarnation of God and the Third Reich was temple and sanctuary of the new deity. A storm was in the making and it was gathering force with every passing hour. It was but a question of time when it would assume the proportion of a violent and devastating hurricane. The sinister mind of Goebbels saw the inevitability of the clash and he awaited a life and death struggle between the Reich and the Church at the conclusion of Germany's present war.

Had the spokesmen of Christianity perceived this fact at the inception of the Nazi movement or in the early years of Hitler's rule the horrendous tragedy of World War II, if it could not have been averted at least would have been enacted on a less colossal scale. For without a concordat with the Holy See the Nazis' acquisition of vast power would not have been as unobstructed and as swift as it was.

The Church voiced its disagreement with the racial theories of the Nazis and on the basis of its contrary teachings made known its displeasure at the disenfranchisement and degradation of the Jews.

Against the Nazi-Vatican Concordat of 1933 we must place the Encyclical "Mit Brennenden Sorge" of Pope Pius XI issued March 14, 1937 wherein the racist creed of Nazism is unsparingly denounced.

"Whoever transposes Race or People . . . from the scale of earth's (sic) values and makes them the ultimate norm of all things . . . perverts and falsifies the divinely created and appointed order of things. . . . Only blindness and self-will can close men's eyes to the treasure of instruction for salvation hidden in the Old Testament. He who wishes to see Bible history and the wisdom of the Old Testament banished from Church and school blasphemes the word of God, blasphemes the Almighty's plan of salvation and sets up narrow and blunted human thought as the judge of God's plans."

The Vatican's condemnation of Nazi ideology spurred the high representatives of the Church in Germany to lift up their voices in behalf of the harrowed non-Aryan victims of Nazism. The names of Cardinal Faulhaber, Bishop (and later Cardinal) Count Klemens August von Galen and Cardinal Count von Preysing and others will ever reflect glory upon Catholicism in Germany in the period of Nazi rule. A citation from a pastoral letter of Cardinal von Preysing and

one from the joint letter of the Bishops issued in 1943 (a
year following that of Cardinal von Preysing) testifies to
the unequivocal wording of their indictment.

"Every human being has rights of which no earthly power
can deprive him . . . the right to live, not to be hurt, to be
free, to own property, to have a family life. These rights
cannot be infringed upon by the government . . . No one
can be deprived of them because he is not of our blood or does
not speak our language." (1942)

"The extermination of human beings is *per se wrong*
even if it is purported to be done in the interest of society
but it is particularly evil if it is carried out against the innocent and defenseless people of alien races or alien descent." (1943)

The degree of opposition varied with individual Churchmen. There were some who considered the acts regrettable
but unavoidable. Others maintained an attitude of neutrality. The majority of the Churchmen of all denominations
pitied the fate of the Jews and did much to help individuals
evade the net which the Nazis had spread for them. Not a
few children were sheltered in Christian homes and mona-
steries and thereby were saved from the crematorium.

"The Catholic Church," wrote Goebbels, "continues to act
in a dastardly way. A number of pastoral letters have been
laid before me which are so unrealistic (weltfremd) and
treacherous that nothing need be added. Nevertheless we
shall not proceed against them. Let the 'skypilots' (pfaffen)
have their say: we'll present our bill to them after the war."

"It's a dirty, low thing for the Catholic Church to continue its subversive activity in every way possible and now
even to extend its propaganda to Protestant children
evacuated from regions threatened by air-raids. Next to
the Jews these politic-divines (Politisierenden pfaffen) are
about the most loathesome riffraff that we are still shelter-
ing in the Reich. The time will come after the war for an
overall solution of this problem. Only one can be the master
in the State, either the Church or the State itself. National
Socialism is faced with the task of establishing supremacy
uncompromisingly over the political claims of the Church."

"I took the position in talking with the Fuehrer that the old Cardinals of the type of Faulhaber and Bertram are much less dangerous than the young reverends who are serving at the front as army chaplains and even wear the Iron Cross of the First Class. *These give us much more trouble, for they rate high with the people.*"

The panegyric which Einstein then paid to the Church, we may conclude, was not undeserved or groundless.

"Being a lover of freedom, when the revolution came in Germany, I looked to the Universities to defend ot, knowing that they had always boasted of their devotion to the cause of truth; but no—the Universities immediately were silenced. Then I looked to the great editors of the newspapers whose flaming editorials in days gone by had proclaimed their love of freedom; but they like the Universities were silenced in a few short weeks. . . .

"Only the Church stood squarely across the path of Hitler's campaign for suppressing truth. I never had any special interest in the Church before, but now I feel a great affection and admiration because the Church alone has had the courage and persistence to stand for intellectual truth and moral freedom."

Chapter 5

TO THE CHURCH, NO MILITARY EXPLOIT
MERITS A BLESSING

Christianity in its Patristic form was an adaptation of Hebrew religion to the Graeco-Roman world and later in the Protestant movement, a readaptation of the same to what we may call the Teutonic Spirit." [1] Santayana

THE question which we must now pose is, "Have we dug deep enough to reach the ends of the roots which tended to feed and sustain the poisonous weed of Nazism? Why had the Church failed to see, until it was too late, the threat which Nazism presented to its teachings and survival as a Free and Independent Institution? Why did it allow *Mein Kampf*, in which the false and vicious creed of Hitler was clearly defined and expounded, to win the esteem of multitudes until it became a rival to Holy Writ? Was it due to inadvertence or are there aspects in the doctrines and discipline of the Church which bear affinity with some professions of Nazism and therefore may have been conducive to its rise.

That an unequivocal answer to the above queries is not to be expected can be inferred from an incident in which I was moved to take a part.

The locale was Hyde Park [in London], which is renowned for its open air meetings where clusters of individuals can be seen especially on Sunday afternoons listening to the expoundings of current issues by the advocate of some party or point of view. Even when the speaker has finished and walked off with his stand and placards the group often breaks up into smaller units.

In my sauntering I stopped at one of these small gatherings. The earnestness of the speaker, as well as his facility of expression and his use of telling figures of speech, attracted the by-passer. The speaker had the rapt attention of the audience and no one seemed inclined to question or challenge his pronouncements and arguments.

After a few minutes of listening, it was apparent who he was and what he stood for. He was a left-wing member of the Labor Party. By his brogue and the rolling of his "r's" one was not running a risk in assuming that he hailed from Scotland.

He was apprising his attentive hearers of the views on religion expressed by Bertrand Russell in his latest book, "Why I Am Not a Christian." I learned that the Scotchman was provoked to take issue with the main speaker who was now gone. The latter had contended that Religion and the Church were bastions offering protection to avowals of conscience and were barriers to the swift and easy spread of totalitarianism. He had cited the Church's opposition to Tito and to the communist wielders of power in Hungary.

"The Church's antagonism to the totalitarians," the de-
bater maintained, "is the result of a second thought and
the realization that the newcomer is not content with a dual
rule but is bent on usurping all power. The Church is not
fighting the despotism of communism because it believes
in the right of the individual to think freely and because it
believes in allowing behavior to be determined by one's
inner conscience. The Church opened the door to the in-
truder but when it found the guest acting as if he were the
host and proprietor of the house, it altered its attitude.

"Far from obstructing the emergence of Fascism and
Nazism, the Church conditioned and fostered their rise. It
is no accident," was his climatic declaration, "that totalitarianism flourishes in lands where the Mediaeval Church
is dominant. In what soil do 'the seeds of totalitarianism
take root?' he asked—and his answer was 'in countries like
Spain, Portugal, Italy, Latin American lands. You don't find
a Mussolini, a Hitler, a Franco, a Peron in Norway, Den-
mark, Sweden, England or America.' "

At this point I was moved to challenge his imputations,
principally because I deemed it unfair to prosecute an Institution like an individual, without the presence of defending
counsel. Perceiving the silence of the hearers, which I considered to be tantamount to assent to the unextenuated and
unconditioned charges, I assumed the role of the 'Fidei De-
fensor,' Vindicator of the Church.

When the speaker finished I posed the question how he
would account for the frequent rise of absolute despots before the Church had come into being or their presence
amongst people of other religions or no religion. I then
cited a string of tyrants who flayed or rewarded subjects
without any check or advice from anybody. Their whim
alone determined their demeanor and there was no demurrer against their caprice before any higher tribunal. I under-
scored the absolute rulers of Asia, the Near East, Ancient
Greece and the Roman Emperors who preceded Constantine
whose displeasure struck terror in the hearts of probable
victims.

I then asked him whether he would attribute the assumption of unbrooked power by Cromwell to any influence of the Church of Rome.

The speaker was visibly taken aback. He seemed lost for a reply. "If your theory is correct," I continued, "why are the Irish, and French and French Canadians immune to dictatorship?"

When I finished, he remained absorbed in thought and refrained from making any reply. After an interval he asked me to give my diagnosis of the causes of the malady of fascism. I replied that it would require more study and brooding than I had given it. When I got ready to go I shook his hand and bade him farewell. I then heard a fellow leftist sneeringly remark in cockney "American papists are no different than the English kind. Their minds are closed. Once a papist, always a papist!"

Chapter 6

THE DELUSIONS OF UNATTAINABLE STRIVINGS

"Hitch your wagon to a star but be sure its wheels are on 'terra firma'." B.H.

As I brooded over the encounter in Hyde Park and pondered over the form of my questions I realized that my examination of the issues was superficial and that the type of debating which I employed was bordering on the specious. I continued to feel that it was baseless and unfair to put the whole onus of all the wars of the post-Christian era on the Church. If the speaker had limited his charge to the bitter intramural sectarian struggles, the Crusades, the wars of aggression against and slaughter of Moslem and Jews whom the Church branded as infidels and a menace to the maintenance of a monolithic Christian Society and

federation of Christian States, then his indictment would
have some warrant. He, however, lumped all forms of warfare, those in which economic and political factors played a
dominant role, and made the hearer believe as if they had
been initiated and promoted by the men who directed the
affairs of the Church.

The doubt, however, persisted in my mind whether a
Spiritual Institution could disclaim all responsibility for
any outbreak of warfare even if the stipulated issues are
declared to be collateral or beyond its domain.

More disturbing than the above doubt was the charge
that with the emergence and spread of the New Dispensation belligerency not only did not diminish but increased.
Furthermore the ferocity with which each successive war
was waged and the cost in lives and the wastage of needed
substance grew and multiplied until today another such
misadventure may spell the end of the human species and
the transformation of the scene of man's endeavors into a
desolate life-forbidding planet revolving in space.

Was the calculation regarding the number and nature
of the wars waged in Europe in the Christian Era the bleary-
eyed version of an agnostic or a virulent opponent of religion?

As I delved into the matter I came across data which was
astounding and depressing. It confirmed the estimate concerning the increased frequency and ferocity of mediaeval
and modern wars. In his volume *The Crisis of Our Age* Peter
A. Sorokin investigated all the known wars in the history
of Greece, Rome and the Western countries from 500 B.C.
to A.D. 1928. The enterprise embraced 967 important conflicts. The author used as a yardstick the duration of each
war, the size of the armies and the resultant casualties. I
quote Professor Sorokin's computation.

"Taking for the measure of war, the size of the casualty
list per million of the corresponding population, the war
magnitude appears as follows for each specific century. For
Greece: in the fifth century B.C. the indicator of war magnitude is 29; for the fourth century B.C. from 48 to 36; for
the third century B.C., from 18 to 33; for the second cen-

tury B.C., from 3 to 3.6. For Rome (Italy) the indicator
is 12 for the fourth century B.C.; for the third century
B.C., 63; for the first century B.C., 33; for the first century
A.D., 5; for the third, 13. If we take the whole Roman Em-
pire, then the respective indicators are naturally much
lower; 3 for the first century B.C.; 0.7 for the first century
A.D.; and 1.3 for the third century A.D. The empire as a
whole, of course, enjoyed the pax Romana. FOR EUROPE
THE INDICATORS OF WAR MOVEMENT AS MEAS-
URED BY THE SAME YARDSTICK—NAMELY THE
NUMBER OF CASUALTIES PER MILLION OF THE
CORRESPONDING POPULATION—ARE AS FOL-
LOWS: FOR THE TWELFTH CENTURY, FROM 2 TO
2.9; FOR THE THIRTEENTH CENTURY, FROM 3 TO
5; FOR THE FOURTEENTH CENTURY, FROM 6 TO
9; FOR THE FIFTEENTH CENTURY, FROM 8 TO 11;
FOR THE SIXTEENTH CENTURY, FROM 14 TO 16;
FOR THE SEVENTEENTH, 45; FOR THE EIGHT-
EENTH, 40; FOR THE NINETEENTH, 17. WHEN WE
COME TO THE TWENTIETH CENTURY, THE INDI-
CATOR FOR THE FIRST QUARTER ALONE STANDS
AT 52.[1]
"ACCORDINGLY THE WAR INDICATOR REGISTERS
A UNIQUE UPSWING: FOR ONLY ONE QUARTER OF
THE PERIOD THE FIGURES EXCEED THOSE OF ALL
THE PRECEDING TWENTY-FIVE CENTURIES WITH
THE EXCEPTION OF THE THIRD CENTURY B.C. IN
ROME. But the Roman indicator (63) is for the whole
century; the twentieth century index is for only twenty-
five years—from 1900 to 1925. If to the European wars of
1900 to 1925 we add all the subsequent wars up to the pres-
ent time, the figures will eclipse even those for the third
century B.C. If, further, we add wars that will doubtless
occur from 1940 to 2000, the TWENTIETH CENTURY
WILL UNQUESTIONABLY PROVE TO BE THE
BLOODIEST AND MOST BELLIGERENT OF ALL THE
TWENTY-FIVE CENTURIES UNDER CONSIDERA-
TION." [2]

Imputation to the Church of responsibility for the besetting sin of war, in which the malefactors were communicants of the Church may be partially justified. However, the indubitably pertinent question is, "Why did not the Church, whose Founder eulogized and fervently advocated "Peace on Earth and Good Will Towards Men" and whose stern warning that "he who takes up the sword shall perish by the sword," succeed in curbing, if not in crushing, the bellicose and aggressive drive of its votaries? Why did the Nazarene's beatification of the weak and the oppressed prove so ineffective an antidote to the prevailing lust for power and dominion?"

If in answering the query the defender of the Church will be prone to enter the plea that the ecclesiastical organizations lacked the influence and strength to cope with this strong and natural impulse, then one must counter with the reply that during the middle ages the Church and its spokesmen enjoyed matchless authority and prestige. Rulers of States and Empires had to kneel before the Pontifex Maximus for His Holiness to place the crown, the symbol of sovereignty, upon their heads. The Church's anathema and excommunication were more dreaded than the infliction of leprosy. The material means at the disposal of the Vicar of Christ made the treasury of any medieval state seem a bagatelle.

Diverse explanations are forthcoming which can account for the Church's failure to have actualized the stated moral and spiritual objectives of its Founder.

It may be argued that the pattern of behavior which was identified with the life and teachings of Jesus was lofty, celestial and beyond the capacity of mortal beings to emulate. The image which the name of Jesus was made to evoke was that of an other-worldly Preacher delivering the Sermon on the Mount with its superbly noble and transcendental dicta. His savings and tenets could be considered suitable as a guide to conduct for angelic characters. A Gandhi could strive and succeed, to some extent, in complying with the doctrine of non-resistance to evil (e.g., the turning of the other cheek, the bestowing of love on those who hate you, the disbursement of one's entire fortune to the poor, the spurning of the legitimate enjoyments of the body and the pleasures of the world and branding them as sensual and carnal and the equating of a passing wish to sin with the actual commission of wrong-doing) but such spiritual and moral prescriptions are beyond the reach of the multitude, the ordinary mortals who make up society. Despite the accolades and paens of praise which are accorded to these exhortations they are tantamount to the request that one crush and extirpate ingrained normal instincts and desires. It is a demand for the complete alteration and transformations of the votary's nature. The metamorphosis would not last, and if it did, the worth of the product would be questionable.

Psychiatry has disclosed to parent and teacher the peril in holding up before their charges an excessively high ideal and unattainable goals.

A man may be subject to a period when he will be disposed to disregard what is practical and realizable, but he will not continue trudging on like the donkey lured by an extended carrot. A high and unrealizable goal may enervate man's determination to press on. It may even generate a corrosive sense of frustration, which may induce a regression from and the repudiation of even moderate attainable values.

If there is no jettisoning of such transcendental aspirations, then the unbridgeable hiatus between the unattainable expectations and what is or can be made actual, may produce a functional disintegration and a form of social schizophrenia, the symptom of which would be a disposition to abide by a dual standard. At that stage the disturbed conscience is calmed and petrified by the verbalizations of belief and the semantics of lofty avowals. The mere profession then creates the illusion of performance. When one is under the influence of such a spell one can assert that "the truth of religion is in the ritual and the truth of dogma is in its poetry."

The Judaic tradition must have been cognizant of the

hazards of postulating unattainable ideals when it warned:
"Be not righteous overmuch, neither make thyself over-
wise: why shouldest thou destroy thyself? Be not over much
wicked, neither be thou foolish, why shouldst thou die before thy time? It is good that thou shouldst take hold of
this." [3]

"No law may be imposed upon the public unless a majority of the people can endure it." [4]

Chapter 7

HEROES WITHOUT MEDALS

"The brave love mercy and delight to save." GAY

THAT there were many in the Reich who were heartsick
over the Nazi brutalities towards the Jews is a conclusion
derived not merely from written accounts of life in Germany but also from events which I witnessed and incidents
which I experienced during my stay in Germany.

As director of the restitution of Jewish Cultural Property (consisting of books, Scrolls of the Law and sacred
ceremonial objects) which the Nazis had looted from liquidated Jewish individuals and institutions, I had to make
my headquarters in Frankfurt-am-Main. There, on Sabbath
morning, I met the gentle and soft-spoken Rabbi William
Weinberg, who endured the ordeal of being a refugee from
Nazism in the land of the Soviets. When the Wehrmacht
advanced to Stalingrad there stared before him the terrify-
ing prospect of becoming captive of Hitler's army and an
inmate of one of his concentration camps. The nightmare
vanished only with the liberation of Germany. Even so he
and his recently wedded wife were bereft of some of his and
all of her kin. The latter were victims of the Nazi crematorium.

I became very friendly with the Rabbi who served as the spiritual guide to the Jewish community of Frankfurt-am-Main. The members of this community, except for the D.P.'s within and outside the camps, consisted mostly, if not exclusively, of elderly men and women who returned to Germany from cities as far as Shanghai because they felt too old or too tired to start life anew in an alien land amidst a strange culture.

I found Rabbi Weinberg to be a fine person. He was well informed and erudite. He possessed an alert mind but above all there was absent from his psychic make-up any form of vindictiveness towards the Germans who were responsible for his ordeals and the loss of his and his wife's relatives.

One day the Rabbi invited me to witness a wedding ceremony at which he was to officiate. It was to be held on a Sunday afternoon (June 2, 1949) when restitutional activities were at a standstill. It was to take place not in Frankfurt-am-Main but in Heidelberg. Its setting was to be the mansion which the American Military Government requisitioned and assigned to the Jewish Welfare Board, a component unit of the United Service Organization catering to the religious, social and recreational needs of the army and navy. The bridegroom, a former inmate of a concentration camp, I was informed, was the brother of a noted East European Rabbi. The bride was the only daughter of a gentleman who belonged to an old and respected Jewish family of Heidelberg. The father of the bride, since his return to Heidelberg, resumed his role as leader of the restored Jewish community. I was also told that this gentleman had inherited from his forebears a fine collection of Jewish books and that he had also added many volumes to the collection. The Rabbi also dangled before me the possibility that, after a meeting with the gentleman on this occasion, it would likely be followed by an invitation to visit his home and examine the reputed collection. Because of all the factors I gladly accepted the invitation.

I arrived at the designated place as the wedding ceremony was about to commence. A brief description of the

scene and setting will help to convey to the reader my feelings as I witnessed the event. It also will offer support for
my inference.

The Jewish Welfare Board Center of Heidelberg, where
the wedding was held, had formerly been the home of an
exclusive student fraternity. The members were mostly
sons of Junkers, children of aristocratic families and
wealthy parents. Until the building was requisitioned and
assigned to the Jewish Welfare Board, probably no Jew had
ever crossed its threshhold.

The edifice was an elegant four-floor, red brick building.
It had in the rear a sloping and terraced garden, in the center of which was a miniature fountain. The first floor presented the appearance of an exotic basement, tea-room and
snack-bar. The second floor consisted of a lobby, reception
and reading rooms. All were most tastefully furnished. The
third floor included a spacious high-ceiling salon and grand
chambers. The fourth or top floor was made into a dormi-
tory where G.I.'s were put up for a night or two, depending
on the length of their leave from camp. The executive director also had his living quarters there. The walls on this
floor were adorned with pictures of former days. One beheld photographs of individuals and groups of Heidelberg
students, with and without their distinctive regalia. Some
were reproductions of renowned duelling engagements.

The wedding ceremony and the subsequent feast took
place on the third floor. One room for this occasion was
made into a banquet hall. The largest room served, for this
as well as previous occasions, as a synagogue. Parallel rows
of chairs on each side of the aisle led to the elevated platform at the end of the room, which was graced by a small
artistically-fashioned Ark containing the Scrolls of the Law
which came from the reclaimed cultural loot of the Nazis.

On the platform in the Synagogue there was an im-
provised canopy. Under it stood the Rabbi attired in his
rabbinic robe and wearing a circular velvet Rembrandt-
like beret on his head. The groom was a tall, slender and
handsome young man about thirty years of age. He wore a
black homburg and a staid dark suit. The bride was a de-

mure, rosy-complexioned young girl, in appearance a typical German maiden. She had big round eyes and was radi-
antly beautiful in her white satin gown and veil that
covered her head of hair and hung on her back.

Everyone on the platform conformed sartorially to the
stipulations of the occasion and recognized conventions.
One could hardly imagine that some of these same folk, a
few years ago, had been living like hunted animals, hiding
in barns and forests, and had inured themselves to subsist
without baths and change of clothes, and that others had
been herded and confined in foul, filthy and vermin-infested
barracks. How quickly they readopted former modes and
procedures and reacquired the social graces!

As the ceremony was being conducted, I noticed, a few
feet away from where I was standing, two women in the
audience. They wore plain but proper attire. Their moist
eyes were fixed on the "dramatis personae" under the canopy. Tears kept rolling down their cheeks as the Rabbi
intoned the traditional Hebrew ritual and as the groom
placed the wedding ring on the finger of his bride, who by
this act became his wife. I was curious to know who these
ladies were, and whether they belonged to the bride or
groom's side and why the copious tears. Everyone to whom
I addressed these queries retorted with a blank stare and
gestures implying mystification. I dropped the matter and
it vanished from my mind.

After the ceremony the Rabbi introduced me to the parents of the bride as well as to the happy couple. All of them
implored me not to leave now that the ceremony was finished but to remain as their guest for the festal repast. I
consented.

After a short interval, which enabled all present to impart their felicitations to the happy newlyweds and to the
beaming parents of the bride, the guests were asked to
seat themselves at the decked tables in the adjacent large
room. The blessing was recited as bread was broken and
the meal was served and much enjoyed. Just before the
Seven Benedictions designated for this occasion were to
be chanted by the Rabbi, the father of the bride rose, os-

tensibly intending to address the guests. After a minute of
waiting the murmuring and conversation of the audience
completely subsided.

I shall endeavor to recall his remarks from the notes
which I had set down in my diary. His talk was in German;
it was elegantly phrased, literary in form and interspersed
with Hebrew terms and expressions.

"Dear and highly esteemed friends," were the first words
that he uttered, after which he stopped and seemed to be
lost for the moment in ruminations. After the brief pause
he resumed in a low, subdued tone. "I wish that I could have
also preceded my remarks with the salutation, Dear and
highly esteemed relatives. Cruel and vicious men have
snuffed out their lives and thus prevented them from being
with us in body. Their spirits, however, I believe are present and share our joy, elation and to some degree also triumph.

"This moment fills my heart overflowingly with gratitude
to the Almighty whose ways are beyond our understanding.
A few years ago my wife and I were in the grip of despair.
Our *days* in this world seemed to have been numbered.
Who could then think of *years?* The Nazi regime, we were
told, was built on foundations which would make it last a
thousand years. Who would then have believed that we
would behold the end and destruction of that evil dominion?

"The Merciful One, for merits unknown to me, designed
to spare my life and that of my devoted wife and that of
my dear daughter. In addition, my wife and I are accorded
the privilege and the joy, that can't be expressed in words,
of seeing her mated to one who, we are sure, will be true
to her and whose family background and traditions will
inspire him to live nobly and exemplify the high moral
tenets of our religion. For all these unexpected good things
I offer the Lord my heartfelt thanks." He then proceeded
to recite the benediction in Hebrew "Blessed art thou O
Lord our God, King of the Universe, who has kept us in life,
and hast preserved us, and enabled us to attain this moment.

"Next to God," he continued, "I must and gladly express my gratitude to two non-Jewish women, who at the risk of their lives concealed my daughter and prevented her discovery and seizure by the eagle-eyed members of the Gestapo. They secreted her in cellar, attic, barn, and stable. They did this not for a week or a month but for two long years. I shall now ask these two heroic and noble women, who are here to rejoice with us, to rise." He then pointed to a table where two women unobtrusively were seated. He signaled them to stand up. This they did hesitatingly. Lo and behold, they were the two women who had stood a few feet away from me when the ceremony was performed and from whose eyes tears of joy trickled down their faces.

I wondered on my way home to what extent Germany's good fortune in escaping utter annihilation and in the emergence of situations and conditions which enable it to convalesce and recover quickly may not have been due to the merits of her rare leaders and their few, if not many followers.

Have I any warrant for such a supposition in Judaic lore? I believe I do, and it is not confined to the sages' avowal of the supreme worth of an individual, a tenet which forms the cornerstone of the philosophy of democracy.

Judaic lore assigns to the righteous overwhelming power and influence. In the heavenly scales, asserted Raba bar Bar Huna, the soul of one righteous person may be equated, in importance and significance with the whole universe.[1] To Rabbi Elazar the creation of the whole universe was warranted if only for the sake of one good and noble individual.[2] Rabbi Hiya ben Aba maintained that the entire universe can be said to subsist even for the sake of one righteous person.[3] He bases his statement on the Scriptural verse which avers that the righteous man is the pillar and foundation of the Universe.[4] One Rabbi goes so far as to state that the righteous can direct and even annul a decree of Heaven.[5]

Chapter 8

JUDGMENT MUST BE WEIGHED

"Be deliberate in judgment." ETHICS OF THE FATHERS

WITH the vanquishment of Hitler's Reich and the occupation of Germany by the Allies, the world at last became apprised of the enormity and frightful magnitude of the crimes of that unimaginably wicked regime. The view, that the heinous acts of the Nazis must be charged not merely to the perpetrators of the iniquity but to the German nation was then widely accepted. Each and every German, it was contended, was to be deemed guilty of the atrocities which had been devised and systematically carried out by the party in power. Changed conditions and circumstances and the passing of time have blunted the sharp edges of the moral indignation which the disclosures had provoked. Expedience, the threat of Russia, and self interest made it advisable to let bygones be bygones. Even so, one not infrequently still hears the view expressed that all Germans are to be held culpable for the extermination of the millions of Jewish victims. Here are some of the arguments that are offered to support that view.

The German people knew, from Hitler's writings and speeches, what he proposed to do; nonetheless they made him Chancellor and gave him unlimited power.

The population was not unaware and surely could have surmised what was being done in the concentration camps. They saw Jews being subjected to heart-breaking humiliations. They were being assaulted on the streets. They had to wear an insignia, the Star of David, and be identified as Jews. They were forbidden to occupy benches in public parks or seats in street cars. Before they were forced to sell

148

their business establishments to Germans, *AT A PRICE WHICH WAS TANTAMOUNT TO CONFISCATION*, they were harassed and boycotted. They saw storm troopers break into Jewish homes and take their occupants into custody. They witnessed Jews forced to trudge to nearby railroad stations where they were packed into suffocating cattle cars and carried off to unspecified places. They saw families broken up and children torn from their parent's side and sent to what they knew was to be their doom. Why did not the average German, they ask, protest against such gruesome behavior? Was not their silence to be construed as an assent?

I propose in this chapter to probe the warrant of the inferences of the previous paragraph. Lest my role be misunderstood, I wish to preface my remarks by emphasizing that it is not my intention to extenuate, in the slightest degree, the guilt of those who planned the Nazi villainies or who freely and directly and knowingly had any part in the program of extermination of the helpless victims. It is my conviction that much leniency was accorded to individuals who were known to have been accessories to Nazi crimes and who claimed to have been coerced into doing what they did. Extenuation has also been accorded to those who professed to have been unwitting adherents of Nazism but who were known to have been devotees of Hitler or were suspected of still being unrepentant. I also do not wish to be understood as exonerating any German from *some* share in the inexpungeable crimes of the Nazis. What the nature of that guilt is, which must be laid at the door of each German, and also of individuals of other nations, will be examined in the succeeding chapter. Here I will but contend that it is unfair and unjust to charge everyone who had cast a vote for a Nazi candidate, before Hitler was offered the post of Chancellor, and especially after the Enabling Act was passed, as bearing the guilt of subsequent Nazi atrocities.

I also dispute the inference that the inarticulateness of Germans in the face of the Nazis' brutal mistreatment of the Jews necessarily signified complacency and approval of such acts.

In brief my aim is not to exonerate or extenuate the acts of the guilty but to vindicate those who are not guilty.

It is not unlikely that even amongst those who shamelessly had given their votes to the Nazis there were some who did it not out of anti-Semitic inclinations. They may have been induced to register their vote with that party because of what seemed to them to be its forthright and aggressive foreign policy. The lure of beholding the transformation of Germany from a vanquished and suppliant people to one strong and perhaps dominant nation, for which Germans did not cease to hanker, was irresistible. They accepted Hitler's promises on faith. Such gullibility is common to no small fraction of voters in all lands, even in the best democracies. As to the Nazis' extreme anti-Jewish, as well as international, proposals, we have seen that many were of the opinion that these were but the bluster and fanciful projections of office seekers who had not yet shouldered the responsibilities of actual government. Even the eminent historian S. M. Dubnow was of the same opinion.

We have seen the chicanery and gangsterism by which Hitler obtained his grant of unlimited power.[1] From then on the German people were mesmerized by stupendous, glamorous government-sponsored Nazi parades and pageants. As if it were insufficient to hypnotize a folk already inured to avoid being critical when it involved obedience to those in office, the continuous appeasement of the Fuehrer by the European Powers, which yielded to the Germans a string of unexpected bloodless victories, was like the injection of dope to a narcotic. They were exhilarated and entranced and were transformed into an amoral people.

Even those who could resist the enchantment of spectacles and remain unawed by them and in addition could maintain their mental stability and assess national ambitions and achievements by ethical standards, even such individuals, unless they were well-nigh moral supermen, were bound to become duped and deluded by the doctored news and the misinformation which Goebbels made accessible to them, *for twelve long years.*

How unreasonable it would be to demand of the average individual to rise up and protest against the existing order, conscious of the peril that such an act would entail!

I shall relate an incident which took place in a non-totalitarian society, which indicates that the policy of expedient silence may shield the individual for a time albeit the nemesis of the act can not be permanently avoided.

In 1917, when the U.S.A. declared war on Germany, I was a student in a theological seminary. When the call for Jewish chaplains was issued I volunteered only to be told that I was too young and that, in addition, only those possessing or who were soon to acquire the coveted rabbinical degree would be eligible. Bent on doing some war work, I applied to the Jewish Welfare Board, which was then also directing the social, recreational and religious activities in the training camps, for some assignment either as a helper to a chaplain or for any other duties.

My offer was accepted by the Jewish Welfare Board. After the preliminary course of instruction, I was sent to Camp Jackson, S. C. The official Chaplain to the Jewish soldiers there was the late Rabbi Jacob S. Raisin. He was a scholar and a noble soul. He was humble, self-effacing and most conscientious. It was inspiring to see how he proceeded from tent to tent distributing writing paper and envelopes or making postage stamps available to the soldiers distantly situated from the Y or J. W. B. Hall. He did this with the zeal and concentration which were evident in the Christian confrères when they were giving communion to their devotees.

One night a non-Jewish soldier panting for breath knocked at the door of the bunker which Rabbi Raisin and I occupied. He informed us that a Jewish lad in the tent next to his was acting queerly, as if he were out of his mind, and that he might do something rash to himself. He was muttering to himself and periodically burst into tears. We all hurried to the tent and there we found a slender lad, in his early twenties, sitting on the edge of his cot, his chin cupped in the palms of his hands and staring blankly out into space. Our entrance did not cause him to change his position, posture, or divert his glare into nowhere. He intermittently muttered something and his body quivered. Pain was registered in his eyes and the muscles on his face began to twitch.

We sat up with this young, and as we realized, very sensitive soldier, till nearly dawn, when out of sheer exhaustion he fell asleep. The next day we saw to it that he obtained all the medical care and attention that were available in the camp.

The cause of the breakdown was a recent and a remote experience. That afternoon he encountered a white sergeant beating up a colored soldier of the Negro battalion assigned to clear a nearby piece of land of tree stumps to extend the area of the camp.

This incident brought back a forgotten horrible experience where he witnessed the lynching of a Negro who was accused of attacking a white woman. He watched, he told us, the infuriated mob dragging the terrified and pleading Negro to the tree and saw how they tied the rope around his neck and then pulled the other end which was over a thick branch until the body was above the ground and was dangling in the air. He had, he said, a strong urge to protest and cry out against the villainy. He repressed the urge, fearing the harm that would come to him. The sight of the bloody face of the Negro who was beaten up by the white sergeant that afternoon, brought back, from what is now termed the limbo of his subconscious, the former scene. The memory continued to haunt him, even to the concluding sentence of his self-indictment, "I was a coward, I was a coward," after which he sobbed bitterly until he fell asleep.

The harrowing experience with this conscience-stricken lad prompted me then and later to think about the perplexing question: to what extent is one bound to protest the commission of wrongdoing? Is one to let one's indignation fulminate when and where it bursts out and be heedless of consequences? Or should one check the urge to denounce an outrageous act and wait for a suitable time and place when the hazards would decrease or disappear? Was Amos, the shepherd of Tekoa, the incendiary from southern Judea, justified in going to the Northern Kingdom and breaking into the festivities of Beth El, the King's chapel and court, and there giving vent to a scorching tirade against their oppression of the poor and their crushing of the needy? Would he not have been more effective if he had planned his criticism of current practices or conferred about the matter with Amaziah, the priest, and tactfully proposed the rectification of the evils.[2]

The more I pondered over the question, the more I found it difficult to arrive at a clear, simple, categorical and all-embracing answer. Each case, it seemed to me, disclosed a different situation with a variant set of problems and issues.

It is difficult to ascertain clearly and unequivocally to what extent the ethics of Judaism enjoin one to endeavor to deter one's fellowman from the commission of a crime by warning him of the evil nature of his deed and the consequent punishment that would ensue to him. The Scriptural passage, "Thou shalt surely rebuke thy neighbor and not bear sin because of him"[3] and the Rabbinic dictum "All Israelites are responsible for one another"[4] lead to the conclusion that the obligation is unconditioned.

On the other hand there are Rabbinic views to the effect that when it is certain that one's warning will remain unheeded, then it is better that the sinner go unwarned. For without warning he is an unwitting transgressor but with it he becomes a deliberate and premeditated sinner.[5] Such views provide a basis to neutralists, or those who are disposed to heed the motto 'mind your own business' to justify their course.

When a severe crime is being committed or is about to be committed the obligation to deter and forewarn the criminal is unshirkable. However if in the specific instance the warning and protest would prove futile and the one uttering the warning would hazard his life by such admonition and outcry, then it would seem that not only would he be exempt from such intervention but that such a

rash and suicidal act would violate the Rabbinic principle
that the observance of the Divine Law is intended to secure
life and not to take it away. This principle the Rabbis based
on the clause in Leviticus reading: "which if a man do he
shall live by them." [6] *The only ones to whom this exemption may not apply are eminent individuals, the elite
of the generation, those to whom all people look up, and
upon whom one would fear to lay one's hands.*[7] *The prescription of any other course for such individuals would
have to circumvent the implications of many Biblical utterances, two of which will be quoted.*

"And it came to pass at the end of seven days, that the
word of the Lord came unto me, saying: Son of man, I have
appointed thee a watchman unto the house of Israel: and
when thou shalt hear a word at My mouth, thou shalt give
them warning from Me. When I say unto the wicked: thou
shalt surely die; and thou givest him not warning, nor
speakest to warn the wicked from his wicked way, to save
his life; the same wicked man shall die in this iniquity, but
his blood will I require at thy hand. Yet if thou warn the
wicked, and he turn not from his wickedness nor from his
wicked way, he shall die in his iniquity; but thou hast
delivered thy soul. . . ." [8]

"Moreover in Jerusalem did Jehoshaphat set up his Le-
vites and the priests, and the heads of the father's houses
of Israel, for the judgment of the Lord and for controversies.
. . . And he charged them saying . . . ye shall warn them,
that they be not guilty towards the Lord and thus shall
you do and ye shall not be guilty." [9]

Chapter 9

THE SHARE OF EACH IN THE GREATNESS OR
BASENESS OF ONE'S PEOPLE OR AGE

"Man is a name of honor for a king." CHAPMAN
"Nations are the citizens of humanity, as individuals are the citizens of the Nation." MAZZINI

IN EXAMINING the degree of moral responsibility which a citizen must bear for the misdeeds of his state, I shall begin with a report of a discussion which I overheard one Saturday afternoon in the summer of 1955 on Riverside Drive. Before I give an account of the discussion it would not be out of place to portray the locale of this episode.

Some years ago there was a popular play on Broadway, entitled 'Grand Hotel.' In it the author (Vicki Baum) skillfully delineated the various backgrounds, differing temperaments and diverse ambitions of the patrons of that establishment. The lobby of the hotel, as well as the privacy of the rooms and suites, constituted the setting for the cavalcade of these common and uncommon specimens of society.

Riverside Drive between 100th and 116th Streets, on Saturday afternoons during the summer and part of the spring and fall, may be termed 'An outdoor Grand Hotel.' One will encounter there contrasting and contrary types of individuals. They promenade its wide sidewalk or sit relaxed on the benches that line its length and face each other.

Traditionally-minded Jews and their women folk, garbed in holiday attire, may be seen strolling leisurely on the Drive. Now and then one may espy a bearded gentleman accompanied by his spouse wearing a difficult-to-detect peri-

wig (sheitel) or having her hair tightly covered with a
silken kerchief. These promenades, when the weather is
balmy and delightful, are deemed to be a part of the 'Sabbath Delight.' Because of this some have jestingly designated the Drive as "Good Shabbos Avenue."

The jesting remark can prove very misleading. For this
esplanade presents an appearance which is the very antithesis of parochialism and provincialism. One sees there,
it is true, a goodly number of Jews on those afternoons but
they are of various shades of belief and no belief, with the
consequent results on their observance or lack of observance of the Faith's rites and practices. Sitting on the same
bench one person may be reading an ethico-religious volume and next to that individual a young girl, puffing non-
chalantly on her king size cigarette, may be absorbed in
Polly Adler's "A House Is Not a Home" or in one of Kinsey's
reports.

Riverside Drive demonstrates more than the toleration
of diversity existing within a specific denomination. The
strollers and the occupants of the benches are far from
being all Jews. The boulevard, furthermore, like the solid
edifice (the International House) that faces Grant's Tomb,
which has been endowed by the Rockefellers in order "That
Brotherhood May Prevail," has a cosmopolitan complexion. Within a short interval one may see passing before one,
Americans, Puerto Ricans, Chinese, Hindus, Koreans. . . .
It is one section of the city where the mating of Chinese,
Negroes and white persons is commonplace and accepted
that when such couples pass, there is no raising of eye-
brows. The languages that one hears on these fifteen blocks
are English, German, Yiddish, Hebrew, French, Japanese,
Chinese, Spanish, Hindi, etc.

One Saturday afternoon a group of Jewish individuals,
some sitting on the sidewalk bench and others standing,
was discussing whether the United States was wise and
justified in initiating atomic warfare at Hiroshima and
Nagasaki. One individual considered it a warranted retribution for Japan's sneak attack on Pearl Harbor. Another

justified the act because it shortened the war and thus saved many lives.

At this point an elderly gentleman in the group put in his demurrer. This gentleman was frail in body. His well-trimmed Vandyke was turning white. A pensive look in his face betokened a kindly and genial disposition. There was a glint in his eye as he voiced his dissatisfaction with the facile conclusions of his comrades. "I have not been in this country very long," he said, "but I love it. I have studied its history. I have read the writings of its great men. America's ideals have been high and her traditions noble. With very few exceptions her actions have always squared with her professions. No other nation can point to three gigantic and costly conflicts (the Civil War, World War I, and World War II) on the outcome of which it staked its fate and fortune, and all was done in behalf of justice and freedom.

"However, I confess, I am ashamed of what we did at Hiroshima. We were too hasty and too eager to bring the war to an end after Germany had capitulated. We failed to reckon with the toll of dead civilians following the use of the atomic bomb, and the comparatively smaller loss had we resigned ourselves to the fact that fighting would have to continue a bit longer without the use of that vastly destructive device. Japan could not have held out much longer. She realized that she was doomed to defeat. Did we have to besmirch our record by the introduction of such instruments of frightful destruction and wholesale murder?

"We committed a great sin, an unwitting sin but a sin nevertheless," he said with a sigh. "God forgive us this thoughtless misdeed for which not merely the President, the Chiefs of the Army and Navy or the abstract entity we call the United States but *each of us must feel morally accountable. What they did they did under our formal authority but not as the instrument of our direct mandate and express will. Yet we are morally accountable not only before the judgment of others but also and chiefly before the tribunal of our own conscience.*

"The Sages tell us that the law or principle of retribution which prevails in God's universe is that a like kind and measure of punishment are to be visited on evil doers.[1] If this be so then we are in for horrible and tragic experiences. Our one hope of avoiding such a fate is sincere repentance and rectification of our ways." He concluded what he had to say with the quotation of the verses from the book of Jonah:

> "Who knoweth whether God will not turn and repent, and turn away from his fierce anger, that we perish not? And God saw their works, that they turned from their evil way; and God repented of the evil, which He said He would do unto them; and He did it not."[2]

After he finished, there was a silent interlude, not the silence indicating agreement with the views which were expressed but rather of awe and reverence for the speaker and the nobility of the ethical precepts which he voiced.

At this moment one of the men pulled out a watch with a dangling fob and after surveying the time announced to his confrères that it was time to go. They rose and leisurely sauntered along. I decided to follow them.

I overheard supplements to the above discussion on the part of two individuals who lagged behind the elderly gentleman and those who walked beside him.

"Who can say that he is sure that the war would have soon come to an end anyhow?" was the comment of one. "War *any way* you wage it," observed the second, "is morally wrong. Once you cloak it with respectability and necessity, then the fiercest means to attain victory seems justified. Moral persons must, therefore, agitate for the abolition not merely of atomic warfare but all and any fratricidal fighting."

The group turned towards Broadway and 110th Street. I continued on their heels. I saw them entering the newly formed synagogue, the founders of which were residents of Luxembourg who fled before the Nazis had occupied their country. I too followed them into the Synagogue and joined the afternoon (Mincha) and evening (Maariv) services. I silently recited the words of the service, but my thoughts were absorbed with these peripatetic moralists of Riverside Drive and the "Sabbath Delight" which they devised for themselves in this new homeland of theirs.

The elderly gentleman, the apparent sage of this small and friendly group, in stating his views gave expression to the idea of the individual's moral accountability for the grave sins of his country, though he personally had nothing to do in planning or executing the misdeed. This precept must be burnt into the consciousness of every German. While the juridical guilt of Nazi iniquities, like the invasion of Poland and atrocities against the Jews, may not be laid at the door of each German, no German can consider himself exempt from *some* responsibility for such acts of extreme wickedness.

This expectation, it seems to me, is neither unreasonable nor unfair. If we are ready and eager to receive the rich legacies of our forebears, we should deem ourselves obliged to assume their debts and attempt to square their deficiencies. Furthermore, since the individual basks in the glory of the corporate achievements of the people of which he is a member, he must be willing to bear the shame of its collective wrongdoing.

No government of today can incessantly defy the attitude of the multitude of its people and long endure. There are clever and seemingly innocuous procedures where one's displeasure with the government's policies and programs could be indicated to members of one's family, trusted friends and fellow citizens. If the disposition spreads and becomes universal no king, no duce, no fuehrer, no almighty commissar would venture to ignore such mood and temper. India, during the English regime, showed that the unarmed and defenseless populace can resort to an alternative other than defiance by means of overt and lawless action or crowd submission to the wielders of whips and guns.

To the German who tries to squirm out of his share of moral blame for Nazi wickedness by professing that he had been only a "little man" with no influence whatsoever, the answer should be given that no individual can live in a community and refrain from making some impress upon it. The smallest pebble that is cast into a pool brings into being not only ripples on the surface, but, if we had a sensitive instrument of measurement, it could be noted that every part of the pool or lake was affected by this small and insignificant vibration.

Lastly, wicked governments come into being not solely because bad men sponsor them but because good men, far out-numbering the bad ones, are content to remain on the sidelines as the tug-of-war is waged between the forces striving for good and decency and those who scheme and fight for the opposite order. There is no exoneration in the statement "I did not vote *for* Hitler or what he stood for." One must also be able to say, "I voted against Hitler and what he stood for." *It is the well-intentioned people who become indolent or lackadaisical on the day of an election who imperil good government in all states, even in the best democracies.*

Justice ordains that punishment should be restricted to the criminals who committed the nefarious acts and to those who were accessories to the crime. Ethical sensitivity and conscience, on the other hand, impute moral responsibility to all whose actions even remotely had tended to cause or influence the culprit to commit the evil deed. The area in the latter widens so that it includes the lowly and the eminent of society, those who are distant as well as those who are near to the place where the evil had been done. Naturally, there are gradations and shadings of moral accountability as the nexus, or chain of causation lengthens and as the periphery expands and becomes all-embracing. The world and mankind, seen through the eyes of conscience, become interrelated and integrated. The parts affect the whole for good or bad and the whole affects the constituent parts. When anything is wrong with anyone anywhere, some guilt is traceable to everyone of us. The words of the poet John Donne are pertinent in assessing the moral responsibility of each individual.

"No man is an *Island,* intire of itself; every man is a piece of
the *Continent,* a part of the maine; if a *Clod* bee washed away
by the *Sea, Europe* is the lesse, as well as if a *Manner* of thy
friends or of *thine owne* were: any man's death diminishes *me,*
because I am involved in *Mankind:* And therefore never send
to know for whom the *bell* tolls: It tolls for *Thee.*"

The Hebrews, even in very ancient days, had a sense of
corporate responsibility for any violence of which even a
single person became a victim. We are told in Scriptures
that when a slain person was found in open fields beyond
city limits, the elders of the nearest town had to bring an
offering as an expiation and after washing their hands,
they had to declare and say "Our hands have not shed
blood, neither have our eyes seen it. Forgive, Oh Lord, Thy
people Israel whom thou hast redeemed, and suffer not innocent blood to remain in the midst of thy people Israel. And
the blood shall be forgiven them. So shalt thou put away the
innocent blood from the midst of thee, when thou shalt do
that which is right in the eyes of the Lord." [3]

Commenting on the affirmation of the Elders "Our hands
have not shed this blood, neither have our eyes seen it," a
Rabbinic expositor astonishingly asks, "Could it possibly
occur to anyone to suspect the elders of murder? No! By this
avowal the elders of the town declare that "he (the slain
one) did not come to us hungry and we failed to feed him:
he did not come to us friendless and we failed to befriend
him." [4]

On this exegetical comment, the late Chief Rabbi of England remarked "Thus did the Rabbis bring home to the
people the great principle of mutual responsibility and
moral interdependence of men and classes."

Chapter 10

THE LIGHT THAT FAILED

"Learning without thought is labor lost, thought without learning is perilous." CONFUCIUS

THE disposition of the average German towards what had occurred is far from what it ought to be, though an improvement has lately taken place. To what extent is the fact due to the incorrigibility of the German and to what extent is it due to the educational failure of the governments of occupation?

The unpopularity of the United States in European countries and the fear and suspicion with which its avowed objectives are regarded puzzle and mystify the average American. Within twenty-five years the United States became embroiled in two conflicts which had been initiated by European Powers. Twice the United States was called to come to the rescue of governments and peoples whose freedom and very existence had been imperiled. Each time she responded to the call, and the cost to her in men and substance was staggering. At no time did she request reparations, either in territorial acquisitions or special privileges for her trade and commerce in payment for the huge sacrifices which she was forced to make. The conclusion of the war did not spell to the United States release from military tasks but rather the assumption of economic obligations to the vanquished peoples as well as to her victorious allies. The flow of gifts of foodstuffs, raw materials, machines and tools and the allocation of dollar-loans after the conflicts had been concluded was continuous.

In the face of such prodigious generosity how does one account for the unpopularity of the United States with the very people who are its beneficiaries?

Each of the many explanations which have been offered partially accounts for the situation.

Not a few attribute the carping criticism and unsympathetic disposition of the European towards the United States to envy. The recent wars have debilitated the formerly-mighty European States and drained their treasuries. The international trade of these countries halted while fighting went on, and at the conclusion their factories were either in shambles or severely damaged. The Unites States, thanks to a vast ocean which separated her from the battle-scarred lands, came out of the conflict with her industries not only unhurt but vastly expanded and more efficient. In a short period a motley of colonies became the World's Croesus and Creditor-Nation. It was as if an erstwhile hawker of wares assumed the role of a proprietor and monopolistic dispenser of the necessities of life. If the Scriptural proverb that "the borrower is servant to the lender" [1] is true, then a sour attitude of the former to the latter is natural and comprehensible.

The economic recovery of Europe which came to it via the Marshall Plan and other forms of aid is noteworthy. In some countries (e.g., Germany) it is phenomenal. When the recipient of help in time of need is expected or imagines that he is expected to acknowledge continually his gratitude to his former or present benefactor his disposition to be thankful is bound to wear thin and there will emerge negative reactions. The ego resents being constantly made aware that had it not been for the aid extended, it would now be in distress or in a state of precariousness.

American-made movies play no small part in generating anti-American sentiment. Pictures displaying indulgence in luxuries in the fabulous and inaccessible paradise known as U.S.A. are bound to evoke compensatory denigrations by terming Americans materialistic and bent on amassing wealth. This denigration tends to allay the smarting pain of the European's inability to satisfy the very same cravings. [2]

The Communists keep fanning these smouldering embers into a blaze. The temper of organized labor in Europe is such that fear and suspicion of every political move which the American government makes easily obtains lodgment in the worker's mind. The communists are dexterous with their whispering anti-American campaigns. Their overt charges that we are economic imperialists aspiring to dominate the world by means of dollar diplomacy are widely believed.

The best evaluation of the United States which may be evoked from the ordinary European is that America may profess high ideals, but that she has failed to exemplify them in practice.

Now, why haven't we succeeded in acquainting the European with our true intent and aim? If there are impediments to their dissemination are they insurmountable and do we lack the ingenuity to overcome them? Why can Americans popularize Coca-Cola with foreign people in distant lands (even in countries where wine and champagne are cheaper than the American drink) and be so ineffective in presenting the democratic ideal in an appealing way? How have such standard American articles as Parker 51 pens become so esteemed and sought for in cities as far as Bombay in the face of the multitude of duplications and imitations?

Educators have long stressed the fact that the good life is conditioned by the adoption of effective means to attain worthwhile ends. Proper techniques are therefore as essential as good goals. The men who were responsible for America's foreign policy during the recent decades amply considered the nobility and high value of the nation's aims. They blundered however and were slipshod in devising the best methods of effectuating those aims. Expediency and temporizing and vacillation marked the course of the United States.

We announced to the Germans after their defeat that we were resolved to *denazify*, to *democratize* and to *decartelize* their political, social and industrial structure. The denazification program took the form of bringing to judgment the political tycoons of Nazidom. The punishment was meted out to the major and most notorious culprits. The precedent was thereby established that henceforth the initiators of a war, like the instigators of a bloody riot, cannot hope to evade responsibility for their actions. Films of the Nuremberg Trials featuring the "dramatis personae" were taken. The testimony that was offered against and on behalf of the offenders was literally recorded. Up to date, however, the presentation of the films has been restricted to chosen and invited individuals. The complete documents were published. Their sale and distribution amongst Germans did not exceed the number necessary to supply criminal lawyers who needed copies for professional use.

The Nuremberg Trials extended over a long period. The interest of readers in the proceedings which were reported in the German newspapers naturally began to wane. The space allotted to such accounts by the editors was progressively diminished. From first page copy they were switched to corners of little perused sections.

In stigmatizing members of the Nazi party there was a failure to distinguish between the following:

1. The Nazi who affirmed that Germany's national interest was above consideration of Right and Wrong; that Ethics and Morality and Truth were to be invoked only when they served the group and could be flouted whenever it was advantageous to the State.
2. The Nazi who repeated the "fashionable" slogans because he lacked the critical acumen to analyze and appraise for himself the dicta of Regierungsbeamter. His allegiance to Nazi ideology was more or less akin to the belief of the American who thinks that a particular brand of cigarettes is the best because it was endorsed by a Hollywood star.
3. The Nazi adherent who joined the party because of his disposition to board the bandwagon of any group which comes into power.
4. The reluctant affiliate who in his heart questioned the validity of the Nazi claims, but realized that without such an identification it would be difficult to obtain a job to support himself, and his family.

Other categories could be cited, but the listing I have made is sufficient to bring out my point that the indiscriminate and slipshod characterization was unfair and unsound. The result was that later, when the American Military Government found it difficult to find individuals who were totally unblemished for posts of teachers, judges, editors, and directors of industrial establishments, they were forced to blink their eyes at their former pronouncement and modify their avowals. Some Germans mistook the action of the Americans as a condonement of Nazi sins and even as a green signal to resuscitate the movement. The cold war with Russia bolstered their belief.

The prodigious generosity of the United States towards Germany (which far exceeded the allocation stipulated by the Marshall Plan) was interpreted by not a few as an attempt to woo them to our side in case of an outbreak of war. Not all Germans have surrendered the hope of the coming of "the day" when Germany will dominate all Europe. (I have been told that in beerhalls and in secret meetings of ex-Nazis the future course for the Väterland is being plotted. It is to get from the United States all that can be gotten in return for implied promises that Germany will be on the side of the United States should she become embroiled in a war with the Soviets. However, should such a war become an actuality they would strive to have Germany remain neutral. Germany then would be content to watch the struggle from the sidelines and at the last moment jump in on the side of the prospective victors.)

We also defaulted in not initiating an effective, all-out campaign of enlightenment which should have convinced the German of the fallacy and baselessness of the Nazi ideology and the speciousness of the claim that Hitler had been Germany's savior at any time or that he had succeeded in fully solving their problem of unemployment when he deprived Jews of their right to pursue their vocations and professions or engage in commerce. All he did was to hand over their places to Aryan citizens. No extra work or wealth had been thereby created.

The increased exports of German products which were fostered by means of the '*Zusatzausfahrverfahren*' or granting foreign purchasers marks at a lower rate and the government making up to the manufacturer or exporter the difference, was equivalent to a rebate which netted profits to the commercial firm but swelled the national debt.

In the secret and subsequent defiant and feverish rearming of the expanded army, navy and air forces Hitler pandered to the vainglory and pride of the Germans. The stupendous program of militarization supplied work and buying power to multitudes. Hitler thereby, however, expended much of the substance of Germany. The prosperity that is the result of a program of militarization is spurious. It expands the national debt.[3]

With our failure to remove the scales from the eyes of the Germans regarding the above matters, is it any wonder that many Germans still persist in believing that National Socialism was a "good idea badly carried out," rather than a vile and vicious aberration? Even as late as 1949, the following paragraph in a magazine of the U.S. Military Government in Germany was allowed to go unchallenged.

"It is important to be aware of the history of the past. For example, Germany after 1918 was faced with a tremendous economic and social problem involving a social revolution with disastrous results to the so-called middle class. Hitler and the Nazies, in the absence of vision and intelligent action on the part of the statesmen in the intervening period, *found a way to solve the social and economic difficulties of the German people.*"[4]

The Nazis made the Jew and his Faith objects of unremitting and relentless attacks. Nothing was too mean and ignoble to deter them from proclaiming or affirming anything which tended to defame the integrity of the Jew and distort the ethical and spiritual character of Judaism.

One would imagine that the gallantry and generosity of the victors would accord in their program of re-education of the Germans some place to the correction of this misinfor-

mation which polluted the minds and poisoned the souls of
the German people for thirteen years, and infected even
the atmosphere of lands that are distant from the Reich.

The woeful neglect of such re-education by the Military
Government was lamentable. The lack of interest on the
part of Jews in this matter was and still is shocking. *Even
now it would not be too late for the sponsors of Interfaith
and Goodwill and Better Understanding to endeavor to
pluck out the weeds that still grow at random in Germany.*

Another and more general default is the result of the
specious notion that democracy, like religion, is caught and
not taught. In an article "Out of the Rubble" which outlines a program for reorientation, Dr. Alonzo G. Grace, Director, Education and Cultural Relations Division OMGUS,
made the following astonishing remarks. "The only certain
method of establishing a society based on the democratic
ideal is to abandon the use of the term and by practice and
precept lead the people to accept this ideal. It cannot be
secured by public lectures or discussions. A society based on
moral principles and spiritual enlightenment is the foundation for world peace. This is the ideology of democracy."

The author like the devotee of progressive education
ignored the distinction between groups of individuals. To
ask for the elimination of the use of the term democracy and
plead for reliance not on lectures and discussions, but on
the contagion of example may be suitable to the attendants
of a New England Town Meeting or a gathering of Quakers
but not to soldiers who have seen their buddies blown to
bits by enemy shrapnel and who now were tempted to give
vent to their wrath against those who had started the war
and disrupted their lives.

Here is another gem in the above article:

"We must not be guilty of attempting to develop the ideal,
which may not have been accomplished elsewhere in the midst
of an environment which generates realism."

Realism (*real-politik*) was a term for which the Nazis
had strong liking. "These are some of the fundamental

principles," our author concludes, "that guide American policy with respect to education and cultural relations in Germany." [5]

The realization of the beauty and goodness of democracy, like religion, seldom comes to an individual or group as a sudden influx of light. It is like a fire of wood which needs kindling and fanning before the flames break forth and shoot upward. True and abiding revelations follow exposition and reflection. The exemplary demeanor of the devotees of the Faith may set the fire ablaze, only after the wood has been assembled and the spark applied to it and the parts had been made to kindle.

We also supposed that defeat in war would be sufficient to convince the Germans of the superiority of their adversary's political philosophy as if might makes right. Physical defeat without an introspective moral accounting for that defeat often spurs the conquered to a more tenacious attachment to their creed. The smart of the defeat is removed by the ego's defiant affirmation of the refusal to relinquish former beliefs. Even a conversion induced by a crisis is not abiding unless it is sustained by a process of enlightenment and a continued deepening of conviction in the truths disclosed by the new outlook. *Spiritual regeneration does not assume the form of a blitz. Democracy, like religion, is firmly established and made secure only after it is taught. The revelation at Sinai did not deter the Israelites from relapsing into the worship of the golden calf immediately thereafter. To prevent a repetition of the relapse Moses immediately proceeded to set before them codes and commandments.*

That the United States woefully neglected a great opportunity to re-educate and reorient the German effectively at a most auspicious moment was evident in the opinions of qualified publicists and journalists.

Robert Haeger in "No More Conquerors" then wrote,

"It is American policy to sell democracy and the 'American way,' but thousands of potential salesmen on the grass roots level never went to work. It's extremely doubtful that the

American occupier, even the reformed, legal and proper occupier of recent vintage, has been of much value in guiding the
German to the path of redemption that the West wants him
to follow." [6]

Robert Lewison was even more severe in his appraisals
of our educational program during the period of our occupation of Germany.

"In 1945, however, the Allies were confronted with a
shortage of teachers. New ones could not be trained over-
night. The French made a beginning, revising thoroughly
the methods of teacher selection and training, but in the
American Zone few teachers are being trained and even
those few are selected and taught by other Germans much as
before. The shortage of teachers in all zones has been
'solved' by taking back the Nazis.

"The United States is lagging far behind the other Allies
in the textbook field. In 1947 a study showed that for each
100 school children in their zones, the French had published
800 textbooks, the Russians 700, the British 400, and the
United States only 150. The American Zone was still last in
1949, with 700 textbooks per 100 students, compared with
1,300 in the French Zone, which led the rest.

*"American policy in Germany, until recently, has given
education one of the lowest priorities among Occupation
tasks.* United States appropriations for 'prevention of dis-
ease and unrest' in Germany for 1947, 1948, and January
to June 1949 were: $1,009,819,691 for food; $113,541,468
for agricultural supplies; $66,625,760 for petroleum, oil
lubricants; $58,018,875 for pay of civilians; $176,690,937
for transportation of goods; $2,172,909 for travel; $5,279,-
228 for incidental operating expenses; and $17,597,756
for 'reorientation and education.' On the other hand, the
French have given education one of the highest priorities.
American educators are now trying to overtake the French,
but they still have too few resources.

"Until 1948 education was not even given the status of a
division in Military Government; it was lumped together
with miscellaneous activities such as roads and communica-

tions. Protest resignations by some of the most talented American educators helped bring about a change and a separate division was set up for education activities in 1949." [7]

Chapter 11

EVIDENCE OF INCORRIGIBILITY

"It is only an error of judgment to make a mistake, but it argues an infirmity of character to adhere to it when discovered." C. N. BOVEE

THOSE who refuse to despair of the power of human reason to tame the wild passions that rage within the realm of the subconscious and assert that only occasionally do they succeed in breaking through their enclosures with fatal consequences on conscious behavior; those who are inclined to the view that man is not innately base but with the talmudic sage assert that man's moral delinquencies are due to ephemeral aberrations and obsessions, these scan the doings and dispositions of the German people to detect signs of remorse for the fiendish acts of the Nazis.

The reports on this matter that come to us are not univocal. They point to the presence of diverse tendencies and they arrive at contrary conclusions.

There are some who maintain that the Germans are impenitent of the national misdeeds. They contend that the miseducation and distortions of the Hitler regime succeeded in making the Germans morally callous and unresponsive to humane considerations, particularly when they involved Jews.

The following testimony is offered to support their claim.

One: The widely current belief amongst Germans that National Socialism was "a good idea but badly carried out."

Two: Evidence of repressed anti-Semitism in the spo-

radic desecration of Jewish cemeteries and in the appearance of occasional letters in newspapers and magazines from
readers (usually assuming a nom de plume like Adolph
Bleibtreu) defending and lauding aspects of Nazism and
appealing to the German to continue to be loyal to Hitler
and what he advocated.

Three: The claim that Hitler's major and ultimate objective was to vanquish the armies of Stalin and thus save
Western Europe and the world from the blight and horror
of rule by commissars. He would have succeeded, it is alleged, had not Poland and England been politically obtuse.

Four: The disclosure of the polls eliciting German opinion that (a) only 2% of the respondents deemed the surviv-
ing Jewish victims of Nazism as having the greatest right to
indemnification for the injuries and losses which they sustained at the hands of the Nazis (49% averred that they were
neither most nor least entitled to prior consideration and
17% maintained that they were least entitled to such assist-
ance) ; that (b) only 20% of the German people would resist with all their might an attempted restoration of
Nazism; and that (c) merely 12% endorsed the agreement
with Israel in which the Federal Government assumed the
obligation to compensate Israel for the cost of transfer to
and settling in its borders half a million Jewish inmates of
the concentration camps.

Five: The resurgence of Nationalist groups with political platforms in which some of the Nazi credos were im-
plicitly if not explicitly affirmed.

Six: The initiation of propaganda that the Nazis had
exterminated not six million but "only a million and a half
Jews." This was stated on the floor of the Bundestag by
A. von Thaddeu, the only remaining member of the former
Deutsche Reichspartei (now posing as independent) when,
on March 18, 1953, he opposed the ratification of the agreement with Israel.

The speciously pious prefatory remark and the sancti-
monious generality which follows the unspecified yet cov-
ertly suggestive estimate of the slain by the deputy merits
citation. "Nobody will be able to compensate or to make

restitution for the persecution by German authorities of five to six million Jews in Europe, of whom more than a million were killed. . . . Murder is murder, whether committed against one human being or against many."

Seven: The trend in German political writing to attribute idealistic motives to the early support which was given to the Fuehrer by the generals of the army and to magnify there later attempts upon his life.

Eight: The displacement of the myth of the infallibility of Hitler by the myth that he solely is to be deemed culpable for the national catastrophe. As a scapegoat, he bears the transgressions of all his aides and the multitudes that exalted him to the status of an omniscient deity. "What remains, then," aptly asserts Gerard Speyer, "is a National Socialism without Hitler, made respectable by decent generals, neutral ministerial bureaucrats, and aristocratic diplomats. The arguments of these writers revolve much less around the political principles of the Nazis than Hitler's military strategy." [1]

Nine: The moral negativism, defiant 'do-nothing' (Nichtstun) and exultant sneering which one finds in popular German works like Ernst von Salomon's "Der Fragenbogen" and Ernest Juengers "Der Waldgang". They mirror not a mood of contrition but a spirit of arrogance and *schadenfreude*.[2]

Ten: The listing of the military blunders of Hitler and the omission of his persistent repudiations of the moral principles and ethical injunctions which had been the lodestars of decent honorable societies and their exemplification, the *goal* of *civilization*.

Against these alibis and evasions, testimony of a contrary nature must also be considered. Testimony will be offered to warrant the belief that remorse was felt by Germans when they became apprised of the villainous acts of the Nazis and that their national mood and psychology evidenced a susceptibility to reorientation and improvement.

While the cited explanations and extenuations are considered by many as unmistakable proof of the absence or

non-existence of feelings of remorse by that nation, some
students of abnormal psychology, on the other hand, arrive
at an opposite conclusion. In the post-war efforts of Germans to deny any and all connection with the Nazi party,
in their disavowal of knowledge of the gruesome acts which
were committed in the concentration camps, in the insolent claim that only a fraction of six million Jews had been
killed by the ghoulish henchmen of Hitler, these students
detect evidence of repressed, concealed and distorted
promptings of guilt-feelings. If the Germans had been
shameless and utterly callous to the misdeeds they would
not have resorted to denials and alibis. Their retort would
have been, "So what?"

Without supporting the charge that the evasions and
extenuations of Nazi crimes by the Germans represent
solid proof of the absence of contrition and remorse over
what had occurred in Germany during Hitler's reign, I
am inclined to reject the reverse contentions and inferences. The arguments, offered to support the claim, constitute, it seems to me, psychiatric casuistry, which is as open
to criticism and as vulnerable to refutation as are the
mental somersaults of Hegelian dialectics.

The alleged reverse-forms of contrition I consider to be
less than worthless. For such masqueraded and undercover
confessions of guilt are as incapable of bringing about the
inner purging which the sinner needs as Lady Macbeth's
frantic washing of her hands was impotent to remove the
bloodstains which her distraught mind perceived on them.
I term the supposed camouflaged remorse less than worthless not only because it will fail to bestow abiding serenity
upon one's conscience but also because a psychic upheaval
is unavoidable when the true facts will, as they must some-
times, penetrate the smokescreen which these individuals
have set up as a shield.

The evidence which will first be invoked is intended to
negate the inferences and conclusions which were drawn
from the aforementioned polls.

The polls in my opinion yield us inconclusive testimony regarding the query which we had set out to answer.

The garnered data shed little, if any, light on the question whether the moral feelings of the German populace (which were perverted and blunted by Nazi ideology), now show signs of resuscitation and responsiveness. Particularly is this so in matters involving their attitude to Jews and to the related question of the government's restitution of the material property which the Nazis took from Jews and the indemnification for the suffering endured by survivors.

There is no disputing the fact that all these polls reveal persistent anti-Semitic proclivities if not avowals. That was to be expected. It would have been extraordinary if such a trend were absent. For twelve years the German people had been exposed solely to Herr Goebbels' interpretations and manipulations of current events. No opinion or account of any occurrence was permitted in the daily press, weekly and monthly periodicals or even on the radio, unless it squared with the ideology and supported the program of the Nazis. The Jews brought on the war, and, in the dual role of unconscionable international bankers and wily proponents of communism, were bent on destroying Western Civilization. So the line ran. And after the defeat the alleged spokesman of American Jewry, Henry Morgenthau Jr. was advocating the demolition of every plant and factory in the Reich so that Germany would be transformed from an industrial state to one whose inhabitants would have to sustain themselves only by tilling the soil and raising cattle.

And topping it all, world Jewry is now demanding and obtaining millions of dollars for property which assumedly had been "legally" acquired and which may have been turned to rubble by aerial bombardment in a war which they had incited. *This was the version of events which was given to Germans during and after the war, and neither the American Military Government nor the private good-will-fostering and truth-dispensing organizations in the United States deemed the correction of these notions a vital and urgent task.*

In a world which is regarded as an indivisible unit, and where communication is swift and easy, hatred of any segment of mankind, fostered in any section, is bound to spread ubiquitously like bacilli which, if allowed to thrive in one organ, infect the entire body.

Considering the circumstances and conditions which the Germans had to face (devastated cities and the inflow of ten million German refugees from provinces which are now Soviet satellites), the fact that there are multitudes of Germans who have not been deluded (and not a few individuals whose sense of right and equity impel them to proclaim Germany's guilt and need for repentance for its past demeanor towards Jews) appears to discerning persons a good omen of the possibility of the moral regeneration of the German nation.

Chapter 12

EVIDENCE OF CONTRITION

He who is penitent is almost innocent. SENECA

AT THIS point, the Court projected in our imagination, will summon representatives of good and morally responsive Germans and ask them to present whatever testimony they can muster which will support the belief that feelings of remorse are not extinct in the breast of the once blind, deluded and drugged German people.

In the evidence emanating from churchmen I will quote from an address of Pastor Martin Niemoeller. Niemoeller was a Captain of a U-Boat in World War I. In the beginning he was not averse to the National Socialism of Hitler. Later he expressed disagreement with the Nazis' denunciation and besmirching of the Old Testament and "Biblical Judaism." At first he did not seem upset over the heartless mistreatment of the Jews, from whose influence, he gullibly believed, the Germans "suffered severely." On January 17,

1946, his erstwhile bewitchment and blindness gave way to keen moral introspection. Addressing then a student audience, he gave vent to the following confession, "I am guilty—I kept silent! I only began to speak up when the Church was affected. I feel that I am guilty."

Hermann Maas, Pastor of Heidelberg's largest Church, was a life-long friend of the Jews and an ardent adherent of Zionism. His utterance, though not constituting a change of heart, nevertheless merits listing. Addressing a meeting of the German Parliamentary society in Bonn he made confession not of Nazi quiet but of *"our guilt towards the Jews."* He said, "Every man is judged in two courts. He defends himself in the first, in the earthly court, in order to receive a lighter punishment. We, even those who were not directly guilty, but who were, and even today remain, thoughtless, silent, or forgetful—have deserved the death sentence even from an earthly judge. How much greater, then, is our guilt in the sight of the Eternal Court."

I now offer the resolutions adopted by the United Synod of Evangelical Churches in Germany held in Schwalback,[1] April 23-27, 1950.

The following constitutes more or less a free translation of some declarations relevant to our inquiry.

"We make confession before the God of Compassion that by our omission and silence we were participants in the outrageous crimes which have been committed by individuals of our people against the Jews.

We warn all Christians that retribution emanating from the Court of God is directed to us Germans for what we have done to the Jews. In that court God's clemency is obtained only by the repentant.

We entreat all Christians to rid themselves of any form of anti-Semitism and conscientiously oppose it when it reappears and to meet Jews and Jewish Christians in a fraternal spirit.

We request Christian committees to look after Jewish burial places in their districts and to assume guardianship over them.

We pray the God of Mercy that He bring forth the Day of perfection in which we with the rescued of Israel will celebrate the Victory of Jesus Christ."

For an illustration of the presence of remorse on the part of devotees of the Church of Rome I prefer to call a layman to testify instead of a prelate.

The incident which I shall report constitutes a discussion between two United States soldiers. One was a humanist with agnostic leanings; the other was a devout Catholic. The conversation was over a table in a restaurant; the place was Frankfurt-am-Main; the time, the summer of 1949. At the adjacent table the noted editor of the Frankfurther Hefte, Eugen Kogon, and I were discussing the future of Germany and the likelihood of any vital Jewish life continuing in the New Germany. The discussion between the two United States soldiers was within the range of our hearing and it attracted our attention.

The humanist seemed to place the blame of the rise of Hitler at the door of the Church. "He was nurtured in the Church, wasn't he?" was his contention. To this argument his Catholic confrère replied, "If you follow that procedure then why don't you attribute the delinquencies of individuals to Nature or to God instead of to thee evil doer? Are not those individuals under the tutelage of either Nature or God?"

The Catholic soldier seemed well grounded in the doctrines of his Faith. We later learned that he had thought of studying for the priesthood before he enlisted in the army. He continued to expound the tenet of free will and indeterminism. An act was ethical only if it was the result of conscious effort and voluntary disposition on the part of the performer of the act. "This power and gift the Church wouldn't and couldn't take away from the individual."

Eugen Kogon repressed his elation at and admiration for the zeal and expository talent of the American fellow-Catholic.

The Catholic soldier mentioned Einstein's accolade to the Church for its refusal to become subservient to the Nazis. This seemed to have exposed the protagonist of the

Church to a strong comeback on the part of the agnostic. "The Church became heroic when Hitler ventured to invade and act as lord in the domain reserved for the Church. Until then Church had no scruples in concluding a concordat with Hitler's Reich."

The countenance of the American soldier who was a devotee of the Church registered discomfiture. He seemed to have been cornered. He made no effort to reply. I looked up to Mr. Kogon and my eyes pleaded with him to come to the rescue of his embarrassed fellow-Catholic. However, his only retort to me was, "I hope that the Church will have learnt a lesson and that no future Vicar of Christ will commit the same blunder." As he made this pronouncement his voice and tone betokened unmistakable evidence of remorse and shame. At that moment there flitted through my mind the dictum of the Italian poet and dramatist Vittorio Alfieri, the wording of which I shall expand, "To err is human, to acknowledge error, when perceived, is superhuman, to make impossible the repetition of that error is nobility bordering on the divine." [2]

The next witness to present testimony to the effect that there are individuals amongst the Germans who are stricken with compunction of conscience over their people's outrageous mistreatment of Jews will be the philosopher and educator, Karl Jaspers. He is singled out not because he is the only one to have voiced the conviction that every living German must bear some share of responsibility for what had been allowed to come to pass in Hitler's Reich. He is chosen as the prototype or examplar of a coterie of morally-staunch and sensitized individuals who now have been given key positions in institutions of learning in West Germany. Karl Jaspers did not impart his beliefs merely to chosen and trusted colleagues. He ringingly proclaimed them in the lecture hall before multitudes of students whose attitudes and behavior he aspired to influence.

On August 15, 1945 on the occasion of the reintroduction of medical courses at the University of Heidelberg, he delivered a discourse on "German Guilt" which was forthright and keenly analytical. The content of this notable address together with other talks are now incorporated in a book under the title "The Question of German Guilt." [3]

Here are some of the author's soul-revealing statements.

"We Germans are indeed obliged without exception to understand clearly the question of our guilt, and to draw the conclusions. What obliges us is our human dignity. First we cannot be indifferent to what the world thinks of us, for we are part of mankind—are human before we are Germans. More important, however, our own life, in distress and dependence, can have no dignity except by truthfulness toward ourselves. The guilt question is more than a question put to us by others, it is one we put to ourselves. The way we answer it will be decisive for our present approach to the world and ourselves. It is a vital question for the German soul. No other way can lead to a regeneration that would renew us from the source of our being. That the victors condemn us is a political fact which has the greatest consequences for our life, but it does not help us in the decisive point, in our inner regeneration. Here we deal with ourselves alone. Philosophy and theology are called on to illumine the depths of the question of guilt.

"Equally vast is the difference and degree of our guilt. No one is guiltless. . . ." [4]

The witnesses to follow are the former President and the incumbent Chancellor of the Bonn Republic.

On the 10th of December, 1949, Dr. Theodore Heuss, the elected head of the new government and the President of the Upper House of Germany's Parliament (*Bundesrat*) delivered an historic address at Wiesbaden. The occasion was a meeting of the *Society to Sponsor Cooperation between Christians and Jews.* That audience was graced by the presence of John M. McCloy, the High Commissioner for the United States Zone.

Dr. Heuss commenced his notable discourse with a deprecation of the widespread habit in Germany to scoff at and belittle the avowals and aspirations of the exponents of the 18th century enlightenment. He termed Voltaire and Lessing path-blazers. He quoted Sombart's view that humanity and nationalism were closely related. This thesis, however, was not substantiated in the Germany of 1933. The Germany of the Third Reich confirmed the observation of Grillparzer "From humanity through nationalism to bestiality."

He then proceeded directly to a discussion of the horrible deeds committed against the Jews. These must be brought into the open, he declared. The world imputes to all Germans the guilt for what was done in Germany. He acknowledged a degree of responsibility for the hellish deeds of the Nazis. More poignant than the imputed collective guilt is the collective shame from which no German was free. I quote two passages from the stirring discourse.

"I know that what I am about to say will anger some people. I shall in all likelihood be the recipient of letters, many letters, even anonymous letters. This is something to which men in my position must resign themselves. We must not forget; we must not forget things which people for the peace and comfort of their souls like to forget. We dare not forget the Nuremberg Laws, the Jew-star, the synagogues consigned to flames, the desecrated cemeteries, the transporting of Jews into exile and death. These things, facts that happened, which we dare not forget because of their disturbing effect upon us. The most terrible thing about these things is that they did not happen under the fanaticism of pogroms like those which took place in Russia or Poland. The worst thing is that *they were the product of a Weltanschauung which took a long time to crystalize.* What kind of a Weltanschauung was it? It was a Weltanschauung which recognized no moral category and no individual values between man and man."

He concluded the address with the exhortation that Germans be bold enough to replace their disposition to hate with the courage to love. "Does love need courage?" he asked at the end of his discourse. "It does," was his reply. "To hate is easy; it is a cheap and light matter to succumb to the indolent inclination of the heart. But love is a daring adventure and he who dares will, in the end, win."

Dr. Heuss voiced the same views when he participated

on November 30, 1952, in the unveiling of a memorial to the 30,000 killed in Bergen-Belsen concentration camp. Dr. Heuss declared then, too, that the Germans must recognize "the enormity of what happened" at the camp. He insisted that the German people knew of the "shameful" crimes which occurred at Bergen-Belsen". . . . "They were a degradation and shame to Germany. *No one can take this shame away from us."*

The last personage to offer testimony is the octogenarian Chancellor of West Germany. Approaching the witness stand is not the expected pliable elderly gentleman who is supposed to have been made soft and tenderhearted by the sorrowful events which he was fated to witness. There looms before the spectators in the court a massive figure who is sure of step and whose voice is firm and resonant. He has become the personification of integrity and selfless devotion to a reborn Germany. The awe and respect which Adenauer evokes have been likened to the emotional response which the name and person of Hindenburg were wont to call forth before he allowed himself to become besmirched by his association with Hitler and his henchmen. The supposed resemblance between the two men is misleading. Hindenburg was deemed incorruptible and his (not inflexible sense of duty served him as a lode-star. A moral imperative, in the mind of Hindenburg, however, was conditioned by its conformity to the interests of the State, a Junker type of State, an Ideal above which nothing was more worthy or commanding. Adenauer is also intensely patriotic and devoted to the Vaterland. But that Vaterland is not extolled above considerations involving the weal of mankind and loyalty to Truth and devotion to one's God and the Abiding Moral Precepts which have the imprimatur of the Holy One and have been also validated by the ages. He is striving to obtain for Germany the recognition due to her not because of what she was but because of what she may become under good leadership which will be imbued with a sound political outlook.

The life story of this great, venerable statesman is already assuming the form of a saga because of his contempt for and defiance of the Nazis, and his deviation from the mode of behavior which the party had prescribed.

In the debacle that followed the Nazi surrender, the elderly and ethically-minded Adenauer forged ahead politically, until the leadership of the nation was proffered to him. He took hold of the reins of government with an undiverted gaze towards a set goal. With a mind ever clear he proceeded to indicate to his people the way out of the quagmire of sullen despondency and the economic depression that tended to demoralize further the vanquished nation.

He refused to be beguiled by Russia's promise of unification of East and West Germany. Nor did he cower before the Soviet reprisals because his Government refused to heed the desires or demands of the Kremlin.

The unprotested acceptance by the Bonn Government of the U. S. Law that Germans restore to the Jewish survivors of Nazi brutality the property or value of the property which the Nazis under the guise of legality had purloined from them is due to no small degree to its stout advocacy by Adenauer. The Bonn Government's willingness to indemnify the survivors for the length of time they languished in concentration camps and especially the agreement to reimburse the Israel Government (in goods to the amount of over $800,000,000 over a period of twelve years) to cover a part of the costs of transporting, feeding and resettling in Israel the surviving inmates of the concentration camps, are acts which could not have been concluded without the Chancellor's determination to have the New Germany mitigate, in some form, the great wrong which was done to the Jews of Germany and Europe.[5]

To gauge the motives of the Adenauer resolve and the moral courage which its execution required one should remember that West Germany at the time of the Israel agreement was in a position to bypass the demand for restitution or to have offered a fraction of the agreed amount. The strained relations between Russia and the United States were near the breaking point and both powers were eager to obtain the support of the Bonn Government. Had the latter been reluctant to make good the extortions, lootings

and confiscation of the disowned and defunct Nazi regime
one may doubt whether pressure would have been brought
by the United States State Department to force the government of West Germany to assume such an obligation. To
this day, East Germany has given no sign of willingness to
make restitution for the looted Jewish property within its
domain and this unconcern we know is not uninfluenced
by the wishes of the Kremlin. (Russia busied herself with
the collection of reparation for herself. This meant the
syphoning of untold wealth from the zones which she occupied to the heartland of the Soviets—Russia.) The U. S. and
Great Britain didn't seem to be upset by Austria's offer of
a ridiculously small token payment for the substantial
property which their Nazis had taken away from Austrian
Jews.

Lastly one must not fail to take into consideration, in
adjudging the Adenauer resolve, the dire threats of unrelenting commercial boycotts which the Arab League hurled
at the Bonn Government if she persisted in going through
this settlement with the Israelis. The Bonn Government
totally defied and ignored the warnings of the Arab Nations, which might have brought down upon West Germany
the hostility of the Moslems not only of the Near East, but
also of the Far East.

The moral courage of the government headed by Heuss
and Adenauer was again displayed in the refusal to go along
with the coterie of nations, amongst whom was the powerful
and munificent U.S.A. They were considering the imposition
of sanctions on Israel when it was reluctant to withdraw
from the Gaza Strip and the Aqaba peninsula without some
assurance that the gorilla attacks and the illegal closing of
international waterways to Israel shipping would not be
reinstituted by a reinflated Egyptian dictator.

Chapter 13

A RENDEZVOUS OF GERMAN YOUTH—
A KOSHER RESTAURANT

"Shall error in the round of time still father truth?"
TENNYSON
"Mistake, error, is the discipline through which we advance."
WILLIAM E. CHANNING

IN DECEMBER 1956 I was scheduled to deliver a lecture to the faculty and students of Johannes Guttenberg University in Mainz. I took advantage of the occasion and revisited Frankfurt-am-Main. While there I was taken to lunch to a restaurant on Goethe Platz which is a few blocks from the Hotel Frankfurter Hof. The window of the establishment bore just the name "Modern Restaurant."

In the main large dining room one saw individuals who were typical Germans sitting and eating at the tables. In the evening the place became filled with German boys and girls who came there for a sandwich and a glass of beer. There was a four piece orchestra playing. In the center was a space vacant of tables where the boys and girls danced to the music. The demeanor of the boys and girls was proper and refined and would have reflected credit on any university whose students they would have been.

The owners of the establishment, a middle-aged couple, were collecting the money brought to them by the waiters for the food and beers which they had served the patrons. They did not seem to be Germans. When I later spoke to them I detected in the interspersed Yiddish expressions and their accent that they were East European Jews. Upon inquiry I learned that they were survivors of a concentration camp. When I asked them whether these facts were known to their customers, the answer was, "Many do know and it does not seem a matter of import or significance to them."

I also noted that in a small adjacent room some Jews with skull caps on their heads were sitting and eating. When the owner noticed the puzzlement on my face, called forth by the sight of Jews with covered heads eating what I assumed was forbidden food, he proffered the information that all the food served in his place was strictly kosher. The following Sabbath I met in the Orthodox Synagogue the reddish-bearded man who supervised the preparation of the food served in the "Modern Restaurant" so that it complied with the dietary laws. Again I asked the proprietor, "Do your patrons know that the food served here is kosher?" His answer was, "I don't make it a point to announce the fact to my German customers. This I can tell you. They like the food and they show it by coming here frequently and in large numbers."

I now present as evidence the story of Arthur J. Olsen (which appeared in the *New York Times* Magazine Section of February 17, 1957) entitled "Anne Frank Speaks to the Germans." In this story he tells of the multitudes that filled the theatre in which Anne Frank's Diary was dramatized. He records the reaction and mood of the audience at the conclusion of the play, as it was reported by one who was present at the premiere in West Berlin's Schloss Park Theatre (October 1, 1956). Here is the quote:

"For a full two minutes there was no sound in the theatre. Then a spatter of hand-clapping began. It was hissed down immediately. Then 700 sophisticated Berliners rose slowly and walked out of the theatre. I saw tear stains on powdered cheeks and men walking as if they were very tired. The people got their coats and went home, still silent. It was like leaving a funeral."

"Four months later," Mr. Olsen writes, "this phenomenon was being repeated two or three times a week wherever 'Anne Frank' was playing. Most managements had inserted notes in the programs requesting no applause at the end. There had been some tense moments between playgoers who wanted to voice their approval and those who considered a whisper tantamount to public insult."

One may consider the dispatch which Mr. Olsen sent to the *New York Times* on March 18, 1957 from Belsen, Germany as a postscript to the magazine article. I quote only an extract from the dispatch:

"A thousand young Germans, shivering in a drizzling rain, placed flowers today on the burial mounds here that cover the victims of a Nazi Concentration camp.

"In one of the mass graves is buried Anne Frank, in whose memory today's pilgrimage from Hamburg was made."

On May 1st, the *New York Times* carried the following (Reuters) news item from Salzgitter, Germany.

"Two thousand young trade unionists marched in a torchlight procession last night to the Salzgitter cemetery where unknown persons had overturned Jewish gravestones and had left behind a swastika sign.

"The unionists, all members of the metal workers union, laid a wreath at the Jewish memorial.

"A wreath has also been sent to Salzgitter by the 2,800 pupils of West Berlin's protestant schools, who have started a collection to help repair the damage done to the graves."

After the completion of my manuscript the well documented monograph of Philip Friedman, dealing with the question, "Was there 'another Germany' during the Nazi Period?", was published in YIVC Annual of Social Science, (Vol. X, 1955). His study, based on much probing and research indicates that an affirmative reply to the question is in place. The proof that he offers is too voluminous to cite. I shall only quote two key passages from his 45 page brochure packed with supporting data.

"Among the most neglected questions is that of the attitude of the German people, of its cultural and religious leadership as well as of the masses, toward Jewish persecution. Were their sympathies with the Nazis or with their victims? If the latter, was their opposition to Nazi barbarism limited to moral sentiment, or extended to open protest and a readiness to aid the victims? What were the at-

tempted or actual achievements of anti-Nazi Germans
on behalf of the Jews? . . . Despite the paucity of research
in this area, much has been written bearing directly or in-
directly on the subject, particularly in German. This ranges
from expressions of regret and repentance to attempts at a
whitewash.—"

"The problems touched upon in this repentance literature are symptomatic of certain post-war spiritual trends
in Germany and are not quite pertinent to our present inquiry. The literature, however, contains ample material
on the Nazi period. These books, pamphlets and articles,
as well as the literature of the resistance, constitute an important source for the study of the attitudes and behavior
of organized and unorganized anti-Nazism with respect to
Jews and Nazi persecution of Jews. Some writers use the
phrase the 'Other Germany' to refer to an allegedly organized anti-Nazi movement. This is not a precise phrase.
To some it denotes organized anti-Nazi resistance; to others
all manifestations of anti-Nazi sentiment or behavior on
the part of the people at large. In the present study, we
have used the term in the second more inclusive sense. We
have also included the material on the anti-Nazi opposition
in Austria after the Anschluss in 1938."

(The above article we are told is part of a larger work on
"The 'Other Germany' and the Jews." It will consist of sections which will deal with (1) "Religious opposition; (2)
Political Resistance Groups and Movements; (3) Opposition within the Wehrmacht; (4) The Anti-Nazi Elements
in the Administration; (5) Attitude of the German Populace; and (6) Literary Opposition." The published monograph is based on the first two sections of the larger study.)

Commenting on the passage in Scripture "Such is the
generation of them that seek after Him. . . ." [1] the Talmud records a difference in exposition on the part of Rabbi
Judah, the Prince and the other Sages. One said "As the
leader so the generation"; the other declared, "As the generation so the leader." [2] The comments that follow these
statements clearly indicate that they were grappling with
the still unsolved question whether the character of a gen-

eration is determined by the kind of leader which it has or whether the leader is the product of and moulded by the generation over which he presides.

It seems to me that there is some basis for each affirmation. Applying the two declarations to the Germany of yesterday and today, one may say that the Germany of 1933 earned the demonic leadership of a Hitler, the blinded and battered Germany of 1945 stood and still stands in dire need of the leadership of an Adenauer. "For as by one man's disobedience many were made sinners, so by the obedience of one shall many be made righteous." [3] The passage in the New Testament can be aptly applied to the leadership of a Hitler and an Adenauer.

Chapter 14

THE TESTS OF GENUINE REPENTANCE

"God dropped a spark down into everyone
And if we find and fan it to a blaze,
It'll spring up and glow, like the sun,
And light the wandering out of stony ways." MASEFIELD

Genuine repentance involves the following:

1. A feeling of shame and regret for the commission of the misdeed.
2. Public confession or acknowledgement of the guilt.
3. A willingness to make all possible restitution to the injured.
4. A determination not only to avoid the repetition of the act but also to rectify the condition which induced or impelled one to commit the misdeed.

Which of these stipulations has Germany complied with and which has she yet to heed?

In considering the first item we must recognize the fact that regret and remorse are mental states. To prove them, one has to be able to peer into the heart and soul of the recanting sinner. Only then can one assay the genuineness of the expression and know whether it presages an enduring reformation. Such a power is available only to God. We humans must draw conclusions as to the sincerity of one who expresses regret and remorse from overt and exterior indications. "The secret things belong unto the Lord our God," Scripture tells us, "only the things that are revealed belong to us and to our children . . ." [1]

I have listed in the previous chapters the signs in contemporary life in Germany which may be said to support, and also other tokens which may be said to refute the thesis that Germany as a nation had experienced a severe shaking of the soul. Considering the character of the men who expressed their sense of shame and remorse over the vile and vicious deeds of the Nazis and the high position which they are permitted by popular suffrage to hold, I am inclined to believe that the seeds for a national reformation and reorientation have been sown and that the tenders of the delicate plant are conscientious and devoted laborers in the vineyard.

In regard to the second requirement, the public confession, it should be noted that its value consists in its pragmatic consequences. Its function is to deter others from venturing on a similar course. The confession also enables the guilt-stricken to translate effectively the feeling of remorse into an act of restitution. It is like the part in an engine which converts electrical energy into mechanical power.

As to the quoted statements of guilt or shame (even if they are not, as some contend, free of material considerations), they have been voiced by men of rectitude and dauntless idealism. That they mean what they said is evidenced by their unwillingness to confess to more than what they feel and what the survivors deem the black deeds demand. That these utterances of morally-elite personages have not swelled to a national lament—PECCAVI—is due no little degree to the tragic sins of commission and omission on the part of the victorious powers who occupied and ruled Germany. The brutality inflicted upon German prisoners of war, many of whom are still unreturned and unaccounted for, and the unrestrained cruelty to and plundering of the population are sins that must be charged to the Russians. The sins of failure to devise an effective program of re-education and purging of Nazi big-wigs and the industrial barons who supplied Hitler with the material means which enabled him to attain power are to be ascribed largely to the easy-going policy of the United States. The inability of the East and West to come to an understanding which will assure to each nation political security and freedom to choose the economic system which it prefers to follow, is a menace, without parallel, to the whole world.

Furthermore, the writer heard the opinion expressed by Jacob Altmaier, one of the three Jewish members of the Bundestag, who is not an adherent of the Adenauer party but is a member of its opposition, the Social Democratic Party, that at the time of liberation, if the Occupying Powers had permitted the German population to take the law into their hands, there would have been about half a dozen hangings of Nazis in every village and hamlet in Germany.

The Bonn Government's resolve to make restitution to the victims of Nazism for their suffering and material losses, while leaving much to be desired, may also be submitted as an indication of contrition.

From an experience which extends to the beginnings of human history, society in every clime and every continent has learned that the way to discourage theft, whether it be committed by lawless individuals or plunder-bent nations, is to penalize the guilty when apprehended and also to see that there should be no profit accruing to the perpetrators of the act. There are some who maintain that if after World War I the barons of German industrial enterprises and banking institutions had been restrained from exploiting the inflation of 1923 to enrich themselves, then the initiation of World War II perhaps would not have been so alluring to German industrialists as well as militarists. For that feat provided the arch-swindler, the high-collared, old-fashionedly dressed and puritan-faced Hjalmar Schacht with the idea whereby under the veneer of legality Germany could expropriate Jewish wealth which enabled Hitler to meet the initial costs of rearming the Third Reich. It was the cunning and craft of Schacht and Funk which made the Fuehrer chuckle on observing a fact which he understated. "In the field of sharp finance," Hitler remarked, "a really intelligent Aryan is more than a match for his Jewish counterpart."

In the matter of restitution and indemnification, the Bonn regime deserves commendation. This is said not without an awareness that in the agreement with Israel the amount stipulated to be given to the newly-established state represents a pittance of what was taken from Jews. The indemnification payments to the survivors are trivial despite their chafing to some members of the Ministry of Finance who are fearful of their possible adverse effect on the stability of the mark. I am not so naive as to assume that the agreement was passed without a realization that Germany would derive substantial advantage from such a step now, and more so in the future. As Israel became more firmly established, she is becoming one of the merchandise marts for the Near and Far East and North and South African countries. As such she becomes a sales agency for the manufactured products of Germany, for which role Jews do not lack the qualification. Restitution to Jews has bolstered the German claim for the restitution of her subjects' property which was seized by the U. S. during the war.

Despite all these qualifying factors which tend to dull the lustre of the Restitution and Indemnification Agreement between the Bonn Government and Israel, history, I believe, will bestow noble motives and a sterling type of patriotic devotion to Chancellor Adenauer's efforts to make some amends for the fathomless injury which the bestial Nazis did to the Jews. The new Germany, as was stated, was not pressured by the United States to propose any financial compensation to the infant State for the expenditures to which she was subjected in providing a haven for the Jewish survivors of the concentration camp.

The recent election of Adenauer by the surprisingly large majority showed that, despite the results of previous polls, the financial arrangement with Israel had been either ignored by the voters or did not evoke their active disapproval.

When we consider West Germany's persistence in concluding the agreement and fulfilling the stipulated obligations (even ahead of schedule) and all this in the face of the threat of an economic boycott by the Arab League we can see how inexact it is to term the action merely expedient.

If the attitude of the New Germany with regard to the first three items which are essential to genuine penitence redound to the credit of the New Germany, there remains, however, much which she must do with regard to the fourth stipulation, namely, the determination not only to avoid the repetition of the act but also to rectify the conditions which induce or impel one to commit the misdeed.

Part V

THE WAY TO REDEMPTION

Chapter 1

MAN—NATURE'S SUPREME BLUNDER
OR MASTERPIECE?

"What a piece of work is man! how infinite in faculty, in form and moving, how express and admirable in action, how like an angel! in apprehension how like a God! the beauty of the world, the paragon of animals, and yet to me what is this quintessence of dust!" SHAKESPEARE

"It would seem that aggression when it is impeded entails serious injury and that we have to destroy other things and other people, in order not to destroy ourselves, in order to protect ourselves from the tendency to self-destruction. A sad disclosure, it will be agreed, for the moralist." SIGMUND FREUD

THE pertinence of our exhortation that Germans endeavor to alter their ways and views or character is conditioned by our appraisal of human nature and our belief in its corrigibility. In this connection I shall relate the following anecdote.

After I resigned my post as director of the Hillel Foundation at Ann Arbor, Michigan, my esteemed friend, Dr. Alexander G. Ruthven, the then distinguished President of the University of Michigan, honored me with an invitation to have dinner with him at his home, to which he also asked some members of the faculty. After we had dined we retired to the spacious living room, where the radio was broadcasting a panel discussion on some social issue. When the program was over our host, after a moment of reflection, addressed to us the following inquiry. "If each of you were given charge of a radio program like the one to which you listened and you were also given the power to bring from paradise or purgatory two eminent personages each to propound and defend the opposite views, which two individuals would you conjure up and whom of the past would you select as a moderator?" Each professor named two individuals in his particular field of study, and explained the divergence of views between them.

The President was considerate enough to put me last on the list and announced that, since I was soon to leave Ann Arbor he would not, in my answer and explanation, subject me to a time limit.

I selected the names of Jean Jacques Rousseau and Sigmund Freud. Jean Jacques Rousseau, I said, declared man to be innately good. Man's corruption he traced to the elaborate institutions of civilization which, he maintained, warped his feelings, befuddled his thinking and dulled his perception.

Rousseau was a romanticist. Nature was to him idyllic. It did not require improvement or embellishment at the hands of man. Man, a feeling and reasoning being, was a part of nature. He was like a seed which contained in itself the power to sprout and grow and blossom into a beautiful plant. If it happened that the seed turned out to be a weed instead of a fragment and beautiful plant, it was so, averred Rousseau, because of the gardener's neglect or misuse of it or because he had allowed heavy stamping feet to trample the soil that held the seed in its tender embrace. To live gregariously, the individual had to sign away his freedom and equality. Rousseau's Social Contract, therefore, commenced with the wail, "Man is born free and everywhere he is in chains."

When I came to expound what Freud's view of man was, I felt myself skating on thin ice. In reading Freud I missed the clarity, precision and consistency of expression that I was accustomed to find in philosophic treatises. The Viennese explorer of the depths of the human psyche resorted to metaphors and often modified his figures of speech. His terminology appeared to me of the hot-house variety.

I tried to get the member of the psychology department, who was one of the guests, to carry the ball for me but he demurred by professing to be a specialist in animal behavior. "My forte," he humbly contended, "is to observe and time-check how long it takes mice to learn to go through certain mazes to obtain their food." With his withdrawal I had no alternative but to proceed. I cast a timid glance at the psychologist whose approving sign was a signal for me to proceed.

"To Freud human personality presents three aspects, the "ID," the "EGO," and the "SUPEREGO." The "ID" is the core and primordial stuff from which the human psyche is forged. It is the reservoir of man's instinctual drives and libidinal urges. The latter emanate from the dark and hidden recesses of our being, the subconscious. The drives break out like the spurting geysers in Yellowstone Park, except that they do not conform to any time schedule or logical procedure.

"If the "ID" makes up so large a part of the human psyche then man, according to Freud, may be described as innately wild, destructive and malevolent. If we may not designate his initial disposition as downright immoral, then we may term it amoral at that stage. But this type of amorality is not the result of staticism and inactivity. On the contrary the "ID" is like an incessantly active volcano.

"To Freud the "EGO" is the aspect of personality of which the individual is conscious not merely as being related to or as forming a part of his psychic make-up but as his very *SELF*. The "EGO" functions not as a mentor but as a tourist's guide, who aids his client in getting to the places he wished to visit.

"The "SUPER EGO" is the social influence and the impacts of man's cultural past and present on the "EGO" and the upthrusts of the "ID." Under it are designated what Rousseau subsumed under civilization and forces and institutions of ordered society. The "SUPER EGO" has the role of moral mentor, approving or reproving the "EGO's" expression or course. Freud identifies it with what is termed *conscience*. It is a check on the "EGO" and the "ID." Without such a check, each individual would be "a wild man; his hand would be against every man and every man's hand against him." [1]

At this point I paused and one of the group asked whether the difference between the appraisal of Rousseau and Freud was factual or merely verbal. I indicated that a more au-

thoritative answer should come from the psychologist. He
replied that he felt that the clash was real and basic. Another member volunteered the view that the difference may
be the product of contrary temperament.

Here Dr. Ruthven, with a sunny smile and a twinkle in
his eye, spoke up. "All the speakers, it is to be noted, failed
to name their choice of a moderator." Then directing his
glance at me he continued, "I will not press each of your
friends to name their moderator and justify their selection.
They are professors and we must reckon with their shortcomings. We can't, however, allow a theologian and philosopher to dodge this part of the query." The group chuckled
and all eyes were focussed on me.

I replied that any acknowledged representative of the
Judaic tradition would make an acceptable moderator since
that tradition, as can easily be shown, would commit him
to steer clear of either extreme position.

"The Jewish tradition asserts that man was fashioned
from lowly dust, yet into those clods there was infused the
"breath of life" and the product "became a living soul." [2]
God created man in His image, we are told. Man was allowed
to sojourn in Paradise. Possessed of soul with a divine spark,
man was not content with a *gift*. He wanted to convert it
into an *attainment*. He craved for knowledge, the personal
experience of what is good and evil that he could not get in
the sheltered, sinecure, temptation-free existence of Paradise.[3] To make himself an ethical being man realized that
he would have to face temptation, struggle, sin, penitence,
anguish of soul, aspiration and only after these, there would
follow spiritual triumphs, and 'the peace that passeth all
understanding.' [4] The seeming paradox of God, the source
and fountain of all goodness, reconciling Himself to the
fact that "the imagination of Man's heart veers towards
evil ever since his youth" [5] finds its explanation in the experience which one must go through in order to become an
ethical being.

"In less poetic form the Rabbis perceived man to be composed of two natures, one disposed to evil and the other to
good. Between the two there is an unending struggle, until

the very moment of the soul's departure from this world. Every decision we make involving a moral issue, adds strength to one or the other. This is what was implied in the statement of Ben Azzai, "Be quick to observe even a light (seemingly-unimportant) percept (commandment) and flee from a transgression; for the recompense of the observance of a precept is the opportunity of observing another precept and the recompense of a transgression is (the violation of) another transgression.[6]

"Lest man appear doomed to moral perdition by his past misdeeds which like snakes entwine the helpless Laocoon, the Rabbis assert, "He who strives to purify himself no matter what his past has been, heaven will extend aid to him." [7] Instinctual as may be man's primordial drives and libidinal desires, he can so sublimate them that he can make himself 'a little lower than the angels.' "

"If I am to single out a particular person to act as a moderator," I concluded, "I would be inclined to choose Hosea, not because there is any uniqueness in his exposition of the Judaic tradition but because his domestic life vividly reveals his realization of the core of goodness that is imbedded in human nature, the contrary grains which can be seen to run through that core notwithstanding. It is known that Hosea loved and was married to a woman who became faithless to him. She left him preferring her many paramours to his singular devotion. Her paramours became as faithless to her as she had been to her husband. She sank to lower and lower levels and then Hosea encountered her a forlorn, pitiable and haggard creature. She had awakened his compassion and rekindled his former love and trust. He took her to his bosom, restored her to her prior glorious self and station.

"I have selected Hosea also because in his wife's easy succumbing to temptation, progressive degeneration and ultimate redemption from sin Hosea saw mirrored the moral tug and tussle to which peoples and nations are subjected. He therefore cites his domestic unhappiness and agony and the crowning reward of his unabated loyalty. Gomer's reformation and rekindled love are made the basis of an exhor-

tation to Israel to repent her misdeeds and return to God,
whose remembrance of the troth in the desert remained
ever fresh and vivid, and Whose arms were outstretched
to receive Israel in love as well as with forgiveness. Hosea
pictures the new reconciliation and restoration of the once
faithless Israel. In a matchlessly sublime scene, and with
meaningful symbolism, he has God saying to Israel, "And
I will betroth thee unto Me forever; Yea, I will betroth thee
unto Me in righteousness, and in Justice, and I will betroth
thee unto Me in faithfulness; and thou shalt know (love)
the Lord." [8]

As I pondered over what the world's disposition should
be to the Germany of Adenauer, this incident in President
Ruthven's home kept bobbing up in my mind. I wondered
whether it didn't point to a course which we ought to pursue
at least until we detect signs which would clearly and un-
mistakably indicate that the German people renewed the
compact which they had with the devil and that our hope
for their redemption was bound to end in disappointment.

The signal and portent of moral recession and self-
debasement on the part of Germans (and of any other people) would be its toleration of the resuscitation of totalitarianism. For a rejection of democracy is tantamount to
the loss of faith in the perfectibility and redeemability of
man *in freedom*. A tyrannic and totalitarian regime comes
into being only after the belief is allowed to grow and
spread like a fungus that self-rule or the non-compulsive
behavior of man is a hapless and hopeless enterprise and
like a rudderless bark in a seething and stormy sea the
venture is bound to flounder.

Chapter 2

MYTHS AND LEGENDS—INDICES OF
NATIONAL ASPIRATIONS

"Primitive man is known to us by the stages of development through which he has passed: that is, through the inanimate monuments and implements which he has left behind for us, through our knowledge of his art, his religion and his attitude toward life which we have received either directly or through the medium of legends, myths and fairy tales—." SIGMUND FREUD

To confirm the thesis, that the German national soul has been a playground and an arena where vicious impulses had been locked and still are locked in a battle and that the triumph of the former over the latter will be decided by self-analysis, deep insight and the resolute determination of the multitude to shed the evil notions and habits of the past, it will be necessary to direct the reader's attention to the role which myths, legends and folklore play in the development of the psyche of a people.

Myths, legends and folklore were considered valuable only in affording us an insight into the mode of thinking of primitive man. They represented, we were told, Man's first venture to account for the 'why and wherefore' of Nature's behavior or the character and particularity of tribal customs and celebrations. Legends and myths were considered signs and indices which afforded us a glimpse into the mentality of primitive man, and the kind of world which he envisioned. As such, they were intended merely to throw light on the past. Their impact upon the ideational, emotional or practical tendencies of the group which conceived or incorporated them into its culture, was supposed to be insignificant, if any.

Psychoanalysts now apprise us that folklore, myths and
legends have evolved primarily not to answer primitive
man's queries or to resolve his puzzlement in regard to
what he saw and felt. These fanciful stories were conceived
or emerged, they say, more in response to a volition involving the present and even more the future. Folklore, myths
and legends are the embodiment of vague wishes and persistent but undefined hopes of the corporate entity, the tribe
or group. They are projections of the group's desires,
wherein we can discern the qualities which they esteem
and which they set up for their successors to emulate. *Legends and myths mirror not so much the character and
psychic dispositions of forebears of the folk as they do the
folk's expectations of those who would follow it.*

"The psychoanalysis of myths," Ernest Jones maintains,
"shows clearly that they represent in a disguised way the
most primitive wishes and fears of mankind. The mechan-
ism of the disguise, as also the motive for it, is extremely
similar to that of dreams, and indeed many mythologists before Freud had pointed out the far-going resemblances between dreams and myths. The energies that could not be
transmitted into the real tasks and interest of life were
expressed in the wishfulness of myths. . . . In short, the
fulfillment of unconscious wishes furnishes the main crea-
tive force in the formation of myths and fairy tales." [1]

The philosopher Alfred N. Whitehead in his little volume entitled "Symbolism, its meaning and effect" maintained that symbolism "plays a dominant part in the way
in which all higher organisms conduct their lives. It is the
cause of progress and the cause of error. The higher animals
have gained a faculty of great power, by means of which
they can define with some accuracy these distant features
in the immediate world by which their future lives are to
be determined." [2] This designation of the import and impact of symbols can equally be applied to legends and folklore.

Legends and folklore at times offer a surer clue to the
character and proclivities of a people than do the avowals
of belief on the part of its spokesmen. Legends and folk-

lore represent the imaginative thought and composite will
of simple folk. Being the product of an unsophisticated
group they are devoid of checks and artful concealments.
Like the speech of children they convey ungilded but authentic desires and feelings.

If legends in general can reveal the nature and disposition
of a people, then the glorified portraiture of its national
heroes are particularly illuminating. For to the lean kernel
of the actual being and life of these heroes there have been
added deeds and incidents which tend to support attitudes
and aspirations which that people esteems.

Such portraitures of national heroes reflect not only a
people's present inclinations and ambitions which they are
prone to project into the past, but those inclinations and
ambitions also become dynamic forces that steer the group
to a future course. A legendary or semi-legendary figure
may play such a potent role in the life of a people that a
full explanation of its behavior can not be attributed solely
to economic or political factors but must be referred also to
the spur and push which follows a people's rapt emulation
of its hallowed heroes. The Duce's determination to make
Italy into a military world power, regardless of the cost
(which of all nations it could least afford and his alliance
with Hitler, whose victory would have reduced Italy to a vas-
sal state and whose defeat would have sounded the death
knell not only to the Duce's dream but to Italy's role as a
European power) cannot be accounted for without a reference to the imperial rule of ancient Rome which in turn
derived no slight encouragement from the contemplation
and emulation of its legendary founders and heroes.

The part that the heroes of Teutonic lore played in mold-
ing the national policy and character of the Germans cannot
be overestimated. That Wotan, Siegfried (with his invincible sword) and Goetterdaemmerung tales played a part in
Hitler's adventure and end can be substantiated by a perusal of "Mein Kampf," the Bible of the Nazis, and the recollection of the weird old Teutonic ceremonies and rites which
they enacted with such solemnity.

A like examination of the delineations of the character

and disposition of Abraham, the father of the Hebrews, will make the contrast striking.

The role of the Jew in the drama of man is exemplified by the figure of Abraham, their patriarch. The aspects of his character and life-goal stand out in bold relief when contrasted especially with the picture of Aeneas, the Father of the Latin people. Both have been glorified by tradition. Both have become prototypes of their respective descendants and devotees. Both are depicted as having been forced to leave the land of their birth and wander in search of a new home. Striking as are the parallels of their history, their differences, however, are even more arresting and illuminating.

In the saga of the Greeks, namely, the Homeric poems, we have a narrative of the exploits of Ulysses or Odysseus, the father and founder of the Hellenic race. The story relates how Menelaus and Agamemnon aided by Ulysses ventured on the expedition to destroy Troy. The destruction of Troy took ten years and it took an equal length of time for Ulysses to return to Ithaca and regain his power. In this epic, lust for a woman plays a notable role. The alliance between Ulysses and Menelaus and Agamemnon was formed in order to recapture Helen, the wife of Menelaus, who was abducted by Paris of Troy. The return of Ulysses is depicted as a struggle of Ulysses for Penelope, his wife, who during his absence encountered (and perhaps encouraged) the many suitors who were striving to win her love. From this legendary account, we can understand the Greeks' regard for external form and beauty. The things pleasing to the eye constituted to them a supreme good. They yearned for them, fought for them and worshipped them.

The saga of the Roman people reveals no less the character of the Latin people. In Virgil's *Aeneid* we have the legendary account of the ordeals and wanderings of that people's Patriarch, Aeneas. Aeneas, we are told was warned by the ghost of Hector of the impending destruction of Troy. To escape captivity, Aeneas, after collecting his wife, son and idols, ventured on the long and precarious journey. He visited a host of places. In every place of sojourn, he immediately proceeded to erect a city. Fate, however, directed his feet to the shores of Italy, where his scions, Romulus and Remus, succeeded in laying the foundations of the metropolis, which, in time, became the heart and center of the vast Roman Empire.

The Roman epic discloses an interest which in one aspect is similar and in another differs from Homer's classic. In the *Aeneid,* we find that the quest of the Latin was not so much for love and beauty as it was for power and political dominion. Aeneas left his city because it was doomed to ruin. He braved angry seas and strange lands in order to erect physical monuments which would attest his strength and power. These monuments he set up primarily for *his* good and glory. If there were any universal and humanitarian considerations, they were only secondary by-products.

In the saga of the Hebrews, we find the account of how God commanded Abraham, the father and founder of that people to leave his country and to sunder the ties of kin and kith and proceed on a pilgrimage through the then known world. Abraham's odyssey was not the result of an untoward event such as the invasion and victory of the Trojans. It was prompted by an inner urge, a call from within his soul. No destination was specified. He was merely told to go out of his land to wander from people to people and from country to country. The one assurance that was given to him was "and thou shalt be a blessing . . . on thee all the families of the earth shall be blessed" . . . This did not imply an exemption from harassment, suffering and servitude for the bearers of this blessing.[3] This divine mandate Abraham obeyed. In each place of sojourn he built, not a city, but an alter to the living and universal God.

It is the realization of this fact, the great influence of legendary heroes and towering personalities on the formation of national character and disposition that evoked from the Rabbis the remark,

"The vicissitudes of the patriarchs are recapitulated in the lives of their descendants." [4]

Chapter 3

THE SHACKLES OF BYGONE CREEDS
AND CUSTOMS

"What we have inherited from our fathers and mothers is not all that 'walks in us.' There are all sorts of dead ideas and lifeless old beliefs. They have no tangibility, but they haunt us all the same and we cannot get rid of them." IBSEN

IN 1834 Heinrich Heine wrote a treatise on religion and philosophy in Germany. In it one will find the following statement which, in the light of the satanic forces which the Nazis unleashed, seems uncannily prophetic. "Some day," predicted Heine, "there will awake that fighting folly found among the ancient Germans, the folly that fights neither to kill nor to conquer, but simply to fight. Christianity has, and that is its fairest merit, somewhat mitigated that brutal German lust for battle. But it could not destroy it; and once the taming talisman, the Cross is broken, the savagery of the old battlers will flare up again, the insane berserk rage of which Nordic bards have so much to say and sing. The talisman is brittle. The day will come when it will pitiably collapse. Then the old stone gods will arise from forgotten rubble and rub the dust of a thousand years from their eyes; and Thor will leap up and with his giant hammer start smashing Gothic cathedrals . . .

Then, when you hear the rumble and clatter, beware . . . Don't smile at the visionary who expects the same revolution in the material world which has taken place in the realm of the spirit. The thought precedes the act, as lightning precedes thunder. True, our German thunder is a German too, and not very dexterous; it comes rolling up pretty slowly, but come it will, and when you hear a crash as nothing ever crashed in world history, you'll know a Ger-

man thunder has finally hit the mark. At that sound the
eagles will fall dead from the sky and the lions in the far-
thest desert of Africa will pull in their tails and slink away
into their royal caves. A play will be performed in Germany
that will make the French Revolution seem like a harmless
idyll in comparison . . ."

The exclamation "A Daniel come to Judgment" may
aptly be applied to Heine, not for having designated and
characterized the exact and well-measured justice that was
in store for the perpetrators of the cataclysm but for his
having caught and appropriated the mood and tone of the
apocalyptic chapters of the Book of Daniel. There is a biblical quality in Heine's vivid delineation of the world-
shaking conflict which he saw coming.

That this Teutonic disposition to be a monster, though
slain, is capable of being resuscitated even in the hearts of
genuinely devout Germans may be inferred from the following prescription of Luther regarding Jews. "He urged
his followers," reports Will Durant, "to burn down the
homes of Jews, to close their synagogues and schools, to
confiscate their wealth, to conscript their men and women
to forced labor." What seems to differentiate his program
from that of Hitler is that he did not prescribe a gas chamber and crematorium for millions of victims and that he left
them a way out, "a choice between Christianity and having
their tongues torn out."

No glib charge of being anti-Semitic or sectarian zeal
can fully account for the tone of such a program. It becomes more a benighted prelate of the Rasputin variety
than the founder of a spiritually vital movement.

Was Heine a clairvoyant? Did he have a mysterious capacity to divine what is to be in the future? Or did he, like
the Hebrew Prophets, entertain an unshakable belief that
the doing of right or wrong was inextricably linked to a
train of consequences and that solely on the basis of the
prevailing creeds and mode of conduct was he sure that a
volcanic upheaval was in the offing?

Heine was not a soothsayer, but a seer. Keen observation,
and sagacity and intense moral convictions, enabled him

to discern the fate of a recreant nation and the doom that
was in store for an errant civilization. The glitter of the
strong and solidified political entities could not conceal from
Heine's keen eyes the virulence of persistent Teutonic and
pagan hankerings. He gauged the fragility of the bonds
which tied the German States to Christianity.

The third Reich's political and military rampage and the
psychologic disclosures of Germanic folklore and legends
afford us ample testimony that a fierce struggle is waged
and will continue to be waged in the German soul. They
attest to the duality of the German character and the schi-
zophrenic symptoms of its national psyche. Teutonic folklore and legend also reveal a propensity for excessive hero-
worship, a yearning for the Superman instead of Man in
his pure and simple humanity and his symbolic groping
for abiding moral values and truths.

The gods of Teutonic mythology, like those of other races,
provide no guide to the good life. These power-hungry and
passion-smitten deities manifest the jealousies and rivalries
and resort to the trickeries of mortal folk.

In due course of time, Christianity was imposed upon the
Teutonic tribes. They were induced to avow allegiance to
it. They incorporated the institutions, symbols and rites
which that religion adopted from current cults or from
Judaism. Christianity's moral stipulations and spiritual
orientation were, however, too transcendent for exemplification by this warlike people.

The churchmen were either not keen enough to perceive
or brave enough to proclaim that the wonted ways and virtues of the Teutonic tribes and the ideals and the modes of
life which the Galilean enunciated were antagonistic. They
failed to provide an effective technique to those who would
not join monastic orders to alter their natures and to sublimate their bellicose dispositions. It did not seem to them
ironic when the latter listened to the reading of the Sermon on the Mount and knelt before the Man on the Cross
while they were clad in armour and with a sword at their
side.

To clarify the point that I am making let us consider the

various kinds of interaction that may occur when two clash-ing cultures meet. The encounter may give rise to one of four possibilities.

One: The capitulation of one to the other. An exemplifi-cation of such course is seen in the choice of some individu-als who veer towards a Bohemian mode of life and others who find peace only in the vows of a monk or a nun.

Two: The mutual adjustment on the part of each cul-ture. This involves an analysis of each culture and the sepa-ration of the elements in each which are congenial. These compatible and congenial elements are then blended in a common avowal and pattern of life, which spells an en-hancement of either of the cultures from which the new one emerged.

The history of Judaism provides magnificent illustrations of such synthetic adjustments between divergent creeds and cultures. The Hebrew Prophets, the lore and labors of the Talmudic Sages, the writing of Philo, Maimonides, etc., may be cited as examples of such syntheses.

Three: The desire to hold onto the two cultures, despite their contradiction and dichotomy. This is done by making them but contiguous instead of homologous. They are thus assigned independent spheres and provided with different criteria by which to test the goodness in each sphere. The early Christian conception that there are two realms, one belonging to Caesar and one to God and that the summum bonum of each need not be identical, or St. Thomas Aquinas' view that what is true in the domain of Faith needs no cor-roboration of the standards of truth which prevail in Phi-losophy are instances of such a morganatic marriage of divergent cultures.

Four: There is the 'pot-pourri' union of cultures. It may be likened to a 'Greek salad' which is made up of dif-ferent vegetables all chopped up or a stew of various kinds of meat-morsels cooked together. The taste and tang of the constituent items would vary, were it not for the dressing or spice which is added to the mixture to give it savor and make it palatable.

The thought and life of the German people of medieval

and modern times fall into the last category. The exalted idealism and ethics of Jesus and the Gospels and the pagan obsession with mundane matters and the craving to gratify sensual passions and the Teutonic love of combat and the extolling of bravery in battle and the Galilean's advocacy of non-resistance and turning of the other cheek are compounded without any attempt to harmonize them. They present not a *fusion* but a confusion of tenets and tendencies.

Weber and Wagner are deemed to reveal the authentic mood and disposition of the German soul. For support of my contention, I shall therefore analyze the plot of Carl Maria von Weber's opera "Der Freischütz" and also some of Richard Wagner's. Of the latter's many notable works I shall single out but "Tannhauser," although similar characteristics are present in the stories of nearly all his other operas.

"Der Freischütz," writes Henry M. Krehbiel, "is spoken of in all the handbooks as a 'national' opera. There are others to which the term might correctly and appropriately be applied, German, French, Italian, Bohemian, Hungarian, Russian; but there never was an opera and there is no likelihood that there ever will be one, so intimately bound up with the loves, feelings, sentiments, emotions, superstitions, social customs and racial characteristics of the Germans. In all its elements as well as in its history, it is inextricably intertwined with the fibres of German nationality." [1]

Here is the plot. A ranger by the name of Max bids for the hand of beautiful and devout Agatha, the relative of the head ranger. To attain his wish, Max must prove his superior marksmanship. Having failed to display his shooting prowess because of 'ill luck,' Max is advised by his sinister confrère to procure magic bullets from the black ranger, Samiel, whose role is like that of Mephistopheles in Faust. Max's desire for Agatha being irrepressible, he consents and at midnight both head for the spot, the terrible wolf's gorge where the magic bullets are cast. He acquires seven, not knowing that one of them was destined to serve him ill in some way.

At the shooting contest over which Ottaker, the Duke of Bohemia, presided, Max was highly successful with the first six shots. When the seventh was fired Samiel directly intervened and guided the bullet towards Agatha instead of the intended dove. The bullet wounded Agatha but she was saved from death by the supernatural powers of the bridal veil which a hermit, the night before, had consecrated and blessed. Casper, the sinister confrère of Max, beholding then the hermit besides Agatha, realized his failure and dies as Samiel was about to carry him off instead of Max. The latter then regrets his misdeeds and confesses before the hermit who is touched by his repentance. The Duke imposes a light punishment and promises that when the period of probation comes to an end he will place the hand of Agatha in that of Max.

In commenting on the plot, Henry E. Krehbiel writes "In the Legend of the Wild Huntsman, who, under the name of Samiel, purchases the souls of men with his magic bullets, the folklorist and student of the evolution of religions sees one of the many evidences of ancient mythology perverted to bring it into the service of Christianity. Originally the Wild Huntsman was Odin (or Wotan). The missionaries to the Germans, finding it difficult to root out belief in the ancient deities, gave their attributes to saints in a few cases, but for the greater part transformed them into creatures of evil." [2]

The above observations are based on facts. One may question the assertion that ancient mythology was perverted. I believe that 'modified' would be a more exact term. One must, however, disagree with the writer's judgment that this kind of modification or perversion of the ancient mythology rendered Christianity any service whatsoever.

The plots and stories to which Richard Wagner joined in wedlock his transporting music reveal even more a mixture of clashing orientations and dispositions than does 'Die Freischütz' of Weber. Traits extolled in a pagan society where brute force and lust are honored above reason and morality, consort with virtues and qualities of soul which have been identified with the humble Preacher of Nazareth.

The parallel musical proclivities of Weber and Wagner are neither casual nor accidental. Their ideologies veered in the same direction and their aims were set to a common goal. In his autobiography, Wagner tells how as a lad his childish eyes would follow with awe the noted composer, the elder Weber, as he passed by the door of his house on the way to and from the theatre. In Weber's "Der Freischütz" and in Wagner's "Tannhauser" we observe the close kinship between the first operatic romanticist and his follower who brought the romantic movement to its zenith.

In Wagner's "Tannhauser," the plot is less complicated, the technique of execution more skilled and the symbolism more lucid and yet the hodge podge in the story is more evident than in Weber's "Der Freischütz."

Tannhauser, a minstrel knight having failed in a singing match sought to shake off disappointment by embracing the pleasures which Venus had to offer. He became a willing slave to the lusts of the flesh.

In due course of time, he felt surfeited with sensual gratifications. He now longed for freedom, spring and church bells. He begged the goddess to let him depart. She, however, maintained her hold on him with her allurement. Tannhauser was then impelled to proclaim that his salvation rested in Mary the Mother of God.

These words broke the unholy spell.

The scene then changes, Tannhauser now is no more nestling beside the passion-exciting Venus listening to voluptuous music as nimble nymphs swirled and danced for his entertainment and displayed their comely and enticing bodies.

We now behold the hero in a serene idyllic but earthly setting. In a peaceful meadow a shepherd sits on a rock and pipes a delightful ode to spring. Near him a wooden post rises from the ground on the top of which there is a nest-like enclosure, the front side of which is open and the figure of the Virgin is visible.

Pilgrims proceed past the motionless Tannhauser who is lost in reflection over his former indulgence. Gripped by a feeling of remorse he falls on his knees in prayer.

While hunting, the landgrave and the minstrels, former companions of our hero, encounter Tannhauser in this mood of penitence. They joyfully welcome the sorely-missed companion and extend to him an invitation to rejoin them. He declines, but later changes his mind when he learns that the song which failed to win for him his sought-for recognition gained for him the heart of beautiful Elizabeth, the niece of the landgrave, who ever since his disappearance had lived in a state of retirement from the world. When Elizabeth becomes apprised of the return of Tannhauser and his participation in the coming song contest, she joyfully agrees to be present at the event.

The scene of the second act presents the impressive hall of the minstrels where the tournament is to be held. The landgrave and his niece Elizabeth occupy the throne-seats. The knights march in battle regalia with sheathed swords. The noblemen come richly attired each with his lady beside him. Each couple is announced by the pages and after their bow before the landgrave and Elizabeth, they proceed to the places assigned to them. Finally the minstrels in a stately manner make their entrance and are led to their positions by the pages.

The landgrave, after welcoming the notable guests and contestants announces that the theme of the prize-song would be "Love's Awakening" and that lovely Elizabeth would reward the winner by granting him his request. Wolfram, who also loved Elizabeth, is picked to begin. With the aid of his harpstring he sings of love, which he likens to a pure stream and therefore says would be placid and unagitated.

At this point Tannhauser bursts in and accords a glowing tribute to sensual love. The audience is taken aback and the other minstrels rise to the support of Wolfram. Tannhauser

with great fervour then sings of the love which is profane
and climaxes his avowal with an admonition that he who
wishes to quaff the cup of love's joys must repair to the
realm where Venus reigns. The assemblage is stunned. With
the exception of Elizabeth, the ladies all leave the hall, the
knights unsheath their swords and are on the point of striking the comrade whose return a short time ago they hailed.
He is saved by the intervention of the heartbroken Elizabeth who notices his penitence. The landgrave orders him
to join a group of pilgrims who are headed for Rome where
he would perhaps obtain forgiveness from the Pope for his
sinfulness.

Elizabeth in the meantime hopes and prays for his return
with forgiveness attained. Encountering returning pilgrims
in the valley of the region, she inquires about Tannhauser.
They have no news for her. She is grief-stricken and after
praying earnestly before the image of the Virgin, she re-
turns dejected to the castle where she dies.

In the succeeding scene Wolfram sees in the valley a tot-
tering individual who turns out to be Tannhauser. He is
weak and wan and his garments are tattered. His steps are
directed to the cavern of Venus where he wishes to drown
his sorrows and disappointment at the Pope's having
heaped upon him a curse instead of granting him the
sought-for absolution.

At that moment they espy a funeral procession descend-
ing the hill. As it nears them, they learn that the bier contains the body of their beloved Elizabeth. As the carriers
set the bier on the ground, Tannhauser, overcome by grief,
throws himself upon the body of the saintly Elizabeth and
implores her to pray for him and with this invocation his
life comes to an end.

A fresh group of chanting pilgrims then enter and announce that the staff of Tannhauser, which the Pope commanded to be erected as a token of his damnation had
sprouted new and verdant leaves, a sign of God's forgiveness to the erstwhile devotee of Venus. With the conclusion
of the pilgrim's paean of praise to God's glory and goodness,
the play ends.

What are the implications of the story? The story of Tannhauser delineates the rival dispositions of the hero and of the other characters of the play. They represent two major quests in life or criteria of what is good. One affirms the necessity and legitimacy of the pursuit of sensual delights and the yielding to the desires and passions of the body. Venus personifies this goal. The other avows the belief that man reveals his true essence and destiny not when he yields to every longing and prompting of his primordial nature but when he heeds the wants and needs of his soul. The doglike snuffings of the trail that leads but to bones will not still the hunger of man's nobler nature: that hunger is evidenced in man's reverence for and the exemplification of a life of chastity and renunciation. Elizabeth is the symbol of these virtues.

Before citing the jarring items that make up the story, I should like to call attention to the fact that while the libretto does not specify the incident which drove Tannhauser to Venus, there are remarks in the script which warrant the conclusion that Tannhauser sought the embrace of the goddess as an opiate which enabled him to escape the depressed mood in which he found himself and as a means of overcoming a haunting sense of frustration.

"Have you so soon forgotten all the black depressions," was Venus' plea when Tannhauser voiced his desire to take leave of her, "which I tempered with joy?"

And in replying to Walter's support of Wolfram in the song contest, Tannhauser asserts:

> "O Walter, you have little learning,
>   Your views of love are all awry.
>   If you are timid with your yearning,
>   You'll find the world has all run dry.
>   If it is God for whom your soul is pining,
>   Look up to Heaven and see the starlight shining
>   Such grace through worship may descend,
>   It was not meant to comprehend.
>   But what will yield to soft caresses
>   Close to your bosom you can hold,
>   What grows from common storms and stresses.

In tender fashion you can mould.
Here there is joy with happy leisure
And love is joyful, love is pleasure!

If Tannhauser's intoxication with the delights of physical
pleasures had been impelled, as the libretto hints, by a desire to escape a downcast feeling and shake off a sense of
frustration then it reveals the hero's indisposition to face
the unavoidable aspects of life, an indisposition which, if
unchecked, may culminate in a form of mental derange-
ment.

The most salient fact about the hero's psyche is its disposition to oscillate from one mood and avowal to its antipodal expression. Tannhauser is enchanted by the goddess
and pledges to her unabated homage. "For you alone I'll
sing of endless glory, And raise my voice in praise to you
alone!" At the very same time he yearns for a liberation
from her allurements by a return to the earth with its sim-
plicities and sanctities and sorrows.

His change, it is to be noted, is not the result of a conversion, the resolution to alter one's self and scale of values
but constitutes an ephemeral preference to move in a different milieu in order to satisfy a momentary change of
taste.

If an oscillation between extremes marks the moral proclivities of Tannhauser, the behavior of the other principals
of the play evidences a disposition to maintain if not all
then many of the mores which are identified with both ethical systems. This is done with complete disregard of their
contrary implications and affirmations.

The poet-composer, Wagner, has the pious God-fearing
minstrels engaged in the chase (hunting), when they
come upon Tannhauser. To the singing tournament, knights
and nobles march arrayed in armor with swords at their
sides to the tune of martial airs.

The grave and shocking sin of the hero, now in the role
of execrable blasphemer, was that he extolled profane love,
for which with unsheathed swords the landgrave, the

knights and the nobles were ready to slay him. These were their words:

> "You all have seen, you all have heard,
> His sin is black in every word.
> This man has known the joys of hell,
> In Venus' arms she let him dwell.
> How dreadful! Ghastly! He's accursed!
> And for his blood our daggers thirst
> We'll send him back again to hell,
> Let him be banned and damned as well!"

One cannot help contrasting a kindred situation when the Talmudic Sages were called upon to adjudge the spiritual value of a literary work, (The Song of Songs) which too dealt with profane love.[3] Instead of cursing the author and anathematizing his views, the Rabbis allowed the Song to be attributed to Solomon and included it in Holy Script.

To Tannhauser's claim that true love is known and fully gauged only by him who had indulged in its baser manifestations, the Rabbis would have given their assent. For it was this very view which made them aver that the place occupied by a repentant sinner is above that held by one who had never encountered and, therefore, never succumbed to temptation.[4]

The proclivity to a dual allegiance in the pursuit of ethical goals is also manifested in the attitude of the German devotee of the Church. The representatives of the Church are the dispensers of absolution, yet even the Pontiff, the Vicar of Christ on earth, is proven fallible. Verdant leaves did sprout on Tannhauser's staff contrary to the predictions of the Holy Father.

The 'pot-pourri' assemblage of the (assumed) Christian virtues of humility, self-abnegation and deprecation of worldly pursuits and the qualities that are extolled and emulated in a bellicose, instinct-heeding and passion-coddling pagan society are not features confined to a single work of Wagner. All the stories of his operas evidence in various degrees all or some of those characteristics. He ad-

mires the robust and chivalrous traits which are embodied
in the pagan myths of the Teutons. He glorified these features that are so outstanding in the Niebelungenlied. This
very same person created a Lohengrin, a Parsifal as well as
a Tannhauser, in which operas obedience, faith, repentance and the orientation on purely spiritual and other-
worldly objectives are given superlative praise.

Chapter 4

THE KEY TO MORAL RENEWAL

"Aromatic plants bestow
No spicy fragrance while they grow;
But crushed or trodden to the ground,
Diffuse their balmy sweets around." GOLDSMITH

IN THE causal explanation of a catastrophe we clearly discern the true nature of the expositor's religious beliefs.

There are some who attribute their trials and tribulations
to the whims of a malicious deity which indiscriminately
picks a luckless individual and then proceeds to torture him
as a wanton child does the fly which he had caught. Others
consider the sufferers as the hapless victims of blind Fate
which dispenses blows and blessings as if guided solely by
the dictates of a throw of dice. The Latin author, Sallust,
characterized Fate well when he wrote, "She raises to emi-
nence or buries in oblivion everything from caprice rather
than from well regulated principles." [1] In both of these
explanations there is no connection or relation between
deeds and deserts.

Other explanations link social incidents, historic events,
even cosmic phenomena which have an impact upon man's
weal to antecedent human actions and strivings. Calamities
are then conceived to be due to human error, miscalculation
of the improbability of their occurrence or a misjudgment

of man's capacity to check or surmount them. This explanation, it will be noted, stresses mental ineptitudes and physical deficiencies which are deemed to have brought on the disaster.

Lastly there is the explanation which affirms that a calamity such as an outbreak of war or an epidemic or even a violent convulsion of Nature like an earthquake or flood has as its basic and ultimate cause a spiritual or moral delinquency on the part of man. These phenomena, it is maintained, are to be accounted for *not solely* by material facts and physical events and mental shortcomings but also by the quality of man's previous or current intentions and interests. Such an explanation emanates from a profound conviction that God exists, that He is moral in essence and aim, that the Cosmos is not neutral or indifferent to the fulfillment or neglect of divine imperatives and that the behavior of Nature is not determined by mere chance, accident or the fortuitous union of forces. Moral principles even more than sheer power determine the flow of events and what some label the 'vicissitudes of fortune,' 'historic necessity' or 'the wave of the future.'

The history of the Jew is punctuated with recurrent disasters and tragedies. Enslavement in Egypt, captivity in Babylon, the destruction of Sanctuary and State by Rome, the expulsion from Spain, the persistent efforts of the Inquisition to suppress any and all belief in and practice of Judaism by Jews, the havoc wrought upon European Jewish communities by the Crusades, the bloody pogroms that stained the pages of Czarist Russia and, eclipsing them all, the systematic extermination of six million Jews by Nazi fiends and their henchmen in Eastern European countries are the most protruding peaks of the continuous chain of vexations and sufferings.

Ordinarily a people subjected to such an interminable series of overwhelming disasters would have sunk into a mood of despair and would have lost the will to live and especially to believe in the worthiness of the pursuit of what it deemed to be true, good and beautiful. Such a fate, however, did not befall the Jew. The blows of misfortune enfeebled him physically for a time, but his spirit was made stout and indomitable by these ordeals.

"The indomitable fidelity of the Jews to their faith in a militantly Christian Europe is perhaps the greatest example of positive non-conformism in history. Its significance looms large since as a sole bastion it upheld and indicated the modern principle of spiritual freedom and freedom of conscience through two millennia of Western development. Such strong faith at all risks, could have been placed only in a strong, convincing system of universally good religious philosophical tenets, otherwise it could not have endured the ordeal of the centuries." [2]

What was the secret which enabled the Jew to surmount tragedy? What antidote did he possess which shielded him from the devastating effects of disasters?

Chaim N. Bialik, the poet laureate of Modern Hebrew asked and proffered an answer to this question in the well known poem, "If Thou Wouldst Know," which was written after the Kishinev massacre in Czarist Russia. I quote a part of it.

"If thou wouldst know the mystic font from whence
   The wretched brethren facing slaughter drew
   In evil days the strength and fortitude
   To meet grim death with joy, and bare the neck
   To ev'ry sharpened blade and lifted axe;
   Or, pyres ascending, leap into the flame
   And saint-like die with 'Ehad' (the affirmation that God is
      One) on their lips;
"If thou wouldst know, O humble brother mine
   Go to the house of prayer grown old, decayed,
   In the long nights of Tebeth (wintry month) desolate,
   Or in the scorching blazing Tammus (summer month) days,
   In noonday heat, at morn or eventide . . ." [31]

Bialik's answer to his query does not, it seems to me, probe the matter to its roots. The Jews' power to survive and surmount disaster precede the emergence of the Synagogue as the institution *par excellence* of Jewish life and antedated the time when Torah-study was the widely-

shared preoccupation (not pastime) of the Jew. *But what
imbued him with the conviction that such a bleak existence was desirable and held out to him the assurance of
brighter days to come?*

The answer, I believe, lies in the explanation which the
Jew was wont to give to account for the catastrophes which
overtook him. The Synagogue incorporated the answer into
its ideology. The answer was permeated with religious
meaning and moral implications. The Jew was taught to
look upon his misfortunes as divine visitations and construed them therefore to be signals calling for the reformation of his individual and collective mode of life. Jewish
spiritual leaders utilized such occasions to ferret out the
moral delinquencies which they were convinced were responsible for the tragic events. They exposed and denounced
their sins.

When the hosts of Babylon, led by Nebuchadnezzar,
stormed the walls of Jerusalem and set the torch to the supposedly inviolate Sanctuary and killed men, women and
children and then carried off into captivity the flower of
Judean nobility, such a calamity, in the eyes of all ancient
people, would have indicated the defeat not only of the
vanquished nation but also of its God. It would have immediately spelled the capitulation and ultimately the total disappearance of that people from the pages of history. Evidence that such views were entertained by some Jews then
is not lacking. The majority, however, were taught to assess
the event differently.

The Seers of Israel affirmed and experienced the reality
of a transcendentally-sublime and moral Deity. His requirement of men was that they "do justly, love mercy and walk
humbly with God." [4] His rites, they maintained, were
subsidiary to Right.[5] His unique relationship with Israel
was not due to any restriction of solicitude for human
kind but solely because He expected the offspring of the
Patriarchs and those who had the privilege of standing at
the foot of Mount Sinai to be a light unto the nations. To
those Seers of Israel, the tragedy was the very vindication
of the power and promise of the God of Israel who

repeatedly announced to them that their security and
prosperity were conditioned by their observance of His
ethical injunctions.[6]

In the Judean rebellion against Rome's domination of
their homeland the poorly-equipped but lion-hearted defenders of the Jewish Commonwealth not only held their
ground in the face of the onslaught of the imperial legions. They also succeeded in initiating effective counter
attacks to a degree that one of Rome's ablest generals had
to be recalled from Britain to direct the campaign against
the "despicable Judean rebels." When the defeat of the latter was achieved and the pent-up fury of the vaunted legions was given free rein to brutalize and brow-beat the
population, the leaders and spokesmen of the obliterated
State did not invent excuses or discover errors of military
tactics to account for the disaster. They preferred to search
for the moral deficiencies of the nation and its members
which, they averred, were the basic cause of the overthrow
of the state.

"Why was the land made desolate?", was a question that
then engrossed the minds of the Rabbis. The assumption
which they propounded attested to their superlative ethical
sensitivity. Jerusalem was destroyed because of the incident of "Kamtzu and Bar Kamtzu," said they. Then they
relate how a man had made a feast for his friends. He dispatched an invitation to a beloved companion whose name
was "Kamtzu." His servant by error delivered the invitation
to one whose name was "Bar Kamtzu," who happened to
be an enemy of the host or had been so considered by the
host. Bar Kamtzu came to the feast. When the host espied
him sitting at the banquet table he ordered him to leave,
despite his ability to explain his presence. "Bar Kamtzu"
begged to be allowed to remain and offered to pay for what
he would eat and then raised the sum to cover half and then
the entire cost of the banquet. The host, however, remained
adamant. Bar Kamtzu abashed at the indignity which he
was to suffer, reluctantly took leave of the distinguished
company. Embittered by the fact that Sages were present

there and did not protest the insult to which he was subjected by the host, he resolved to malign them to Caesar.

The Talmudic Sages cite other acts of individuals which
appear trifling but as judged by their ethical sensitivity
loomed large.[7]

It was this disposition to assign a moral basis for private
and public affliction that made the Rabbis assert:

"Seven kinds of catastrophes come to the world for
seven transgressions." One of these sayings is particularly
pertinent to our time. "The sword comes into the world for
the delay of justice and for the perversion of justice and on
account of the offense of those who interpret the Torah not
according to its true sense." [8]

The traditional Jewish reaction to affliction inspired a
Talmudic Sage to formulate the admonition: "If a man sees
trouble coming upon him, let him examine closely his conduct (whether he is guilty of sins of commission). If he discovers nothing that was wrong, then let him consider
whether he had neglected the study of the Torah (whether
he is guilty of sins of omission). If he does not find himself
derelict in this respect, then may he consider that his sufferings are chastisements of love." [9]

I contend that it was the religious explanation of the
cause of recurrent disasters which gave to the Jew the will
and zest to endure the forbidding present and even to exact
from the ordeal a blessing as did his father Jacob from the
angel with whom he wrestled.

How was this possible?

With a religious explanation the door is ever open to a
rectification of conditions. The unbearable factors in a situation can be mitigated and even eliminated by the sufferers.
If the Exile was brought on by Israel's sins then the repentance of the sins can bring about the penitent's redemption. No army, vast as may be its numbers, great as may be
the quantity of chariots and battering-rams, can have
dominion over conscience. At this point, physical power becomes powerless. If however defeat is due to military superiority, if disaster is the result of vagaries of nature a sense

of gloom is unavoidable. The antidote which the Freudians
advocate, namely acceptance of one's limitations and adaptation to external realities, is but didactic advice which
can appeal only to the morally blasé.

An individual and a people are more likely to take defeat
and disaster 'philosophically', that is with equanimity or
in their stride, if they endow the experience with religious
significance and implications. With such a disposition and
mood, *tragedy* can be transmuted to *triumph*.

Endowing the vicissitudes of history with religious significance and meaning involves, beside the correlation of
suffering and sin, also the conviction, warranted by the
observation of nature's ways and the initially destructive
prelude to the emergence of beneficent results, that pain
and suffering are the unavoidable price we must pay before
we scale the mountain peaks of moral vision. "Only the man
who knows bodily suffering is truly a man"; wrote Heine,
"his limbs have their Passion-history, they are spiritual-
ized."

This penetrating perception of the prerequisites and
quintessence of spiritual sensitivity and maturity has been
vividly delineated by Deutero—Isaiah in his portrait of *"The
Servant of the Lord"*.[10] It has also been enacted in the
unending trials of the Jew and the part which this whole
"people on the crucifix" played in the march of civilization.

Why it should be so remains a mystery to man. Calvary,
and the millennial torment to which the Jew was subjected
baffle the inquiring mind, except those who in their smug
and arrogant affirmations believe that with their puny
mortal ken they can comprehend the Infinite and can apprise
themselves fully of His Will.

Chapter 5

VICTIMS OF MISINFORMATION

"By education most have been misled." DRYDEN

W HILE I was in Germany I had the opportunity of meeting and becoming acquainted with a sincere, pious and well-intentioned Protestant Pastor. He was a man in the forties but looked much older. In World War II he had been a chaplain in the armed forces on the Eastern front. I was told that he came near being courtmartialed because of the doubts that he, at times, voiced about the wisdom and humaneness of some of the military orders that emanated from headquarters. The prescribed disposition towards the civilian population of the conquered regions was to him brutal. The wanton sacrifice of men to attain a designated objective at a given time appeared to him shocking and murderous.

His pastorate in the concluding months of my stay in Germany was a hamlet in the northern section of Germany. We corresponded by means of letters. When I had to go to Hamburg to see that a shipment of crated books and ritual silver objects went off to designated libraries and museums (in Israel, European countries other than Germany, the U.S.A. etc.), my friend went to the expense and trouble of meeting me in Hamburg. We dined together and conversed for hours, after which we strolled through the streets of that famed port city. Heaps of broken brick and chunks of twisted steel and rusted iron beams were on each side of the now cleared streets. Surveying the jagged walls of bombed buildings on each side I had the eery feeling that I was passing between and inspecting columns of skeletoned gargantuan soldiers who became petrified while standing

at attention. It was then that our conversation veered from
the moral nihilism of the Nazis, the extent of the average
German's unawareness of the heinous crimes of the Nazis
and the degree of responsibility which each German must
bear to the speculation of the length of time that will be required to heal the breaches made by the sinister regime of
Hitler.

Pointing to the mounds of rubble and the grim remnants
of walls of shattered and roofless buildings the pastor retorted to my last remark, "The restoration of these edifices
and the erection of new residential quarters will constitute
the easiest task for us Germans. The more difficult job will
be the rectification of the damage which Nazism did to the
minds and souls of countless individuals. Can they be made
sound and wholesome?" When I proffered the opinion that
this task was not insurmountable and that it presented a
challenge to educators and particularly to Churchmen, I
heard him heave a sigh which was followed by the statement, "They too, need healing. For up to now we were
'blind leaders of the blind'. And until our vision is restored us by God's Grace the questions of our Lord, "Can the
blind lead the blind? Shall they not both fall into the ditch?"
are apropos." He continued, "More formidable that the restoration of bombed buildings and the evoking of a desire
on the part of the German to regain his blighted sense of
right and wrong is the urgent task to effectuate a reconciliation between the aggrieved Jewish survivors of Nazi
atrocities and those of my people who are aware that they
have been duped and made unwitting accomplices of Hitler's malevolence."

I was curious to ascertain what he meant by "reconciliation". Before I solicited information on this point I ventured
the opinion that the attainment of this objective too ought
not to be insurmountable in view of the small number of
Jews who are now in Germany. The Jewry of Germany has
been decimated from 600,000 to about 20,000 souls consisting mostly of elderly folk.

"By a reconciliation with Jewry" my friend was quick to
explain, "I do not refer merely to Jews who now reside in

Germany but also to their kin and coreligionists all over
the world and also to those who are to be born as well as
those who are now alive."

When I asked him to specify the impediment to which he
was referring, I was amazed and saddened by what I heard
coming from the lips of that genuinely devout and penitent
soul.

"Jews avow a belief in revelation that is confined to the
Old Testament. They reject the teachings of our Scriptures,
the New Testament. The God of the Old Testament to whom
the Jews pay homage and whose attributes they emulate is
a God of vengeance. He does not forgive or forget wrongs
done. He commanded the Israelites to annihilate the entire
population of Canaan because of their unwillingness to surrender their homesteads and national patrimony to the in-
vading Israelites. On their Purim festival they commem-
orate the wanton destruction of thousands of Persians as
well as the downfall of Haman. The most telling point in
Goebbels' propaganda was his dire warning that the German Nation was locked in ceaseless life and death struggle
with international Jewry and that a truce would be unfeasi-
ble and deceptive. Critical as I am of the facts and contentions of the Third Reich's Minister of Propaganda, do
not the proposals of American Jewry's spokesman, Henry
Morgenthau, warrant our belief in and fear of the Jews' un-
mollifiable vindictiveness?

"We can now strive to make the Germans see the evil of
their former ways. We can make them feel remorseful and
induce the government to return the property and the
wealth which the Nazis illegally took from Jews. Who, however, will make the Jews see that the New Dispensation is
to be heeded rather than the Old Testament injunction
stipulating 'an eye for an eye'? Who will convert aggrieved
Jewry to the Nazarene's teaching to the effect that forgiveness knows no bounds or limitation?"

For a moment I was speechless and the silence seemed to
my friend an awareness of the colossal difficulties of the
task and solutions which he posed. When I managed to regain my serenity and disposition to retort I began my in-

tended reply with the remark "You know that I am a Jew," at which point the pastor interposed the comment "Yes, I do, but you are only a nominal Jew. In belief and disposition I find you to be a Christian. Your God is not the one delineated in the Old Testament but the One revealed by His Son and by the tenets which He enumerated in the Sermon on the Mount. What a chasm there is between Moses' assertion on Sinai that God is "a jealous God, visiting the iniquity of the fathers upon the third and fourth generation" and Jesus' sublime declaration "Blessed are the merciful, for they shall obtain mercy" or the explicit and implicit teachings in the narrative, "Then came Peter to him and said, Lord, how oft shall my brothers sin against me, and I forgive him? Till seven times? Jesus saith unto him, I say not unto thee, until seven times but until seventy times seven."

I wanted very much to show and to convince my friend, then and there, that he was laboring under benighting misinformation and conceptions. It was, however, then past midnight and I had an all night drive ahead of me in order to get to Wiesbaden, where I had an appointment with an A.M.G. official the following morning. So after registering a verbal demurrer to his version, and after inquiring from him whether Lord Vansittart and Stalin, who prescribed a more severe and restricted economic procedure for Germany than the alleged program of Morgenthau, were Jews I bid him 'good night'. I promised to send him a lengthy letter in which I would point out the inexactness of his premises and the fallibility of his conclusions.

When I returned to the United States I began thinking about the promise that I made to my friend, the German pastor. I proceeded to examine the notations that I had collected which I thought would have some bearing on the subject. I also kept an eye open in my reading of current magazines and news items in daily papers for pertinent data. Unexpectedly I found that the notions of the German pastor (who, like his eminent confrères, Martin Niemoeller, Hans Christian Asmussen, Karl Barth and other Protestant clerics and theologians, was once favorably disposed to Na-

tional Socialism but later repented his erstwhile attitude)
were extensively held by men in the United States. They referred to the current notions as if they were well-substanti-
ated facts. And the men who subscribed to them were not
illiterate rustics but famed attorneys and men of letters including even a winner of a Nobel Prize for literature. I shall
cite only a few examples.

Some years ago, Donald R. Richberg, then general counsel of the National Recovery Act, expounding the significance of the law concluded his address with this fervid peroration; "This is a war—a war on poverty, a war without
precedent in history—a cruel war it might be called to save
ourselves from deceptive forces within our own nation. It
is not a war of man against man. It is rather a war of ideas
—the cooperative idea against the unrestrictive competition—the idea of national welfare against the unrestricted
self-seeking—the New Testament—The Sermon on the
Mount against Mosaic Law." [1]

A few years ago the play "Harriet" (depicting the life
of Harriet Beecher Stowe, the author of Uncle Tom's
Cabin) was presented on the Broadway stage. In the early
part of the play Harriet, longing for serenity and quiet so
that she may be able to write, relates to her brother Henry
the reasons impelling her to accept the offer of marriage
from Calvin, a bookish kindly widower and professor.

Harriet: Yes I hated the noise, the arguments and confusion.
Squalling babies, children and animals underfoot.
William and Catherine always crusading for some
cause; and brooding over it all, father's horrible
gloomy God.

Henry: Harriet.

Harriet: Oh come, Henry. You don't believe in father's God—
a sadistic monster who condemns his people to eternal
torment. I am through with all that. I am turning
my back to the Old Testament and putting my faith
in the New.

Near the end of the play Harriet, now a renowned author
of the then best seller, "Uncle Tom's Cabin," a book that

fanned the flames of a conflagration (the Civil War) is
temporarily gripped by a realization of the meagre result
even of the coming of victory, asserts:

"Years ago I turned from father's Old Testament God
of wrath and created a God for my own worship—a God of
tenderness and compassion. This war has killed that illusion
too." [2]

Similar animadversions on the concept of God and ethical
teachings of the Old Testament will be found in the works
of Aldous Huxley, Irving S. Cobb, James Truslow Adams,
not to mention the writings of various American theologians
and in the sermons that are delivered in American pul-
pits.[3]

In William Faulkner's prize winning novel, "The Fable,"
the power of love in human relations is extolled. Faulkner
describes the opposition between narrow nationalism and
universal brotherhood, between force and solicitude for
mankind. These opposing attitudes he identifies respec-
tively with the allegedly stern, decree-promulgating God of
the Old Testament and the gentle compassionate Christ of
the New.

This notion seems to have become an obsession with
Faulkner. For, in a letter to the *New York Times* some
time ago, he dragged it into a discussion of the cause of a
plane crash at Idlewild. He imputed the tragedy to the
pilot's (and modern man's) reverential awe for gadgets and
their infallibility. We are not concerned here with the merits of his explanation but with that part of his letter where
he gratuitously asperses the God of the Old Testament. Here
are Faulkner's words: "He (the pilot) dared not to flout
and affront, even with his own life at stake, our cultural
postulate of the infallibility of machines, instruments, gadgets—A Power more ruthless even than the Old Hebrew concept of its God, since ours is not even jealous and vengeful,
caring nothing about individuals."

One more example. Benjamin Fine, an authority on
schools and educational programs, wrote a timely book dealing with the current outbreak of juvenile delinquency. In
this book "1,000,000 Delinquents" the author pleads for a

thorough study and treatment of the alarming social malady. He criticizes the disposition to lecture at the youthful
violators and then deems the task as having been performed.
He termed the procedure as throwing "the book" at them.
In reviewing this book in the New York Times, John Dollard pounced on Mr. Fine's metaphor and gave it his own
interpretation. "We throw the book," was his comment, "but
it is the wrong book—the Old, not the New Testament." [4]

Letters of readers were subsequently published calling
the reviewer's attention to the baselessness of his contention
and to the empiric refutation of his premise in the fact that
though the Jews of New York City constitute 30% of the total population, they have but 5% of the delinquents and even
less among those who come from strictly observing orthodox
homes where the Old Testament is highly revered.[5] Mr.
Dollard's reply to his critics reveals the characteristic Christian misconception of the Old Testament. While admitting
in his answer that he is not a Biblical scholar and that he is
ready to defer to expert opinion, he continued to justify
the use of his amended metaphor with the following arguments:

"Both the legalistic talion tradition, as in Leviticus, and
the message of love, brotherliness, as in Amos, Hosea and
Micah, are offered in the Old Testament. Indeed, the medi-
ating Apocryphal manuscripts seem directly to prepare the
way for the message of Jesus. The question then becomes a
matter of emphasis. It is my personal opinion that, taken as
a whole, the austere and talion tradition is more characteristic of the Old Testament and the love-brotherhood tradition more characteristic of the New." [6]

I believe that not a grain of malice prompted the authors
to resort to the above phrasings and comparisons. They
were merely conveying an opinion that was current and to
which was attributed unquestioned validity. The generaliza-
tion was a stereotyped judgment based on only a fraction of
the evidence, with a mass of other data being entirely ignored. Such depreciating characterizations, I knew, were
the product of conventional Christian teaching that the Old
Testament had been superseded by the New Gospel.

I shall now recast the form of my reply to my German friend so that it may constitute a general refutation or clarification of the current appraisals of the two Scriptures.

A reading of the Old and New Testaments reveals the inaccuracy of these characterizations. The Old and New Testaments are both collections of utterances and writings by many men of radically different backgrounds and cultural attainments. The books selected for each collection were not written at one period or at one place. In the Old Testament we have books or sections of a book which reveal the imprint of a nomadic outlook, primitive customs and creeds. We have, moreover, in the same collection legal injunctions, prophetic exhortations and psalmists' meditations, whose ethical and spiritual orientation often makes ours seem crude and morally blunt by comparison.

These changing influences are reflected in various concepts of God. In the same anthology where God is referred to as "a man of war" [7] we also find the vision of Isaiah of the day when men "will beat their swords into ploughshares and their spears into pruning hooks; and nation shall not lift up sword against nation, neither shall they learn war anymore." [8] Within the covers of the Old Testament you have the command that the firstling of the womb be set aside for the Lord; and you also have Micah's sublime definition of religion "to do justice, to love mercy, and to walk humbly with thy God." [9] The settings of the Old Testament range from the simplicity and barrenness of sandy deserts to the luxury and bustle of metropolitan communities. Its writings cover more than a thousand years.

The New Testament possesses, to a certain degree, similar attributes. Between the teaching of Jesus and the latest writing in this collection there is a span of nearly a century.[10] In it are mirrored the deeds, attitudes and aspirations of the other-worldly Essenes; the conscientious law-abiding Pharisee; the proud Roman official with his sense of power. Here one beholds the disciples of Jesus who adore and hail him as the long-awaited Messiah and those who, in moments of danger, desert and deny him. We see Paul expounding the doctrines of the Gospel in the streets and synagogues of

Judea, Rome, Corinth and Galatia in a manner with which James and Peter, and hosts of unnamed disciples, must have expressed emphatic disagreement. The New Testament is far from being a homogeneous product.[11]

There are instances in the Old Testament where God is delineated as a Father with unmeasured compassion and love for all mankind as well as for Israel. On the other hand, God in the New Testament does not always appear in the role of a kind, tender and ever-forgiving Father. Not infrequently He is pictured as stern and implacable, as the incarnation of unquenchable wrath specifically on the day of judgment. His fierce anger is directed not only against those guilty of moral and social infractions but also against the "worshippers of the image," false prophets, and all unbelievers. In the apocalyptic visions, scenes are drawn of lakes of fire and brimstone in which sinners will be subjected to everlasting torment. The sentence "There shall be wailing and the gnashing of teeth," [12] and the phrase "eternal damnation" [13] occur with great frequency.[14]

This delineation of God is not characteristic of a Christian conception of any particular period. The APOCALYPSE OF PETER (one of the apocryphal Christian books of the second century) contains the most lurid descriptions of the detailed tortures and sufferings to which various types of sinners are doomed in hell. The descriptions are not only horrifying but revolting. Yet this book was read in churches on Good Friday up to the fifth century.[15] These harsh conceptions of the deity do not preclude the inclusion in the New Testament of noble descriptions of God; Christians, however, have identified the God-Idea of the authors of the New Testament solely with this latter treatment.

A study of the Jewish Scriptures will disclose to any open-minded person that the predominant concept of God is precisely opposite to that which has been identified with the Old Testament by its unwitting or witting detractors. God calls forth to many psalmists the image of a kind and solicitous Father.[16]

This picture supports the prophet's plea for amity between human beings: "Hath not one God created us? Why do we deal treacherously every man against his brother?" [17]

The Psalter is permeated with the avowals of the goodness and lovingkindness of a Divine Being "who forgiveth all thine iniquities, who healeth all thy diseases, who redeemeth thy life from destruction, who crowneth thee with lovingkindness and tender mercies." [18]

Instead of a harsh and vindictive deity, the reader finds the conception of a God who yearns to forgive the misdeeds of persistently wayward children: "Thou art a God ready to pardon, gracious and merciful, slow to anger and of great kindness." [19]

Such phrases as "eternal torment" and "everlasting damnation" are conspicuous by their absence in the Old Testament. Some of the writers picture the divine anger provoked only by man's evil deeds, as lasting but for a moment.[20] In Isaiah, the way to penitence is never closed, even to the infamous sinner.[21]

In Jeremiah, God's tender feelings are like those of a mother for her child,[22] and in Hosea, the picture of divine love is as stirring as it is vivid. Even in the earliest portion of the Old Testament, God is not conceived as an implacable deity.[23] In the same section of Scripture where one finds the command against making and serving idols with the warning that the Lord is a jealous God "visiting the iniquity of the fathers upon the children," [24] one also reads passages which endow Him with attributes of a very different strain. "The Lord, the Lord God is merciful and gracious, long suffering and abundant in goodness, and truth, keeping mercy for thousands, forgiving iniquity, transgressions and sin." [25] Even in passages where God's sternness is emphasized He is conceived as dispensing justice according to measure.[26]

Judaism from its very beginning deemed justice and mercy to be inseparable rather than mutually exclusive aspects of Divine Nature. In accounting for the names, JHWH and Elohim, which Scripture assigns to God, the Rabbis assert that the former appellation designated His attribute of mercy and the latter His attribute of Justice. A stable, healthy and normally advancing society is possible

only when the two concepts are cojoined and integrated.
The two dispositions are perceptible in divine law manifested not in some special and selected tradition, but by the
consensus of universal man.

In concluding this chapter I wish to emphasize that my
aim is not to contend that One Testament is superior,
equal or inferior to the other. If there are men who find
themselves stimulated to lofty behavior and belief by one
Testament in preference to the other then that Testament
may be said to possess superior value—*but only for them.*
A grievous moral violation is committed when one distorts
facts or allows facts to be distorted even for a laudable objective. For Christians to resort to such methods in order to
exalt their faith is both ungallant and unnecessary.

Furthermore the denigration and maligning of the faith
by which one lives may not be termed a primal cause for hostility to those who profess that creed. It surely constitutes a
factor which may condition one to be prejudiced against
that person or persons when a disagreement arises or some
grating incident occurs which otherwise would have been
passed over.

"Trifles unconsciously bias us for or against a person
from the very beginning" was the observation of Schopen-
hauer.

The German pastor's acknowledgment of my letter was
heartening. He was most gracious with his appreciation of
my effort. He concluded his missive with this statement of
his realization that, in the emergence of the ideology of
Nazism, German Bible Scholars, the so called Higher Critics
and those theologians whose zeal blurred their perception
of what was true, were not exempt from some responsibility.
He ended his letter with two New Testament quotations.
(The first he slightly altered, the second however was unvaried.)

"Father, forgive them for they *knew* not what they *did.*"

"And forgive us our debts as we forgive our debtors . . .
For if ye forgive men their trespasses, your heavenly Father
will also forgive you. But if ye forgive not men their
trespasses, neither will your Father forgive your trespasses." [27]

Chapter 6

THE MYTH OF JEWISH VENGEFULNESS

"The object of punishment is, prevention from evil; it never can be made impulsive to good." HORACE MANN.

DURING our walk through the streets of Hamburg with its piles of assembled rubble and grim remains of bombed buildings my friend the German pastor had voiced doubt whether contemporary Jewry would be amenable to a reconciliation with the German people, even after the latter had evidenced remorse over the enormity of Nazi crimes and were willing to acknowledge their share of responsibility of the ghastly acts. He based his doubt on the assumed divergence of teachings of the New and the Old Testament regarding what one's disposition should be towards aliens and enemies.

Is there a warrant in fact for such skepticism and negative belief? The moving story of the Good Samaritan has made the average individual identify the advocacy of extending aid to strangers and of being magnanimous to adversaries as salient and distinctive tenets of the New Dispensation. A dictum attributed to Jesus, the exact reporting of which is questionable and its implication baselessly defamatory, fortifies that supposition.

The literature of the Old Testament, as was noted, extends over a vastly longer stretch of time than does the contents of the New Testament. The initial recording in the former coalesces with bedouin customs and life. It would therefore be extraordinary if there were not imbedded in the Old Testament collection of books incidents and narratives which would fall short of the standards and practices which we extol. Nonetheless, the Old Testament is not devoid of sayings the nobility of whose ethical teachings are com-

parable to those found in the New. And that applies also
to what one's attitude should be towards outsiders and one's
enemies. *What is even more significant is that this disposition is incorporated and concretized into laws and statutes,
as well as narratives and casual sayings and declarations.*

The commandment to the Israelites not to oppress the
stranger in their midst, but instead to accord to him equal
justice and kindness when in need is a recurrent refrain in
the Pentateuch: "And if a stranger sojourn with thee in
your land, ye shall not do him wrong. The stranger that so-
journs with you shall be unto you as the home-born among
you, and thou shalt love him as thyself for ye were strangers in the land of Egypt; I am the Lord your God." [1]
Not only is rejoicing to be eschewed where disaster over-
takes one's enemy but the enactment of the Jewish Scripture
is clear and unmistakable as to what one's obligations are
on such occasions.

"If thou meet thine enemy's ox or his ass going astray,
thou shalt surely bring it back to him again. If thou see the
ass of him that hateth thee lying under its burden, thou
shalt forbear to pass by him; thou shalt surely release it
with him." [2]

Samuel, the younger, taught, "In the downfall of thy
enemy do not rejoice and in his stumbling let not thy heart
be delighted, for the Lord will see it and it will seem evil
in His eyes and will direct His displeasure towards you." [3]

The Rabbis of the Talmud admonish solicitude for and the
bestowal of charity upon the poor of non Jews as well as
Jews, *for the sake of peace* as well as the fact that all human
beings, having One Father, must therefore be accorded
the treatment due to brothers. This attitude was not relinquished during the time when the Crusaders, in the name
of Him who would not crush a broken reed, slew Jews and
pillaged their possessions and attached sanctity to their
misdeeds.

The charitableness of present day Jewry, in whatever
land it had planted its roots, is marked not solely by concern for their needy, a charge that could be shifted to the
government for the social welfare program of which they

are taxed. Jews also extend the prodigality of their contributions toward the support of non-sectarian and sectarian institutions and causes other than their own.

I propose in this chapter not to marshal easily-available
data to substantiate the claim that Jews are no more disposed to be vindictive than are Christians but to relate an
incident which I witnessed and which reveals the dominant
sense of fairness, and spirit of forgiveness in the attitude
of ordinary Jews.

Recently a friend, the author of well-known books, and
I decided to visit the lower eastside in New York. The day
was unusual for the latter part of the Fall. The sky was
cloudless and the temperature was mild. The time being past
the noon hour our initial stopping place was a kosher deli-
catessen establishment on Houston Street. We then directed
our steps to the bookshops on Canal Street and its vicinity.
Lastly we meandered along Rivington Street surveying the
wares that were piled on the rows of stands along the walls
and on the pushcarts at the edge of the pavement.

When my friend began to feel fatigued, I suggested that
he rest himself on one of the benches in the newly-formed
tree-lined esplanade on Allen Street while I completed some
necessary shopping. I returned after a short interval and
found him engaged in a lively conversation with an elderly
man. The latter was short, a bit round and stocky. His
clothes were shabby. He wore a shirt without a tie.
He held a crumpled paper-wrapped bundle under his arm. I
was later told by my friend that the elderly man had
informed him that he had lost his wife, that he had no
children, that he lived in a rented furnished room in the
neighborhood and that he sustained himself on the monthly
social security check that he was receiving.

My friend introduced me to the elderly man whom he
called 'the diplomat'. When I inquired of my friend why he
gave this title to the elderly man he, with a gleeful mien,
hurled at me the question, "Can you tell me how much the
up-keep of royalty cost the British?" I was taken aback by
the sudden and unrelated query. "I don't know," I replied,

after a moment's pause. Then pointing to the diplomat, my friend, in a raised voice said, "He knows and can cite the source of this information." Other queries phrased in the same manner followed, to all of which I could only give a negative answer, and after each the hand of my friend was raised with the forefinger pointing to 'the diplomat' followed by the refrain-like remark "He knows."

I then asked the gentleman how he obtained these facts. "I read the papers. "Der Forwards" and "Der Tag," [4] and each afternoon and evening, except when the weather is bad, people gather in groups here, on Delancy Street and in Seward Park, and they discuss everything under the sun, especially world events." His reply was in Yiddish which was interspersed with English words and phrases.

"What is your opinion of the regime in Russia?" I asked.

A simultaneous wave of the hand and a facial contortion were intended to show not only his disapproval but his disgust with the whole matter. When I pressed him for a verbal reply he remarked, "From the very beginning the Bolsheviks showed themselves to be cruel and bloody monsters. Consider," said he, "they took the Czar, his wife and children and had them slain in cold blood *without* a court trial, without witnesses, and without testimony. Barbarians and cutthroats act that way, but not social and political reformers, alleged heralders of a messianic era." Knowing the extent of the Czar's guilt in his failure to try to stop the pogroms of his day, I was taken aback by the proffered illustration of Communist wickedness.

It then flashed through my mind to ask the diplomat's opinion of the attack by the armed group of Israelis on the inhabitants of the border village of Jordan which resulted in a frightful death toll of over fifty Arabs, many, if not all, of whom may not have been implicated in the border crossings and slaying of members of the nearby Jewish settlements.

As I was stating my question the countenance of the old fellow seemed to register pain. He heaved a sigh and there was no mistaking that the emotion provoking the sigh was sincere and keenly felt. "This question is being discussed and debated," he said, "on every corner and in every park in the East Side. Some brand the act as shameful and assert that no amount of provocation can justify it. Does such behavior become 'merciful children of merciful forebears'? Others are more inclined to the view that it was the only course which would put a stop to the endless chain of sneak attacks and killings of peaceful, hard-working pioneers in that region by Arab marauders. These killings numbered over 400 and they were all perpetrated within a year. Amongst this stern group I didn't come across one Jew who didn't regret and lament the necessity of such a deed. I assume that you read that Abba Eban, the Israeli representative to the U.N., had immediately voiced his government's sense of remorse and emphatically disclaimed that it had any hand in the incident."

At this moment a bearded man very close to the three score and ten was coming slowly toward us and unceremoniously sat down beside the 'diplomat', who was still holding forth. The newcomer immediately became engrossed in the discourse. He leaned on the handle of his cane and seemed to drink in every word. His half-closed eyelids and his large furrowed brow indicated that he was concentrating on what was being propounded. Since he made no comment I assumed that he was a good listener and not disposed to reflect or to share his opinions with his friends.

I continued to address my remarks to 'the diplomat'. I told him that thus far he had apprised me of the views of others and avoided telling me whether he personally censured or condoned the attack. I was curious, I said, to know where he stood.

"How can anyone with a 'Gewissen' (conscience) condone a reprisal? In a reprisal you do not inflict punishment on those who had been guilty of the designated crime. A reprisal is an outburst of unchecked anger. It is letting loose a passion for revenge. At best it is intended to forestall a repetition of the crime by intimidation and the spread of fear and terror through the indiscriminate killing of individuals who are related to the criminals but who are completely innocent of the misdeed.

"The condemnation of the evil by persons residing in New York City, Rome or London who are totally immune from the continuous and fatal assaults of Arab marauders does not require moral courage and is not a proof that, were they in the position of the condemned, they would have acted differently.

"What I do censure is the United Nations' refusal to condemn the many murders by the Arabs which preceded and provoked the regrettable attack and its spineless indisposition to command, or even to recommend, that the Arab representatives sit down with Israel's spokesmen and strive to hammer out a 'realistic' peace agreement.

"An armistice" 'the diplomat' continued "has always been deemed a prelude to peace. A perpetual armistice which is used by one side as a scheme to ward off a crushing defeat when it perceives itself to be in a difficult position; an aristice which is admitted by one side to be only an interval to replenish its depleted strength in order to be better equipped for a renewal of the combat, when the resumption of the fighting would be to its best advantage, such an armistice is a strategy which is associated with the communists in Korea but certainly does not merit the sanction of an august body like the U.N.

"The ungallantry and unfairness of the Arab-Israel armistice is glaring. Israel is expected to abide by stipulations that she refrain from making available the use of Hebrew University buildings and the Hadassah hospital on Mount Scopus, for which there is a crying need and for the regaining of which she does not lack military power, but Egypt can go on defying the U.N. and not allow vessels of nations carrying non-combatant goods, even food-stuffs, to Israel to pass through the Suez Canal. And now these Arab politicians, who seem more eager to preserve the feudalism of the region than to better the lot of the fellahin, are brazen enough to demand that the U.N. prevent the new but Sovereign State from clearing its marshes and providing

water for the irrigation of its arid lands on the basis of un-
substantiated claims that such efforts spell injury to them
or until, mind you, they, the intractable opponents of Israel,
will consent to those improvements."

My friend and I cast glances at each other as we marveled
at the information and the intelligence displayed by this
individual who could from external appearance be mis-
taken for a habitué of the Bowery. (There flitted through
my mind the apocryphal statement attributed to some Jewish worthy of New York City to the effect that the difference
between a modern uptown Rabbi and the Eastside Jew of the
old school was that one had a pulpit and the other had
none. I wondered whether a like characterization could not
apply also to professors of political science in some of our
colleges and 'the diplomats' of the Eastside.)

At this point 'the diplomat' turned to the newcomer and
addressing him as 'Reb Moshe,' said: "What answer would
synagogue-Jews (shul-juden) give to the question of our
uptown visitors?" He then repeated my question to him.

The silent Reb Moshe meditated for a moment and then
instead of holding the handle of his cane with both hands
and resting his chin on them, he released his left hand and
began to stroke his beard with it. It was evident that he was
searching for the correct reply. He then began as follows:

"In the portion of the Torah which was read the previous
Sabbath we had the story how Shechem, the son of Hamor,
the prince and ruler of the region, enticed and defiled
Dinah, the daughter of Jacob our father. When the patriarch
and his sons were apprised of the vile act of Shechem they
grieved. The brothers' anger was uncontrollable. Employing
a ruse, Simeon and Levi armed with swords, ventured forth
when the culprit and his father and the male population of
the city were physically debilitated and could not offer resistance and slew them.

When they brought the news to Jacob he lamented the
horrible act with these words, "Ye have troubled me, to
make me odious unto the inhabitants of the land, even unto
the Canaanites and the Perizzites; and, I being few in num-

bers, they will gather themselves together against me and
smite me, and I shall be destroyed, I and my house." [5] And
the Bible tells us that the only retort they could make to his
reasoned rebuke was the exclamation, "Should one deal
with our sister as with an harlot?" [6]

The Patriarch was unable to forgive or forget the provoc-
ative but brutal deed, even to the moment of his last breath.
Before his death he called his sons to his bedside to bless
them. When Simeon and Levi came forward expecting a
benediction from the dying father, what words did they
hear him utter?

> "Simeon and Levi are two of a kind
> Weapons and violence mark their kinship
> Let my soul not come unto their council
> Unto their assembly let my glory not be united.
> For in their anger they slew men,
> And in their self-will they houghed oxen
> Cursed be their anger for it was fierce
> And their wrath, for it was cruel: . . ." [7]

The great commentator Ibn Ezra specifically asserts that
the Patriarch's harsh words at this moment were prompted
by the lingering remorse over his sons incensed retaliation.

For days this incident lingered in my mind. I was
tempted to send the account of it to my clerical friend in
Germany. I desisted lest he would construe it as an endeavor
to obtain from him an admission of error which he had already made in a previous missive.

Chapter 7

JEW AND GERMAN, ANALOGUE OR OPPOSITE?

"Das Jüdische Volk hätte immer sehr grosse Wahlverwand-schaft mit dem charakter der germanische Rasse. (There was always a close affinity between the Jewish people and the character of the German race.") HEINE

"Deutschland aber ist das Mutterland der Kultur für seine europäische Judenheit uberhaupt. (However Germany is the cultural mother land for European Jewishness.") HERMANN COHEN

HITLER branded the Jewish people as the natural adversary of the herrnvolk and declared the ambition and goal of the collective group and its constituent members as the antithesis of what the Germans longed for. Ever since the Nazi creed was proclaimed to be the authentic expression of the German spirit Jews rightly assayed this manifestation or eruption of Teutonism as antipodal to the basic principles of Judaism.

Was the Nazi myth of an innately malicious international Jewry with its breed of greedy and wily individuals true to fact? Was Hitler and Nazism the genuine and abiding embodiment of the German mood and spirit or were they but a transient convulsion brought about by a trauma and cyclonic attack of a fierce neurotic anxiety? Must these two peoples and their cultures be deemed to be at war with each other because of their innate irreconcilable natures and dispositions? Is one to be viewed as black and the other as white? Or are they both shades of gray, appearing to one as 'lightish black' and to the other as 'darkish white?'

Students of social psychology could make out a case in support of the claim that there is an affinity between the German and the Jewish ethnic character. Before the ogre of Nazism defiantly raised its ugly head, German Jews, among them the eminent philosopher Hermann Cohen, were proclaiming this thesis. Paul Tillich, a very incisive theologian hailing from Germany, is inclined to this view and expressed it recently in a series of addresses which he delivered in Germany.

Without denying the presence of common traits in the psychic make-up of those two peoples and some parallel trends in the events of their respective histories, the differences, I believe, far outnumber the similarities. To pursue this subject, with its baffling aspects and ironic results, would lead us far afield of the main objective of this book. This much, however, one must note that in the history of no people do you see the continuous confrontration by each of a choice between the *Ideal* and the *Expedient* and what is designated as *good* and *evil* and the tug and pull of the contending forces in each being so nearly evenly matched as was the case with the alternatives which the Israelites and Judeans of bygone days had to face and those which the Germans had to choose.

The parallel ends with the advent of Hitler, who managed to wrench the Germans from their orbit. After that Germany descended to unfathomed depths as no other people did with such lightning speed.

That the soul of the Jew was exposed to tests and temptations from the very moment he stepped on the stage of history a reading of the Scripture discloses. In the Old Testament delineations of the people of Israel (and this applies. also to their most revered heroes) the see-saw swings between good and evil are set in bold type. At one moment we see their trust in Moses and their faith in God's providence and power conjure up a pathway of dry land in the midst of a turbulent sea and a little later we hear them complain that the waters of the spring are bitter to their palates.[1] At one moment they are overwhelmed by an awesome theophany at Mount Sinai and reverently accept the Divine Decalogue with the acclamation, "We shall do and heed," [2] and a little later we behold them pressing Aaron, the High Priest, to fashion for them a new deity and hilariously caper around the Golden Calf.[3] At times they hear lawgiver and prophet term them "a kingdom of priests" [4] and "a light into the nations" [5] and they cherish these designations and enshrine them in the Sacred Lore, and a little later they pollute the land of spiritual promise with all kinds of heathen altars and revolting rites, as if their God required of them these practices instead of doing justly and loving mercy and walking humbly with Him. The Rabbis, noting the duality of their nature cryptically comment, "Appeal to them for the Golden Calf and they will give lavishly of their substance, ask them for the building of a Sanctuary and their generosity will be equally prodigious." [6] In another place the Rabbis assert that when Israel aspires, his goal is the stars of heaven; when he is morally on the downgrade, he will not reverse his course until he is deep in the mire." [7]

With the Hebrews of olden days the combat between the sense of duty and the inclinations of the heart, a combat, the arena of which is every human soul, was aggravated by another poignant dilemma. These Hebrews became settlers in a region whose indigenous population's mode of life and prevalent views differed greatly from those to which they and their forebears had been accustomed. These Hebrews had formerly been a desert folk, who wandered from place to place with their sheep and goats in search of water and some pasture land. Now they found themselves in the midst of an advanced civilization, the economic basis of which was agriculture and trade. To adapt themselves to the new environment necessitated the acquisition of the techniques of sowing, planting, reaping, the bartering or selling of the surplus produce and the replacing of tents and temporary shelters by permanent abodes made of stone. The doing of all these things, the old inhabitants informed the Hebrew newcomer, would not necessarily make him a successful farmer. He must become like the natives, a true Canaanite. To that end it was advisable that he discard the primitive and outmoded beliefs and behavior of the bedouin and adopt the customs and creeds of the indigenous populations, whose gods had dominion in that region and who dispensed the rain and regulated the fertility of the soil. Jehovah with his rigorous, life-negating desert-morality must give way to the up-to-date, life-affirming practices of Baal and Dagan and their kindred deities.

The newcomers were not deaf to the admonitions of the native. They were allured by the new environment, its culture and the unrepressed inclinations of the population. The simple and puritan ways of the desert seemed to them narrow and cramping beside the libertarian and elegant living of the land-tilling dwellers of the region. The pleas of Moses, the examples and insights of the desert, the memorable experience at Sinai, the hopes and expectations of the ancient patriarchs, all became dim in their consciousness. They were bewitched by what they saw. The excitations of the current licentious mode of life which were termed the new freedom debilitated their power to reason and to apply tested moral standards to the prevailing creed and conduct.

For a time the Hebrews of both the Southern as well as the Northern Kingdom appeared doomed to a course of spiritual self-annihilation. How close they came to such a fate may be inferred from the denunciations of Ezekial, especially those of chapter sixteen wherein the nation is likened to a frivolous capricious and narcissistic courtesan.

Israel and the inhabitants of Judea suffered severely for their spiritual failings and moral instability. Such conduct brought them afflictions and agony. They witnessed heartbreaking national humiliation. They saw their State and Sanctuary twice destroyed by nations whose ways they courted and copied. Twice they were led into exile in strange and foreign lands.

Only then did they begin to reflect and reassess their former creed and mode of life and resolve in the future to abide by the time-tested hallowed ideals of their seers and sages. This introspection, revaluation and reorientation transmuted physical defeat into spiritual victory. The Good overcame the Evil within them. The blandishments of the current culture were not allowed to go unprobed and unchallenged. The civilization was assayed and its merits and virtues were separated from the chaff and the weeds. Even then the desirable items were refashioned and made to conform to the abiding principles of the faith. Only then were they deemed worthy of adoption and incorporation into the tradition and spiritual treasures of Israel.

The moral achievement of the Jews in distilling from a catastrophe the potion for spiritual purging can and should serve as an example to the German nation, whose disposition and demeanor, it is averred, strikingly resemble (in many aspects) that of Israel and the Judeans. If the German nation would only ponder its catastrophe and deem its latest disaster a signal for an inner catharsis then one would be warranted in fancying that the blood of the millions of Jews who have been cruelly slain by the Nazis would cease to cry from the ground for retribution and justice. For then the spirits of the martyred would perhaps feel that their deaths had not been in vain.

Part VI

GERMANY AT THE CROSSROAD

Chapter 1

THE FUTILITY OF UNIMPLEMENTED PROFESSIONS

"Avowals are often not signposts but decoys" B.H.

THE ethics of the Sermon on the Mount with its lofty and super-excellent dicta gave rise to a dual pattern of behavior—a twin conception of what was required of a devotee of Jesus. A stern discipline involving the negation of physical cravings and worldly ambitions was set up by the Church for priests, monks and nuns. They solemnly vowed to literally emulate specific sayings of the Nazarene. The vast multitude of ordinary adherents of the Church, the laity, was granted exemptions and indulgences. Except for displays and poses of fidelity and homage to Jesus on stated occasions, the followers of Christ were allowed to cling to attitudes and practices which were more like those of their pagan forebears than the manner of life adhered to by the spiritually élite. The divergent indices to and tests of what is a good Christian were also made necessary by the extension of the small coterie of Galilean disciples to the empire embracing and later world-encompassing Catholic Church.

The churchmen honestly believed this accommodation to have been essential and unavoidable. Jesus had come, they averred, to save mankind and not merely the Jews. The chances of inducing a pagan to conform to the celestial tenets of the Nazarene as promulgated in the Beatitudes were slim, even if the erstwhile adherent to paganism manifested a concern for his moral well-being and spiritual destiny. Re-education by stages must have seemed to them prudent and preferable to excessive demands which were likely to terminate in total failure.

Their error was not in their adopting a step-by-step procedure in the advocacy of moral and spiritual advancement but in their making the dual allegiance a fixed and

*permanent principle and an abiding criterion of what was
proper and right.*

"Give unto Caesar that which is Caesar's and unto God
what is God's", was never intended to bifurcate life into
two independent and unrelated domains, terming one temporal and the other spiritual. To Judaism there is no demar-
cation between the sacred and the secular. All needs and
authentic expressions of life were endowed with divine significance. All Israel was destined to become "A Kingdom
of Priests" and all mankind "a Holy Nation."

Was the thinking and line of action of the Church following Emperor Constantine's arrogation of the role of
being protector and patron a course without an alternative?

A perusal of the history of European peoples during the
medieval and modern periods amply confirms the view that
there was but a nominal alliance or tangential contact
between the life-renouncing, excessively-idealistic ethics
enunciated on the Sermon on the Mount and the mores,
habits and strivings of the nations who extolled these
teachings in Cathedrals and Abbeys but ignored them in
every-day practice. Actually they but typified the norms of
behavior of their belligerent and plundering forebears and
of the pleasure-loving and luxury-craving patricians of
Rome.

This tenuous alliance between these diverse dispositions
and cultures made it difficult for each to interpenetrate or to
temper the excesses of the other to any great extent. The
medieval Christian outlook and the German's demeanor,
before and during the Hitler regime, were in need of a
corrective synthesis. Judaism, as we shall see, could have
shown them the way to such a wholesome synthesis. Without such an abiding and reciprocally-rectifying synthesis,
Christian civilization swung from one extreme profession
and practice to its opposite with deleterious consequences
at each stage to itself and the world.

In the laboratory of a chemist one encounters elements
each of which in its pure and isolated state could be in-
jurious and may even be fatal to living beings. However,
when one such element is compounded with a different but

equally baneful substance, then the compound paradoxically turns out to be beneficial and even essential to the maintenance of life. Sodium and chlorine singly administered to man might have a deadly effect. Both combined in a certain way, according to a stipulated procedure forms salt. The union of hydrogen and oxygen resulting in water, without which life is impossible, is another example.

Social theories and ethical philosophies are like chemical elements. Presented as a one-sided set of beliefs, conceived as a rigid and inflexible pattern of life which will not tolerate any exception or modification (no matter how much conditions may warrant an alteration or suspension of some of its prescriptions), a social theory or ethical philosophy is bound to have unfortunate consequences. An ethic which prescribes the renunciation of the natural yearnings and physical needs of its spokesmen (though not of all its followers), and enjoins its devotees to turn their back on what it terms worldly concerns, a moral system which brands the former as carnal and the latter as mundane, is bound to be inept. On the other hand, a libertarian ethic which sanctions any and all gratification of sensual desires and lascivious indulgence, and which conceives the hereafter to be a valhalla, where divinities carouse and satiate themselves with nectar and are as little exempt from gusts of passion and jealousy as are mortals, and like mortals resort to cunning and trickery to attain their ends, such an appraisal of life and human destiny is equally noxious.

The ethics which Judaism evolved manifest, to a signal degree, a sense of realism and a wholesome regard for human wants and values. When the stipulation of articles of beliefs and dogmas was the fashion of the day, the most eminent of Jewish philosophers, Maimonides, was not deterred from asserting that the literal meaning of Biblical Writ may and should be made subsidiary to the imperatives of reason.[1] Equally so were the expositions of God-given law made to reckon with the conditions and needs of time and place and the prodigious sacrifice which their strict observance would necessitate. The Torah or Moral Law was made for man, the ethics of Judaism maintained. Its objective was to enable man to live fully but on a plane higher than the one on which animals move.

In the ethics of Judaism, the world and man are conceived to be essentially good. Judaism took notice of Nature's seeming indifference to moral values and the unconcern of its forces with moral deserts. It was also keenly aware of the wayward inclinations of the untutored heart of men. One may discern foreshadowings of the Freudian "ID" in the verse in Genesis.

"The imagination of the heart of man is evil from his youth," [2] and also in the observation of Jeremiah "The heart is deceitful above all things and desperately corrupt wicked." [3] Despite the moral negativity of Nature's forces (whose harmful behavior was construed to be the product of man's moral fall) the Sages of Judaism affirmed that the world and man were predominantly good. The evil in the world and in the heart of man was rectifiable.

Conceived in that light the goodness of man and the world could not be considered to be beyond improvement. Endowed with a nature which is weak and waywardly-disposed, man has the opportunity to exercise choice and attain self-mastery. By redirecting his primordial propensities toward good ends he justifies his claim to being a moral person. In a universe which is malleable and unfinished man can thus attain the role of being a partner in Creation with the Almighty.

In the ethics of Judaism, natural instincts and cravings were not deemed to be intrinsically and irremediably bad. Judaism refused to brand bodily urges and impulses as carnal. The Sages of Judaism would have recoiled from Paul's exhortation to his followers: "Mortify therefore your members which are upon the earth." [4] They deprecated and condemned celibacy and the spurning of the legitimate enjoyments of life even for those who aspired to dedicate their lives to the service of God. They never proposed the suppression of human inclination and impulse. They advocated only that the impulses and desires be channeled to worthy ends. They stressed the moralization and sanctification of human impulses and dispositions. Their prayer was not "Eradicate or destroy" but "bend and turn our inclinations to serve Thee." Commenting on the verse wherein God looked on the finished work of Creation and termed it "very good," [5] Rabbi Samuel ben Nahman asserted that this referred specifically to the evil impulse. For "were it not for the evil impulse no man would build a house, nor marry a wife, nor beget children, nor engage in trade." [6]

They denounced the indulgence in the then current masochistic practices of bodily flagellation. They looked askance even at the taking of Nazarite vows. "Are not the things prohibited you in the Law enough for you, that you want to prohibit yourself other things?" remonstrated one Rabbi. Such abstainers were termed sinners. [7] A noted Sage (RAB) even maintained that "A man will have to give account on the judgment day for every good thing which he might have enjoyed and did not." [8]

Had not Eve extended the prohibition against eating of the fruit of the tree of knowledge to include also the mere touching, the violation of the former might not have led to the violation of the authentic command, is the opinion of a Rabbi. What an amazing feat, if not a peerless achievement, for a Faith that stressed observance of the Law to accent, to no small extent, latitudinarism and flexibility. To the saying, "Make a fence around the Torah," [9] I maintain, has been given a meaning contrary to what it was intended to imply. Its counsel was not to restrict the range of freedom but to extend it. The former connotation is contained in the phrase "To keep a man far from transgression." [10]

"Make a fence around the Torah" is a corollary of the rabbinic policy to widen the area in which one may legitimately browse. Actually it resulted in bringing to bear the beneficent and liberating influence of the Torah to an extended domain of life. The peregrinations and the reconnoitering, of course, were not to disregard reasonable bounds. "Amplify the law but not beyond a set terminus" was the intent of the admonition.

Chapter 2

LAW—THE INSTRUMENT FOR INDIVIDUAL
AND SOCIAL BETTERMENT

"Think not that I am come to destroy the law or the prophets: I am not come to destroy but to fulfill." MATT. V:17

"But we know that the law is good, if a man use it lawfully." I TIMOTHY I:8

THE dicta of the Sermon on the Mount were quoted and given an aura of sanctity and ineffable worth, but their spirit was not implemented by and incorporated into forms, habits, rules and disciplines. For that a stipulated regimen of procedure in the every day demeanor of Christians was essential. The will to peace, as well as all other spiritual strivings needs to be translated into concrete deeds. As electricity surcharging the atmosphere during a storm has to be caught and transmitted through wires to glass bulbs with filaments before it can be made to kindle and glow, and thereby replace the darkness with light so must our noble aspirations be channeled to pragmatic behavior and overt acts. *The unimplemented pronouncement of noble avowals tends to anesthetize our acumen and critical faculty. It fosters in one the illusion that the recital of a spiritual intent and moral aim is tantamount to its actualization.*

One can also venture the view that the pre-eminence which the ideology of the Early and Medieval Church gave to *FAITH* over and above *WORKS* was also responsible for the hiatus which was evident between the profession and the practice of Christians. Avowals of belief are not as potent in moulding human nature as are stipulated modes of behavior. Modern pedagogy stresses the fact that children

learn by doing things. Didactic instruction is replaced by
assignments of tasks and projects. "Habits," the psychologists tells us, "determine character."

The author of the sayings in the Book of Proverbs must
have been cognizant of this fact when he admonished,
"Train up a child in the way he should go: and, when he is
old, he will not depart from it." [1]

The much maligned legalism of Judaism is a consequence
of the realization that regulated and rational behavior is
vital to the mastery of one's whims and impulses. The voluntary compliance to significant and beneficently-intended
injunctions and laws, whether instituted by others or ourselves, is a basic prerequisite to the development of a mature
and wholesome personality, as well as the making of a stable and good society. The libertine, the egotist and the criminal, resent enactment of laws. However, it should not be
necessary in a society where the ceaseless promulgation and
accumulation of laws and ordinances make the sea of the
Talmud seem like a shallow pond to argue for the need and
value of rules, traditions and laws. I record here another
comment of a keen-minded and learned reader of this manuscript. "If religious development in Christian Europe had
retained, instead of abrogating their basic concept of the
law, the Church's educational influence on the civilization
of all Europe, including Germany, would have proven in-
comparably more sound and effective than it actually
turned out to be." [2]

Christians were, and some still are, prone to term the distinctive method and technique of Judaism in implementing
its spiritual and ethical professions as *legalism*. That the
denigration of its procedure is unfair and even slanderous
has been amply indicated in the writings of George Foote
Moore and T. H. Herford who are Christian scholars.

"The idealistic character of much in rabbinical juris-
prudence" declares the former, "is an inheritance from the
Law and the Prophets. . . . Intelligent and religious men
could not have spent their lives in the study of the Scriptures without recognizing and approximating this spirit,
and interpreting the law in it. The Law was not for the

Jewish Doctors of the Law merely a Corpus Juris, a volume
of statues on all kinds of subjects, ritual and ceremonial,
criminal and civil; it was—to give it modern expression—
a revelation of God's ideal for men's conduct and character." [3]

Judaism (together with Christianity and other high religions) aspires to ennoble and spiritualize the individual,
the group of which he is a part and society as a whole. It has
developed a 'modus operandi' which has been for centuries
misrepresented and vilified. Judaism sincerely believed
that the best way to attain its aim was through the observance of stipulated laws and commandments. These were not
meaningless orders, unreasoned decrees of a despot to be
blindly obeyed. They served a purpose, their ultimate aim
is the weal and happiness of man. When conditions altered
and changes were demanded for the good of the individual
or society, then those laws were, in due course of time, modified or replaced by others.

The Torah (the body of laws which commences with the
injunctions and commandments of the Pentateuch and is
continuously being augmented) is to the Jew what Jesus
and His sayings are to the devout Christian-compass and
lodestar to guide him past the shoals of life. The faithful
Christian maintains that the meditation and emulation of
the actions and attitudes of the Nazarene offers a SURE
KEY to the solution of the problems that vex individuals
and nations in all ages and under all circumstances.

Jews and Judaism have been and are skeptical as to the
adequacy of such a claim. Judaism deems the contemplation
of the life and spirit of any of its Seers as incapable of offering an unequivocal and certain index to what is right and
good in a controversy where the issues are complex and
debatable and the contending parties are remote in time
and the civilization of one radically differed from that of
the other. One must be extraordinarily naive, or totally
devoid of critical acumen, to assume that the contemplation
and emulation of an action of a shepherd or a tiller of
the soil, however exemplary and edifying it may be, can

solve the problems which worry individuals and nations in an atomic and nuclear age.

Judaism has a different method. It prescribed what its sense of equity and fraternity decreed to be right in a concrete situation, in a plain and primitive social setting. From that ruling it inferred what should be right in a more complex and involved affair. That procedure helped it to build up a body of laws which yielded precedents and principles enabling its authorized spokesmen to dispense justice in developed societies and in intricate circumstances.

Did this technique prove effective in spiritualizing Jewish life or did it but foster the punctilious observance of the letter of the law?

In answering this question, one is disposed to point to the devoutness of the medieval Jew. In the face of his confinement to a ghetto, and stigmatization by a yellow badge and frequent subjection to the pyres of an auto dé fé, bloody pogroms, vile calumnies and heart-breaking discrimination, the branded obduracy and stiff-neckedness of the medieval Jew was the exemplification of a singular fidelity to an Ideal. The exclamation of Job, "Though He slay me yet will I trust in Him" [4] aptly befits his demeanor. His thirst for the knowledge of God was never slaked. An erudite man was not called a Sage but a wise student (Talmid Chacham). The Jew's devotion to his family, his high regard for domestic virtues, the comparative chaste life which he then led, his sense of social responsibility and obligation to less fortunate kin which make him willing to share with them, not merely material possessions, but his VERY home—all these facts can be marshalled to refute the imputation that Jewish legalism proved less successful in spiritualizing the life of its devotees, than was the case with the distinctive procedures of Christianity.

Chapter 3

THE PENITENT'S CLEANSING TEARS

"Who errs and mends,
To God himself commends." CERVANTES

"To do it no more is the truest repentance." LUTHER

"ALL things come alike to all," declared the author of Ecclesiastes, "there is one event to the righteous and to the wicked." [1] The Sages of the Talmud rejected this supposed Solomonic notion of Nature's indifference to the performance of good and evil by man, even though they decided to include the book which harboured this and like views in the Holy Canon. "Abandon not the belief in retribution," [2] "Faithful is thy employer to pay thee the reward of thy labor," [3] were admonitions which they proffered to their disciples.

Both Judaism and Christianity accent the doctrine of retribution. Moral defection, they aver, gives rise to consequences which are deleterious and painful to both the culprit and the society which bred or tolerated such evildoers.

The dire consequences of wickedness which they envisaged were not restricted to the infliction of physical pain. A diseased body, a rainless sky and a dry and parched earth were not the sum-total of punishments in store for moral transgressions. Evil deeds and habits are followed by a deterioration of character and a disfigurement of the divine in man. The addict and the inveterate criminal become bereft of the power of reason, human feeling, faith and courage. "You will eat the flesh of your sons and the flesh of your daughters," Scripture warned those who would persist in defying the commandments of God. "You will be-

come faint of heart. The sound of a shaking leaf will terrify
you. You will flee as if from brandished swords wielded by
pursuing enemies until exhaustion will overtake you, when
in reality none have pursued you." [4]

The drama of history and life, wherein men select and
are given specific roles to play, testify to the presence of
untold mentally-deranged and conscience-stricken Mac-
beths and Boris Godounoffs. The array of kingdoms and
empires which waxed mighty and rich and imagined themselves incorruptible as well as invincible only to decay and
decline and disappear is long. Isaiah's stigmatization of
Babylon applies to all the Powers, States and Dominions
who made the Chaldean Empire their model.

> "Now therefore hear this, thou that art given to pleasure,
> Thou that sittest securely,
> Thou that sayest in thy heart:
> 'I am, and there is none else besides me,'
> Neither shall I know the loss of children
> But these two things shall come to thee in a moment,
> In one day.
> The loss of children and widowhood
> In the full measure shall they come upon thee,
> For the multitudes of thy sorceries
> And the great abundance of thy enchantment.
> And thou hast been secure in thy wickedness.
> Thou hast said, 'None seeth me.'
>
> Thy wisdom and thy knowledge
> It hath perverted thee." [5]

Emphatic as is the avowal of the Synagogue and the
Church that "as a man soweth so shall he reap," equally so
their affirmation that man (who is subject to temptations,
aberrations and defections in varying degrees) is not ines-
capably doomed to suffer the consequences of his misdeeds.
Both Judaism and Christianity assert that the sinner by
means of repentance (remorse, abandonment of his wonted
way and rectification of any injury done to his fellowmen)
can stave off physical retribution. And what is even of

greater import, the repentant sinner can in a mystic way transmute the gashes of his disfigured soul into marks of transcendent glory and beauty.

Resh Lakish held repentance in such high esteem that "sins antedating repentance are accounted," he said, "as though they were merits." [6]

"Whence do we know," asks another Talmudic sage, "that if a man repents he converts into pious deeds even the many sins of which he may be guilty? Because it is written, 'And when the wicked turneth from his wickedness and doeth that which is lawful and right he shall live THEREBY' (namely by the misdeeds which he now repudiates." [7]

Rabbi Simeon ben Halafta taught, "All the good things, blessings and consolations which the prophets beheld in this world were intended for the repentant: but as for him who never experienced sin in his lifetime these visions and experience are withheld." [8]

Jesus' espousal of unabated patience with sinners who repeatedly transgress and seek forgiveness must have been prompted by his realization of the precious results of sincere penitence.[9]

Not all the evaluations of repentance, however, are commendatory. Some notable thinkers have deprecated it. Spinoza, for example, deemed repentance to be a fatuous mood. He conceived the actions of men to be determined by the impact of past events and contemporary forces no less than is the case with the movements of physical objects. A chain of causes make the events in question inevitable. Regret over their occurrence is, therefore, pointless if not idiotic.[10]

This supposition of Spinoza clashes with man's sense of actuality, namely the inner conviction and empiric assurance that he is free and that he chooses his course of conduct despite the fact that his freedom is not totally uncircumscribed and unconditioned. If freedom is an illusion then Spinoza's exhortation (in the concluding propositions of his Ethics) that man seek the good and strive for truth is of no avail.

Many noted contemporary psychologists are also inclined to view the attitude which is associated with penitence as unwholesome, if not actually hazardous to mental health. "All schools of psychiatry agree that behind every anxiety-neurosis is a sense of guilt." In the terminology of Freud and his "orthodox" apostles and even those psychoanalysts who are known to have deviated from some of the master's pronouncements the word 'repentance' is conspicuously absent. In its place we find the terms 'anxiety' and 'guilt-feelings.'

I believe that the testimony which the religionist can muster regarding the heart-lifting and purging-power of repentance far exceeds the exceptional clinical specimens which psychoanalysts may bring as witnesses to the contrary. The moral seers of mankind whose visions and inspiration emerged from their sense of spiritual inadequacy and short-coming are legion.[11]

The commission of sin, when followed by sincere penitence, far from marring and degrading the sinner's character tends to refine it. The Hebrew verb —'CHATA' to sin (in the piel and hith-pael forms) has the meaning also to *cleanse* and to *purify*.

Chapter 4

THE GLORY OF THE REDEEMED

"I have blotted out, as a thick cloud, thy transgressions,
And, as a cloud, thy sins;
Return unto Me, for I have redeemed thee." ISA. XLIV

PEOPLES and nations are subject to spasms of moral degeneration and through repentance are capable of spiritual regeneration no less than are individuals. In stating this view one is not indulging in wishful thinking and idealistic speculation. Here history, too, supplies us with an array of testimony to support our claim.

The great prophets of Israel were fully cognizant of this fact. When they saw their people steeped in quagmires of moral degradation they did not allow themselves to become overwhelmed with despondency. They experienced such moods but they managed quickly to free themselves of them. They were aware of inherent latent spiritual potentialities in that folk. The Patriarchs' discovery of and their peerless devotion to the GOD of Truth and Righteousness, they were convinced, had left a deep impress upon the collective subconscious, if not conscious mind of that people. The recollection of those exemplary figures was dim but not dead. They were the victims of moral amnesia which the Prophets were sure would soon pass.

The literary legacies of the group wherein its destiny and character were foreshadowed could not remain ignored. For it was the product of a nascent national spirit and corporate will. The heritage would haunt them, paradoxically, to the degree that they were indifferent to it. But one day, they felt, the lettering of these documents would appear distinct and their meaning unmistakable and their worth incalculable.

Only one with the foresight and faith of an Isaiah could join such divergent moods and dispositions as are evidenced in passages like the following, which are part of the same discourse:

"Hear the words of the Lord,
　Ye rulers of Sodom;
　Give ear unto the law of our God,
　Ye peoples of Gomorrah:
　To what purpose is the multitude of your sacrifices unto Me?
　Saith the Lord;
　Bring no more vain oblations;
　It is an offering of abomination unto me:
　They are a burden unto me;
　I am weary to bear them
　And when ye spread forth your hands,
　I will hide mine eyes."

Despite the above fulmination the Prophet continues:

"Wash you, make you clean,
  Put away the evil of your doings
  From before mine eyes.
  Cease to do evil;
  Learn to do well,
  Seek justice, relieve the oppressed,
  Judge the fatherless, plead for the widow.

  Come now let us reason together
  Saith the Lord;
  Though your sins be as scarlet,
  They shall be as white as snow;
  Though they be red like crimson,
  They shall be as wool." [1]

One finds the mood of gloom giving way to a feeling of
elation and sanguine hopefulness, characteristic not of one
but all the Prophets. This is true even of Jeremiah whose
name came to connote lamentation and doleful prediction.

"Be astonished, O ye heavens, at this,
  And be horribly afraid, be ye exceedingly amazed,
  Saith the Lord.
  For my people have committed two evils:
  They have forsaken Me, the fountain of living waters,
  And hewed them out cisterns, broken cisterns,
  That can hold no water.

  And now what hast thou to do in the way of Egypt,
  To drink the waters of Shihor?
  Or what hast thou to do in the way of Assyria
  To drink the waters of the River?

  Thine own wickedness shall correct thee,
  And thy backslidings shall reprove thee";

"For though thou wash thee with nitre;
  And take thee much soap,
  Yet thine iniquity is marked before Me
  Saith the Lord God.[2]

Israel is the Lord's hallowed portion,
His first-fruits of the increase;
All that devour him shall be held guilty
Evil shall come upon them,
Saith the Lord." [3]

The most notable aspect of prophetic teachings is not that they extolled abstract principles of justice, righteousness and mercy. One may find injunctions in earlier biblical books and codes which evidence not merely such beliefs but even stipulate the action which such avowals make necessary in specific situations.

Nor does the signal feature of prophetic affirmations consist in their proclamation that there prevails in the moral realm what Emerson called the Law of Compensation, that every moral deed or misdeed is linked with a specific sequel no less than there is to every action in the physical world an unalterable reaction. All the books of the Pentateuch reiterate the warning that retribution is in store for all moral violations.

The keynote and salient point of the Prophetic Message is its perception of the redeeming power of suffering, which comes to one who becomes aware of guilt and shortcoming and is contrite and penitent over its commission. With a firm will to rectify the evil that had been done and an unbending resolution to avoid its repetition a moral victory may be wrested from such physical ordeals and defeats.

It was the Prophets' faith in Israel's latent capacity to convert physical tragedy into spiritual triumph, as well as their belief that God assigned to their people an eternal role in the drama of man, that made them proclaim the indestructibility of Israel.

"When thou passest through the waters
I will be with thee
And through the rivers, they shall not overflow thee,
When thou walkest through the fire, thou shalt not be burned
Neither shall the flame kindle against thee." [4]

"Thus saith the Lord
Who giveth the sun for a light by day

And the ordinances of the moon and of the stars
For a light by night,
Who stirreth up the sea, that the waves thereof roar,
If these ordinances depart before Me,
Saith the Lord.
Then the seed of Israel also shall cease,
From being a nation before Me for ever." [5]

The capacity for spiritual self-renewal was not conceived
by the Seers of Israel to have been confined to Hebrews.
They deemed it a latent attribute of all men and peoples.
The story of Jonah and the Rabbis' inclusion of the book
bearing his name in the Canon are the result of that conviction.

The book of Jonah affirms the universal solicitude and
compassionate nature of Israel's God. It also gives us a character study of a prophet who needed to be purged of his ego-
centricism no less than the inhabitants of Nineveh had to
be cleansed of their sins. Jonah's demeanor provides us
with a vivid illustration of the observation of one of his
more dedicated and gifted colleagues, "Who is blind, but my
servant? Or deaf, as my messenger that I send?" [6]

The outstanding pronouncements of the Hebrew Prophets and their successors, the Talmudic Sages, succinctly
stated, are:

1) National disasters and tragedies are the consequence
   of the repudiation or neglect of moral principles.
2) Calamities so judged can function as shock-treatment
   which may restore insight and emotional health to a
   mentally-confused and morally-callous folk.
3) Political collapse and military defeat can then be
   made the prelude to a notable spiritual victory.

That these precepts are validated by historic events a
perusal of the annals of ancient people amply confirms. The
reflection over and moral explanation of the vicissitudes of
fortune of some contemporary nations, to the fateful occurrences of which this very generation had been a witness,

corroborates and fortifies the affirmations of the Jewish Seers and Teachers.

For illustration of the abiding truth of the Prophetic teachings I cite some contemporary instances of states whose ambition-obsessed rulers or knavish political leaders have led their nations to a military adventure which terminated in defeat and debacle. The catastrophe seemed fatal. The nation, it was maintained, was doomed to decay and disappearance and the preparation of an obituary for it was believed to be in order. However, the prediction was not fulfilled. On the contrary, the nation was regenerated and reinvigorated after the disaster. A new leader with a new group of followers got hold of the reins of government. They had perceived the mistakes and sins of the former regime. They correctly appraised the present situation and its requirements and succeeded in reorientating the wishes and hopes of the people to a sound national but non-imperialistic goal.

Even before World War I began Turkey already had been dubbed the sick man of Europe. The Ottoman Empire was in a state of visible decrepitude. Energetic land-lusting European Powers were surveying it as a vulture does a dying body from which life is fast ebbing. Hungary, Serbia, Bulgaria, Montenegro, Greece, Austria, the Danubian principalities of Wallachia and Moldavia (which later constituted a part of Roumania) and Italy tore off chunks of the prostrate body without waiting for it to become cold and totally inert. Even the nation which pledged itself to come to Turkey's aid if attacked was not altruistic in her promise of protection.

Turkey was a backward unprogressive state with an absolute ruler at its head. Its population was illiterate. The people were bound by oriental customs and creeds which were deemed to be heaven-ordained. The masses were poor as well as benighted. Their condition was that of serfs and servants. Landowners and employers exploited them. Petty civil officials, aping their baksheesh-demanding superiors, tyrannized over them.

With indigent, fatalistic and enfeebled subjects and corrupt self-seeking officials and the head of the state, who at
one moment deemed himself to be the incarnation and the
voice of Mahomet and at another assumed the part of an
all-wise and powerful sovereign, it was not difficult for the
crafty diplomats of Europe to bring about the disintegration of the Ottoman Empire and reduce it into a congeries
of small, rival and jealous Balkan kingdoms; they became
the tinderbox where a spark could and did start a world conflagration. Except for the city of Constantinople and a bit
of land to the west of it, Europe became "Turkei-rein."

Rankled by the thought of the foul and flimsy excuses
that the predatory nations offered for the dismemberment
of the Empire, and dazzled by the martial demeanor and
dynamism of the Teutonic armies, the Sultan in November
of 1914 cast his lot with that of the Central Powers. One
could have been justified in equating this step with an act
of suicide. Turkey was, it could have been said, nailing its
own coffin.

Unexpected results, however, followed the defeat of the
Central Powers as far as Turkey was concerned. With the
Peace of Versailles, the ancient Ottoman Empire disappeared. The house of Osman, which had ruled the Turks for
seven centuries, went the way of the Hohenzollerns,
Hapsburgs and Romanoffs. A Republic came into being
headed by a vigorous leader, Mustapha Kemal Pasha. He
became their 'Moses,' who not only emancipated them from
the thraldom of the dark past, with its archaic and degrading restrictions, but he also kindled their will to survive
within the prescribed boundaries as a virile Westernized
nation. He devised for them a constitution. The institution
of the Caliphate was abolished. The Promised Land which
he envisioned was to be a Commonwealth where Church and
State were to remain separate and independent. Social reforms, equal rights for women, the State's duty to provide
education and opportunities for professional pursuits to its
youth, the encouragement of the development of industry,
the organization of workers and the protection of the public
from the abuses of both capital and labor are items which

are now evident in the social and political structure of Modern Turkey.

Japan offers us another example of the capacity of a people, after experiencing an unexpected and stunning shock, to change its wonted course and alter its character (in certain respects even in a diametrically opposite way).

The Japanese for centuries led a sheltered and secluded existence in the elongated islands separated by sea and ocean from the mammoth mainland of Siberia, Manchuria, Korea and China.

Their social organization and forms and modes of thinking were of a feudal mould. A small group, the nobles and the 'Samurai,' the fighting men, moved on an exalted plane. They lorded it over the multitude who were tenant tillers of the land and the fishermen who had to hazard daily the dangers of the storm and sea in frail craft in order to sustain themselves and their families. The select few were accorded homage and tribute by the fear-ridden and subservient multitude. The élite behaved like petty deities and considered themselves above the law.

Separated from the mainland, and rarely visited by ships of distant lands, both the common folk and the élite remained unaffected by 'winds of doctrine' which here and there moved the dispossessed and the down-trodden to ameliorate their condition. Gripped by fear and suspicion of what was strange and foreign, they were content with their indigenous and revered manners.

When in 1854, after the failure of previous ventures, Commodore Perry fearlessly directed the ten amazing ships propelled by steam and equipped with big guns into Yedo Bay, the inhabitants, rulers and ruled, were paralyzed by consternation and fright. The Commodore landed with a guard of five hundred sailors. They marched through the streets and headed for the palace of the ruler. They demanded no tribute or special privileges. All they asked was that the door to Japan be unlocked for trade and commerce. The request was granted and this marked a new era for the secluded Japanese people and islands.

The impact of that event is not overstated by H. G. Wells, despite his propensity for popularization and literary embellishment.

"The humiliation of the Japanese by these events was intense and it would seem that the salvation of peoples lies largely in such humiliation. With astounding energy and intelligence they set themselves to bring their culture and organization up to the level of the European powers. Never in all the history of mankind did a nation make such a stride as Japan then made. In 1866 she was a medieval people, a fantastic caricature of the extremist romantic feudalism; in 1899 she was a completely Westernized people, on a level with the most advanced European powers, and well in advance of Russia. She completely dispelled the notion that Asia was in some irrevocable way hopelessly behind Europe. She made all European progress seem sluggish and tentative by comparison."

Dazzled by her industrial and commercial achievements, inspirited by her waxing military might, the guides and rulers of Japan became obsessed with the belief that Fate had destined them to exercise hegemony in her hemisphere and to play also a dominant role in the affairs of the whole world. This obsession seduced them into war with China and even into stooping to the craven attack on the United States fleet at Pearl Harbor.

The Nipponese people paid dearly for the folly and infamy of their politicians and war lords who brought the nation to the verge of ruin and annihilation.

In December 1956, I was privileged to deliver a series of lectures on the Philosophy and Ethics of Judaism before the faculty and students of Keio, Waseda and Nihon Universities in Tokyo, Japan.

I also was privileged to address two meetings of a growing sect, formerly carrying the designation of Christian Brethren, but now connected with its professions by tenuous bonds. This group of Japanese display a greater esteem for the Old Testament than for the New Gospel. The singing of Psalms makes up the hymns of their Liturgy. They, as well as the intellectuals who make up the academic echelon, are very much attracted to the tenets of Judaism and are most sympathetic to Jews.

Why this is so and how it came about are matters that lie beyond the scope of this book.

My conversations and discussions with these people and the individuals whom I met on the street and in public conveyances led me to the conclusion that the Japanese had sloughed off the militaristic traits and imperialistic ambitions which had earmarked their national character up to the tragedy of Hiroshima and Nagasaki when they realized their helplessness before a nation which was capable of using atomic bombs for warfare. I found this people unrevengeful and forgiving. Their defeat spurred them to scrutinize their former aspirations and actions. They perceived that what had been done to them was only the retribution for their own iniquitous deeds.

The shock of unexpected defeat dispelled their enchantment and shattered their illusion of invincibility and predestined glory. It impelled them to reexamine and assess anew their aims and ideals. It evoked, it appears, a sense of regret and remorse over their behavior. They resolved to begin to write a new page in the history of Japan. And if signs are not misleading, they will not falter in their determination to display to the world the truth that glory and greatness can come to a people who had been vanquished in battle but is resolved to be industrious and genuinely peace-loving.

The cited instances of national spiritual regeneration that followed a stunning catastrophe inclines one to wonder whether the future conduct of the Germans will earmark them as a *prodigal people*.[7]

Chapter 5

SHOALS AHEAD

"The first and worst of all frauds is to cheat oneself." P. J.
BAILEY

"WHO is a hero?" a talmudic sage asked. To this query
he offered the answer, "He who can subdue his (evil)
disposition." [1]

A Welsh poet some four centuries ago wrote:

> "Summe up at night what thou hast done by day;
> And in the morning what thou hast to do;
> Dresse and undresse thy soul; mark the decay
> And growth of it; if with thy watch that too
> Be down then winde up both; since we shall be
> Most surely judged, make thy accounts agree." [2]

If ever a nation needed to heed that advice and show the
world that it can be truly heroic by discarding aberrations
and vices that it was wont to extol, it is Germany.

What specifically are the errors and forms of wayward-
ness against which the New Germany must be on guard?

First: Germany must revise her notion of what constitutes an elite people. The economic comeback of West Germany since 1949 is phenomenal. The aid which she received
in various forms from the United States partially accounts
for her amazing recovery. The industriousness and intelligence and skill of her people are important factors in ex-
plaining her phoenix-like rise from the ashes of her destroyed cities and factories. These traits presage also a
notable advance in the realm of invention, science and art.
The question that disturbs one as he peers into the future
is "will these achievements again inflate the national ego

of that gifted people and lure them to worship the old idols? Or will they now in humility take to heart the saying of Goethe "Die gaben kommen von oben herab in ihren eignen gestalten: gifts come from above in their peculiar form?"

Will the Germans conceive the possession of wealth and wisdom as a trust to be used for mankind's best interest and welfare and not as a justification for pride? Will service to others and not the enslavement of others be the consequence of their possession of extraordinary talents?

Second: Will Germany beware of the possible abuse of the dogma that the Weltgeist finds embodiment in the course of German history and in the progress and development of *its* cultural expression? The belief is not without potential moral value. If the nature and objective of the Weltgeist's manifestation are not primarily to endow a nation with power and splendor but to disclose to it attributes of compassion and the beauty of holiness, then an identification of a people and its way with a Supreme Plan and Will may tend to exalt that people's existence and make it more regardful of the things it should seek.

A people which is inclined to equate its actions and ambitions with the cosmic and historic process must however be doubly on guard against the supposition that its course and behavior are without any alternative and therefore that its people is exempt from blame, or is to be deemed above the ordinary criteria of right and wrong.

The metaphysics of Hegel was made, we have seen, the foundation of Germany's national consciousness and ambition. In his scheme the interests of the State would warrant, it was believed, a suspension if not renunciation of prevalent moral principles and precepts. In the light of the Ultimate or the Absolute, human standards and criteria, it was reasoned, are woefully inadequate and inconstant. Why then should momentary dots of light emanating from fireflies darting hither and thither be preferred to the Lamp whose incandescent brilliance was reckoned to be beyond measure?

The notion that the course of history is decreed by a

Transcendental Power and that it is to conform to a Predetermined Plan may rob a man of his freedom. For in reality his sense of freedom is but the projection of his imagination and the product of wishful thinking. There is a Cosmic
Drama to be enacted, the view contends. Its performance is
under the aegis of an Invisible Director. To us, human beings, roles are assigned and we have our stipulated pieces
to recite. Not only have the lines been composed for us
but we are also commanded to speak them with certain
inflections and gestures.

Byron characterized this credo of inevitability.

> "For I am a Weed
> Flung from the Rock, on Ocean's foam, to sail
> Where'er the surge may sweep, the tempest's
> breath prevail." [3]

The Judaic tradition, noteworthily, set up safeguards
against the siren assumptions of specious deductions that
man must jettison the notion that he is a free and self-
directing being. When the Talmudic Sages affirm that "everything is conditioned by Heaven but not the fear of
Heaven" [4] they caution their devotees against the view
that man is the puppet of fate or that he is 'as a driven leaf'
at the mercy of every gust of wind or as an eddy of a current.

The affirmation or implication that man's role is only
that of a marionette is not confined to a region or a period
of time. It is evidenced when slavery or the belief in the
right of the white man to rule and dominate his dark-
skinned brother on the alleged ground that such a practice
or attitude was ordained by Nature or Holy Writ. It is evident when a strong power justifies its aggressive invasion
of the territory of a weaker neighbor by the contention that
it is impelled to that action by its "manifest destiny." It
can be discerned when toleration of and amity with Hitler
were advocated on the presumption that Nazism conformed
to the "wave of the future." In all these instances we witnessed Man's capitulation of moral responsibility against

the doctrine of inevitability. Benjamin Disraeli and James Anthony Froude, the English historian, made the following observations (both being good Jewish doctrines): "Man," declared Disraeli, "is not the creature of circumstances; circumstances are the creatures of Man." [5] "Our thoughts and our conduct are our own" [6] proclaimed Froude.

Third: Will the New Germany unreservedly acknowledge the sovereignty of the Moral Law which cannot be rescinded or even temporarily suspended or modified by the needs and interests of the State? Moral principles must be as sacrosanct as the law was to the King of Israel, upon ascending the throne. "And it shall be, when he sitteth upon the throne of his kingdom, that he shall write him a copy of this law in a book . . . And it shall be with him, and he shall read therein all the days of his life; that he may learn to fear the Lord, his God, to keep all the words of this law and these statutes to do them." [7]

Fourth: Germans have been a discipline-minded folk. They were disposed to consider obedience and submission to authority a well-nigh axiomatic virtue. All one needed to deter a German from a certain act was to say "Est ist verboten."

One can speculate how it came to be that the German evinced such awe of authority. His apotheosis of authority, it is maintained may be traced to doctrines embodied in the Pauline injunctions, "Servants obey in all things your masters according to the flesh." [8] "Obey them that have the rule over you and submit yourself." [9]

It can also be contended that this trait was the product of Prussian militarism. After Prussia's crushing defeat of France in 1871 and Bismarck's unification of the separate German duchies and states into not merely One Great European Power, but into an expanding Empire, soldier-like demeanor and army officialdom were glorified. To heed unquestioningly commands of those who are higher up and to goosestep were tokens of manliness and patriotism. The latter explanation appears to me to accord more with actuality.

Worthy of note is the ironic fact that in the land where Luther unfurled the banner with the inscription 'conscience above (ecclesiastical) authority' 'heil Hitler' and cheers for waving swastikas, the emblem which proclaimed that the dictates of the State and political authority transcend the promptings of conscience, succeeded in infecting the minds and souls of the majority.

Germans, if they are to be immune from another Nazi nightmare, must strive to think independently. If a conflict should arise between their sense of what is right and that which political officials maintain is their duty they must be strong and courageous enough to assert, "The Lord our God will we serve and unto His voice will we hearken." [10]

The verses of Shelley deserve to be engraved in the mind and heart of every German.

> "Power like a desolating pestilence
> Pollutes whate'er it touches; and obedience
> Bane of all genius, virtue, freedom, truth,
> Makes slaves of men, and of human frame
> A mechanized automaton." [11]

Fifth: Will the New Germany unremittingly maintain a watchful eye against the inclination to revive Prussian militarism, which nurtured and fondled the belief that Germany was an Army possessing a State instead of a State having an Army? Sovereignty has now been restored to Germany. She can, and she is now urged to raise an Army. The size and strength of her military establishment, it is true, are restricted and will also be integrated into the contingents of the North Atlantic Treaty Organizations. The question, however, arises, "Will the restored Germany under the successors of Adenauer remain content with the small army and with the modest role assigned to her? Will she strive to imbue the national slogan 'Deutschland über alles' with the old meaning? Will she be tempted to defy the imposed curbs openly or secretly or circumvent them by means of some legal technicality?

(The realistic fact must be faced that the Bonn Government cannot now be prevented from bolstering Germany's war potential beyond the set mark should she desire it. The green signal for unrestricted industrial expansion and production given to West Germany practically eliminates the curb on that country's military potential. For the conversion of one to the other, we have seen, is not so difficult. It is better and safer for the world, Europe, and particularly for France that the defensive measures against Soviet aggression on the part of the nations of Europe are regulated and coordinated and placed under an over-all command. Even so, it is important that Germany's contingent be not officered by Prussian or Nazi-minded generals . . . lest they may induce their followers to resume the worship of old gods. With our failure to reeducate and to extirpate the lingering aberrations and misconceptions of erstwhile adherents of Nazism the hazards of a return to former ways have not been eliminated.)

Sixth: Can the Germans be made to realize that the successful outcome of a venture is not proof of its justness and goodness? Many Germans perceive the error of Hitler's ideology and the viciousness of the Nazi program but their sense of right and wrong was benumbed by the victorious outcome of his every political move and coup d'état up to 1939.

The spiritual religions have declared their heroes to be not the dominating lords of the earth, but those who, to the mundane, seemed to be failures. In this connection the words of the former President of Harvard University and erstwhile Ambassador to the Federal Republic of Germany are pertinent.

"If I may speak personally, for me the whole story of human history would be only a 'tale told by an idiot' and my life and yours would be totally devoid of meaning if the prime significance lay in the visible results of an individual's or a nation's actions. In terms of my faith it is unthinkable to say, as some have said, that men died in vain in certain wars because the proclaimed objective was never won. To me whether a man lives or dies in vain can never be measured by the collective activity of his fellows, never

by the fruits of war or peace. It can be measured only by the
way he faces his own problems, by the success or failure of
the inner conflict within his soul. And of this no one may
know but God." [12]

Lastly, citizens of the New Germany ought not to look
down on or shy away from "politics," lest it becomes the
plaything of power and profit-seeking individuals and
groups. Politics should be the concern of all citizens. It is
the duty of all to see that the best government shall prevail
and that truly public-minded persons be at its helm. The
"Ohne Mich, Without Me" movement that was in vogue in
Germany for a time, when it came to political action, must
be totally discredited and the sooner the better. For Man,
as Aristotle observed, is by nature a "homo civicus." "Separate not thyself from the community," [13] taught the gentle Rabbi Hillel. In another place he admonished his devotees: "In a place where there are no men, strive thou to be
a man." [14] Elsewhere he pithily sums up his conception
of the individual's obligations to himself and to society, and
the urgency of their fulfillment. "If I am not for myself,
who will be for me, and if I am only for myself what am I,
and if not now, when?" [15]

Epilogue

SURVEYING THE ROAD TRAVERSED

" 'Tis well said again." SHAKESPEARE

BEFORE reiterating the major theses of the book I should like to retrace the course which we have followed. The subsidiary observations and reflections will then be seen to fit in and support the consequential admonitions and warnings. This review will make more apparent the unity and continuity of the chapters' themes, which may have appeared to the reader collateral and even digressional.

We began by noting that Germany seems to be simultaneously favored and frowned upon by Fate. It was admitted that she was a singularly gifted folk. Her astounding attainments fostered the belief amongst her subjects that the Germans were a Chosen People, chosen however not to serve but to be served.

The Weltgeist it was assumed had selected German history and culture to mirror what is universally desirable and good. These views engendered national arrogance and a supposition that moral principles may be subordinated to the weal and the manifest destiny of the State. The consequence of all these aberrations was two cataclysmic World Wars. At their termination Germany presented the appearance of a mangled and moribund body with a waning promise of her recovery and restoration to her former robustness.

In a short period of time, however, this inert lump of bones and flesh acquired a new lease on life. The prostrate body rose as if from the unclosed grave and proceeded to walk with firm foot and head high as if it had never suffered a staggering calamity and a paralyzing shock.

In surveying the fortunes of Germany we asked the key

question, What made this nation topple from the dazzling heights to the abysmal bottom of a steep and gaping gorge? What brought this cultured and keen-minded people to the point of being willing to replace a Goethe by a Goebbels?

Political and economic conditions were shown to have been direct factors. A program of mis-education, extending over a long period of time in which the guides and tutors of the nation were philosophers, historians and publicists as well as generals constituted a secondary cause.

The ineptness of the Church in bringing about a wholesome synthesis of ideals instead of a mere welding of the sacred to the secular and a tangential contact of the claims of God with the claims of Caesar, which resulted in the bifurcation of life and the toleration of alternate dispositions and the validation of dual criteria of what was required of a follower of the Nazarene . . . all these were imperceptible factors in the Church's lack of success in halting the German moral collapse. Concretely and specifically stated, the daily demeanor of the Christian individual and nation gave evidence not of the exemplification but the repudiation of the Beatitudes of Jesus. The over-extolling of Faith and Obedience as superlative virtues and their designation as prerequisites for salvation, to some extent conditioned the devotees of the Church to be receptive to the protagonists of totalitarianism and to the demands of Fuehrers and Duces that they be given unquestioned trust and blind obedience.

In contrast, attention was directed to the purview of the ethics of Judaism. Instead of shuttling between the antipodal extremes of pursuing mundane and hedonistic goals to the avowal of belief in other-worldly objectives and striving for ultra-spiritual attainments, the Judaic way of life was content to extract the worthwhile elements of each and to blend them in the proper proportions to make the product unique, wholesome and not beyond the reach of normal beings.

The prevailing misconceptions and unconscious misrepresentations of the precepts and the procedure of Judaism deprived it of a chance to be fairly considered and ap-

praised. One does not have to belabor the fact that the understanding of and respect for a people are heightened by the
comprehension and proper evaluation of the Faith which
that people professes and practices. All these considerations led me to make excursive expositions of some of the
teachings of Judaism and the parallel or divergent doctrines
of the Daughter-Faith. These expositions, as was noted in
the preface, came within the scope of the book.

In citing the course of Jewish Ethics and suggesting that the
insight which it reveals and the technique which it evolved are
matters worthy of consideration by this distraught and schizo-
phrenic generation I trust that I will not be considered a
proselytizing zealot. Religious truth is too recondite and elusive
for any parochial group to maintain that it has a monopoly of
it. Each Faith and Tradition at best may lay claim to a partial
insight of the Divine Being and what His Will is. Each has a
distinct place and function in the Mosaic of Religious Expression. Christianity stands in need of Judaism and Judaism
can be enhanced by Christianity's distinctive orientation and
accent. What I do feel, and this was the intent of critical estimate of some of the churches' avowals and practices is THAT
THE TIME HAS COME WHEN ALL RELIGIONS MUST
TAKE STOCK AND EXAMINE THEIR OBJECTIVES AND
COURAGEOUSLY ACKNOWLEDGE THEIR FAILINGS
AND SHORTCOMINGS. ONLY AFTER SUCH AN HONEST
SOUL-SEARCHING INTROSPECTION WILL THE CHURCH
AND THE SYNAGOGUE AND THE MOSQUE AND THE
TEMPLES OF EASTERN RELIGIONS BE ABLE TO
SERVE MAN AND GOD MORE EFFECTIVELY.

With seizure of control of the government by the Nazis
the demoralization of the German populace plunged further downward until it touched the nadir of spiritual
insensitiveness and moral callousness. The guilt of various
groups and individuals, it was shown, was not to be considered equal. Although the entire nation was to bear the
shame of the crimes of the Nazis, the peccability and responsibility of each had to be differentiated and graded. TO
THIS CONCLUSION I WAS LED BY THE EXPLICIT
AND IMPLICIT TEACHINGS OF JUDAISM AND NOT

BY A REGARD FOR THE POLICY OF OUR STATE DE-
PARTMENT.

Has the German people been taught a lesson? Does it now
perceive the error of its ways? Or is it doomed by the blood
corpuscles which flow in its veins or do the behavior-
syndromes which it cultivated ordain it to be insensitive
to moral appeals and influences? Or has some evil spirit or
malicious deity decreed that it trudge a circuitous path
proceeding unendingly from achievement to failure and
failure to achievement?

Neither Judaism nor Christianity maintains that a man
or a people, having grievously sinned, is doomed to a life
ineradicably smudged by past misdeeds. That *man* and *nations* can alter their ways and transmute their character,
both Faiths affirm. This is not a mere theoretical postulate.
It is an observable fact.

Such a reorientation and rebirth are most likely to take
place after a severe set-back. The triumphant allies failed,
however, to remove the obstacles that blocked the way to
Germany's spiritual regeneration. We also have been derelict in helping them to see the light of the yesterday and
tomorrow. Considerations of momentary expediency seem
to direct our course. However, it is not too late to rectify the
omission.

THIS BOOK HAS BEEN WRITTEN WITH THE HOPE
THAT IT WILL AID THE PEOPLE OF GERMANY AND
THE WESTERN NATIONS TO PERCEIVE THE TASK
WHICH IS BEFORE THEM AND TO REALIZE THE
POSSIBLE FRIGHTFUL CONSEQUENCES OF THE
CONTINUED NEGLECT OF AN ABIDING REORIEN-
TATION OF THE THINKING OF THE GERMAN PEO-
PLE. WITHOUT THE RE-EDUCATION OF THE AVER-
AGE GERMAN, THE POLICIES INITIATED BY ADE-
NAUER ARE LIKE FOUNDATIONS SET IN SHIFTING
SAND DUNES.

The best prophylactic against relapses and disillusionment of naive wishful thinking is the continuous and wid-
est dissemination of undistorted truth and the unflagging
advocacy of a program of humanist education. Only then

may one concur with Dr. Theodore Heuss' conclusion of the address that he delivered on June 5, 1958 before the joint session of the Congress of the United States that, "All that is required is to set in motion some of the all-pervasive forces inherent in human nature: reason, a sense of proportion and perhaps a little love."

The supreme import that is attached to the unhampered pursuit and acquisition of knowledge is presupposed in the dictum: "ETERNAL vigilance is the price of liberty."

A Postscript—THE POLITICAL RUMINATIONS
OF AN AMATEUR

And a young man came running and informed Moses that Eldad and Medad were prophesying in the camp (without authorization). "Imprison them," was Joshua's advice. And Moses said unto him, "would that all the Lord's people were prophets." Lev. XI:27-30.

WITH the passage of time and the waxing of her productive industrial capacity, bolstered by a growing sense of political independence and power, West Germany and the western world are bound to find themselves on the horns of a tantalizing dilemma.

West Germany will be as nonplussed as the weary wanderer at the crossing of the roads with no abode in sight wherever he turns. Which way is he to choose? In what direction is he to go? What is to be his destination? With such questions West Germany will have to grapple. And the answers that will be forthcoming will always be tainted with doubt and uncertainty and no little fear.

What are some of the alternatives that face West Germany?

(1) It is not impossible that a radically-minded group may appear in Germany, and grow strong enough to lead that government within the orbit of the Soviets. Such an occurrence, though improbable, cannot be ruled out. Germany's short-lived compact with Russia on the eve of World War II and the ease with which Czechoslovakia was maneuvered to join the Soviet satellites do not indicate the event to be beyond the bounds of possibility. Who would have predicted when the elder Masaryk and his co-worker Benes had been at the helm of that democratic state that a misalliance of that country with Russia would ever take

place? Such a step could be brought about by the appeal and lure of the bright-colored paper in which the meretricious tenets of Communism come wrapped. The inveigling of free men to become helots of a totalitarian regime is couched in idealistically-sounding phraseology "to everyone according to his needs and from everyone according to his abilities." The Germans could also succumb to the spell of Russia's stated or hinted promise to allow the sundered sections of West and East Germany to be joined together if and when the Bonn Government will ally itself with the allegedly peace-loving Soviet States. Russia in the role of buyer of German-made goods may also prove an inducement to closer collaboration.

Should Germany take this fateful step, she would commit the most colossal political blunder in her already notoriously blundering career. That step would prove more fateful to Germany than was Mussolini's alignment of Italy with Hitler's ventures. For the Kremlin would not hesitate to exploit, if not actually to appropriate, the industrial skill and military aptitude of this people to communize Europe and the world. Whether the procedure would be climaxed by blitzkrieg assaults against weak countries, or whether the Kremlin would remain content with gradual infiltration and subversion by means of a fifth column strategy, is a secondary consideration. The ultimate intent and goal are matters of transcending importance and concern.

What must be done to forestall such an event?

The average and ordinary German should be made aware of the inescapable consequences of such a procedure. The laboring class can be made to see:

(a) that the right of the individual to choose the type of work for which he feels he is best fitted or the factory he desires to work in and the city or region in which he prefers to reside are all jeopardized in a totalitarian society. Every distributor and producer of commodities, aye everyone engaged in private enterprise, could be made keenly cognizant of the ineluctable fact that in the Soviet scheme there is no such thing as the voluntary contribution of services for which one receives recompense without the intermediation of a governmental agency. Every individual is forced to become an employee of the State which is dominated by a group of erring mortals, even when they should be idealistically motivated. The individual was bound to find himself enmeshed in the tentacles of a mammoth bureaucracy. His economic security would now totally depend on the whim, mood, or disposition of a commissar. To stay away from work, to protest against a promulgated ukase, to strike, could subject one to imprisonment if not a firing squad.

(b) Such a compact, it must be shown would be the death-knell of freedom and liberty as they are known in western lands. For wherever the shadow of the Kremlin would fall there the individual would be deprived of his God-given right to think for himself and to have access to information which is not distorted or doctored by considerations of party interests and decisions of the ruling junta.

(c) The religiously-minded German must be apprised that the apotheosis of a set of economic dogmas propounded by the supposedly infallible Marx and Lenin and pontifically interpreted and concretely applied to specific situations by the then secretary of the small Communist Party wielding unchallenged power are an admixture of evils which would make the worst abuses of all the religious fanatics of former times appear trivial. The discipline and obedience demanded by the Kremlin are also a repudiation of inherent and inalienable rights of man to which he is entitled by his kinship with God.

The Russian Communists have fashioned a pagan deity, a New Moloch to whom they offer, I suspect, faked panegyrics. The uncritically-minded may deem their prostrations and praises as sincere expressions. The countless multitude apes its obeisance because of fear and intimidation.

In the Gospel of Marx and Lenin religion ironically is termed "an opiate of the people." They correctly discern religious teaching to be the deadly foe of its materialistic credo. And though they may tolerate the presence of a restricted number of synagogues and churches their system of education dooms the growing generation to become fanatic disbelievers in the existence of God and fierce opponents of or scoffers at all forms of religious expression.

(d) The moral nihilism that is an inextricable component of the communist ideology must be clearly exposed to high-principled and ethically-sensitive Germans. In the metaphysics of Soviet theoreticians Truth, Justice and Virtue have no objective reality independent of the mind that thinks them. Their validity is therefore conditioned. They are conceived, say the communist theoreticians, by individuals and society. The extent of their currency is to be determined by their expediency and utility. When their function comes to an end they may be discarded without the slightest compunctions.[1]

The fact is to be noted and stressed that the Kremlin's reappraisal of Stalin is not the result of a new insight and inner illumination, a recognition that what they had been doing or allowed to be done by the generalissimo, whose wisdom and goodness they superlatively extolled, was evil but solely because the ruling clique concluded that conditions called for an altered strategy. There is lacking a note of penitence in their recantations. They are not confessions of contrite souls. They are but declarations and announcements of a new policy.

(e) Lastly, the German populace must be made to realize that the Soviet leaders, knowing that they would have access to the output of Germany's farms and huge industrial plants, may not recoil from making an aggressive move against the West, which would transfer the cold into a shooting war, with no holds barred. The indignation against America for its entry into World War I and II, which deprived Germany of what would have been victories, is not entirely expunged from the consciousness of Germans. It may have been mollified by the post-war generosity of the United States, but its subconscious rankling could be brought to the surface by skilled Russian propagandists. Such a contingency must not be lightly dismissed.

This fact must be burned into the consciousness of the

entire populace of Germany, particularly the young, who have not known the retribution that was visited upon the Germans when Hitler believed he could vanquish his opponents with lightning speed and thus attain victory before they could flex their muscles and corral their strength.

Germany in such a war would be made a target of attack. Bombers, jet planes, and guided missiles would make of the country a smoldering heap beside which the desolation of World War II would appear like a scratch on a coat of paint. Germany would be annihilated if Russia (with whose fate she would cast her lot) were vanquished. Germany's survival as a nation, with a pyrrhic victory of Russia, would also be problematic. The condition of her people who managed to escape death would be most pitiable in either circumstance. Unimaginable privation, horrible deformity and unbelieved slavery would be the reward of her alliance with Russia.

Who should sponsor the work of such education and what line should it take?

The task of making clear and vivid to the German workers, tradesmen and all religiously and ethically-minded individuals the grave and terrible consequences of an alliance with Russia should not to be undertaken or sponsored by the State Department or any United States agency. It will be more effective if it is done by private organizations. The task offers a challenge and an opportunity to labor unions of America and to the various educational foundations. The service which labor would render to their fellow workers in lands other than the United States would be incalculable. The bond that they would establish with their confréres in foreign countries would tend to foster peace in the world and thus assure the values of modern culture and its institutions from utter destruction.

(2) Another alternative which Germans may believe is before them is the possibility of remaining neutral. Such neutralism was being advocated by the Social Democrats, the party in opposition to the policies of Adenauer and his

Christian Democratic Union. They were and many still are averse to West Germany's re-armament within the North Atlantic Treaty Organization and reliance on the Big Three (the United States, Great Britain and France) to effectuate reunification of former Germany. The negotiations of the Three Powers with the Soviet Union, they believe will prove futile. The party's socialistic leanings incline them to look upon the closer approach to Russia as an expedient and wise course.

Notwithstanding Adenauer's reelection the stalwart Chancellor's failure to make headway towards the reunification of East and West Germany is bound to make the steering of the Ship of State more difficult for its pilot.

In addition the fact must be kept in mind that the respected and venerable Chancellor is eighty-five years old. After he relinquishes the reins of government, persons espousing differing policies will be prone to agitate vigorously for their adoption. As time passes the benefits and contributions which the United States had made available to a restored and prospering Germany will be eliminated. There will ensue a lightened dependence upon America and a lessened reliance on its support. Competition and rivalry for foreign markets between German and American concerns are bound to appear. All that may revive the agitation for the neutrality of Germany, if not for a closer cooperation with Russia than with the West. When Russia will perceive that her display of military might and advancement in science are incapable of intimidating the Western Powers she will luringly dangle before them trade pacts.[2]

With regard to reunification would it not be wise for the advocates of such a course who are fervently devoted to the democratic procedure to consider the following possibilities?

Assuming that Russia would genuinely be willing to allow East and West Germany to become reunited without conditioning its National Sovereignty (except perhaps by the stipulation that it cease to be associated with NATO) then there are still grave questions which the Bonn government must answer before she takes the fateful step. Will not West Germany be imperilled by the alliance with East Germany

before the latter has come out of the stupefaction or the
state of hypnosis in which she was put? Does East Germany
now realize that the communist concoction, despite its
sparkling and bubbling, is not champagne but a bitter,
nauseous drink which may have enabled Russia to vomit
forth Czarism but does not quench thirst or stimulate the
appetite for genuine democratic political expression? Is unification *NOW* worth the price which Russia will demand or
expect? Will it warrant the hazard to the freedom of her
people which the step will entail? Will not East Germany
continue to be a puppet of the Kremlin even as part of the
United Germany (or an agent provocateur)? Before she
becomes disillusioned and disgusted with the nostrum of
Marx and Lenin will not East Germany at best be a chunk of
yeast in the German dough?

*Can Germany be neutral in a war between Russia and the
West?*

Germany's ability to remain neutral would seem to be
possible if the U. S. alone were the opponent of Russia.
There would be no overwhelming inducement to Russia to
invade Germany. She could siphon German industrial production better if she respected her territorial boundaries
than if she violated them.

Such reasoning, however, is fondling an illusion. Even
if the U. S. alone were Russia's antagonist the latter would
have her agents infiltrate Germany for whose products the
U. S. would vie. Russia would not be content to stand by and
see a flow of goods from Germany to her adversary. The
least she would resort to would be sabotage.

In a war between the U. S. and Russia there would also be
some elements in Germany which would be pro-American,
not necessarily because of national sympathy but because
of their preference of the ideology identified with America.
Would Russia then refrain from an endeavor to squelch such
sentiment in a State so near its border?

In a conflict between Russia and the United States which
would be sparked by ideological differences it is most unlikely that the U. S. would not be joined by those democratic
States to whose aid she came when they were in such a

predicament. England and perhaps France also would be found at the side of the U. S. In such an eventuality Germany would have as much chance of maintaining her neutrality as Belgium had in World War I and II or Holland did when Hitler was bent on obtaining a speedy victory. Germany is not only the heartland of Europe but she is also the corridor through which the Soviet armies would have to pass to reach the channel ports, from where Russia may want to supplement her missile-thrusts launchings of aerial attacks against England and submarine expeditions against American shipping. At any rate the Russian armies would have to guard the coastland to prevent beachhead landings of the enemy.

Let us assume that in an Armageddon between the Soviet States and the Democratic Countries Germany's neutrality would be respected, would Germany cease to be a problem? Would she not at the termination of the conflict present an even greater danger to both the victors and the vanquished?

I contend that in such a conflict an unreformed Germany would be as much a peril to the world as Kaiserism and Nazism had been. In a gargantuan struggle between East and West with Germany assuming and maintaining the aloofness of a neutral she would be bound to become prosperous and powerful while the contenders would emerge from the death fray pitiably weak and economically ruined. Germany without having participated in the war would be in a most commanding position. She would be the dominant nation in Europe, if not the world. Would she then serve the stricken nations or would she have them serve her as had been her desire and ambition in former days?

(3) The last alternative to be considered is West Germany's affiliation with North Atlantic Treaty Organization (NATO). Will West Germany's entry into NATO increase or diminish the chances of an outbreak of war between the East and West? The writer is convinced that NATO is but a defensive measure.

Totalitarian regimes respect power more than moral principles or spiritual ideals. Would not the U.S.S.R. be deterred from undertaking any aggressive military venture upon realizing that the nations whose economic system the Kremlin considers anathema are strong enough and determined to block and strenuously oppose any such maneuver?

If Germany would be utterly devoid of military strength, if she would propose to be neutral, a condition which, as was shown, would be unlikely of attainment in a conflict between the East and the West, would Germany then play a part in preserving peace? Would she not in that case invite invasion or infiltration? Would not her entry into NATO be equivalent to a declaration (which Russia will not fail to note) to the effect that if she initiates an attack West Germany pledges her newly acquired military strength and her growing industrial power to the side of the attacked?

Will it not also be a warning to the Kremlin that all the nations of NATO will come to the aid of Germany should Russia venture to go beyond the boundaries of the territories which she now provisionally occupies?

To fully convince the people behind the Iron Curtain that NATO was not brought into being with an aggressive intent, it may be advisable, though needless, for each of the constituents of NATO to pledge and declare that in the event of an unprovoked offensive attack upon Russia by the United States (or any other member or group of members) the other constituent members of NATO would be absolved from coming to the aid of the aggressive nation or nations.[3]

"What effect will West Germany's entry into NATO have?"

Germany's limited contingent will be integrated with the joint forces of the NATO members. Germany's military strength will then be under surveillance and kept in check.

"Is a clash between the two rival economic ideologies unavoidable?"

The proponents of each system contend that their political and economic creed and programs are intended only for the States which willingly desire to adopt or experiment with them. They aver that they do not wish to impose their doctrines and procedure upon another State either by force or cunning. If these protestations are sincere and genuine and if their professors would solemnly pledge that *any voluntary surrender of freedom* of *expression* and *restriction of economic procedure on the part of a State would be revocable whenever the citizenry of that State would have a change of heart, then coexistence need not present insurmountable obstacles.* The tension and the vast expenditures of wealth, which could be relegated to medical research, the building of schools and hospitals, would then be acts of insanity and border on being criminal.

Israel offers factual evidence of the possibility of peaceful coexistence of diverse economic systems. For in that tiny land you have *Collective Settlements* (*Kebutzim*) where private possessions are predominantly eliminated and the motto "To everyone according to his needs, from everyone according to his ability" is followed. All property is owned collectively, all tasks are assigned or voluntarily assumed. In these communes, each individual and family are given suitable living quarters which belong to the collective. All eat in a common dining hall, where the food is prepared by members qualified for such work. The children are taken care of in the collective's nursery and playground by trained personnel while the parents are at work. Parents and children are united at the end of the day's work. Family life is lived as in our society where private property is the keystone of the system.

In Israel you have also *Cooperatives*. Here the homestead and the little farm are the possessions of individuals. The expensive machinery to till the land and the trucks to carry the produce to the market or the shipper, are collectively owned by the unit. The members also buy their needs and sell what they cultivate 'en masse.' Each pays for what he gets and receives payment for what he has given.

Finally you have the merchant, the owner of a factory, the builder of stores and dwellings. They conduct their businesses as *Private Enterprise,* subject, of course, to government regulation when the weal of the populace is involved.

There are no fratricidal conflicts between the proponents

of each of these economic procedures. *The policy is to accord to each the right and freedom to live in a miniature society which is to his liking and which, he believes, will accord also the maximum material return to the greatest number. Here you see the dictum, "One for all and all for one" actually put into practice.*

Now, if a tiny commonwealth like Israel can tolerate and encourage the coexistence of such diverse economic systems, why can't the procedure be practiced everywhere, especially in lands where national resources and opportunities for individual development are limitless? The devotees of Israel, who perceive it to be a laboratory for social justice and a pilot-experiment for peaceful coexistence of radically differing economic procedures, are not unwarranted in their conviction that the future is destined to give new content to the prophetic utterance "Out of Zion shall go forth Torah, and the word of God from Jerusalem." (Micah 4:2, Isa. 2:3)

In 1924 after my first trip to Europe I wrote a series of articles for a local newspaper which were later, together with other reflections, embodied in a book. Its title was *"A Harvest of Weeds,* or the European Observations of a Peace Advocate." In the chapter "Germany Between Two Fires" I displayed the[4] audacity of youth and took issue with a then renowned publicist and authority on current European events and movements. I quote from that chapter.

"Karl Von Wiegand, a noted foreign correspondent, stated in a recent article in the *New York American* (Sept. 16) that the French policy is speeding Germany to a red regime. That this may prove ultimately the precipice for the German people I do not wish oracularly to deny. It seems to me, however, that if Germany is pushed to that extreme the fault of it should be laid at the door not only of France, but of the German capitalists as well.

"Personally I feel that the Germans are more likely to turn to the extreme right of monarchism as a result of French imperialism rather than to the left. If the Brest-Litovsk Treaty, and the military defeats, and their post-war economic suffering and starvation were unable to convert them to communism then I feel that they will continue to be immune to it. Secondly, the German does not possess the temperament necessary for the communistic gospel. Communism needs a free and emotional nature, one that defies restrictions and dominations. It must be the psychology of rebellion. Now the German has been for decades taught to obey. The military tradition and training has inculcated discipline into his mind and soul. A man with a sense of order and discipline is unlikely to be swept away by a passion of rebellion as were, for example, the Russians. Thirdly, the German is a patriot. He still loves his Fatherland. He is anxious to have its soil cleared of the foreign invader. Should Germany turn communistic, France would then capitalize the change as an excuse for her large army and its presence on German soil. She would justify her presence in Germany and even claim for herself the gratitude of the world. She would then crown herself as the defender of western civilization and its institutions. Such a possibility is an additional factor in keeping the German people away from communism. The German, it should be remembered, is a political student and thinker."

In quoting the above statements I do not pretend to lay claim to the possession of any power or gift of political clairvoyance. I cite the opinion because I felt strongly then that Germany and the allies were at the fork of the road . . . I feel it to be the case even more now. The nations of the West and also Russia are in the throes of making a most momentous decision. The fate of the world and the survival of man on the planet hang upon the right choice and resolve.

The people of the Western World are tormented with indecision as they become aware of the ominous consequences of Western Germany's being drawn into the Soviet orbit and yet they dare not blink their eyes to the fact that weeds of Nazism have not been uprooted.

Germany, too, faces a dilemma and a challenge. Will she continue the role she selected for herself in days gone by? If so, another misstep by her may spell her extinction and the devastation of the continent of which she is a part. If she decides to cast away the idols she formerly worshipped, if she resolves and strives to reorient herself and set her sites on moral and spiritual goals, she will not only then make amends for her past national sins, but she may be an impetus toward mankind saving itself. For she may be the *fulcrum* and *balance* between the nations of the East and West.

The warning and the admonition of Moses to the Israelites, as they were on the verge of entering the Promised Land, can be made to apply to the nations of today.

"I call heaven and earth to record this day against you that I have set before you life, and death, blessing and cursing: therefore choose life, that both thou and thy seed may live." [5]

Notes

NOTES TO PART I

Chapter 2—SEEDS AND ROOTS

[1] Isa. XLII:19.
[2] Matt. IV:1, Mark I:13, Luke IV:1-2.
[3] Isa. I:18.
[4] Gen. I:27.
[5] Ps. CXXX:I.
[6] Measure for Measure, Act II, Sc. I.
[7] Amos IX:7.
[8] Isa. XXIX:25, Jer. XLVIII:31, 36, 47, XLIX:1-6, 11, 39, Jonah I:2, II:2, 10, III:10-11.
[9] Isa. LIII:3-8, 10.
[20] Deut. VII:7-8.
[11] Deut. XXVI:17-18, XXVIII:9.
[13] B. Talmud Meg. 31 a.

Chapter 3—MALT IN THE DEVIL'S BREW

[1] Nietzsche, Genealogy of Morals (ed. Alex Tille) Foreword p. 9.
[2] F. C. S. Schiller, Humanism, Philosophical Essays—Preface p. XXVII, see also F. C. S. Schiller, The Riddle of the Sphinx, Chapter VI.
[3] F. C. S. Schiller, Humanism, p. 273.
[4] William James On some Hegelianism in "The Will to Believe," p. 293.
[5] Morris R. Cohen, article on Hegel, Encyclopedia of the Social Sciences, Vol. VII, p. 313.
[6] Marvin Lowenthal, The Jews of Germany, p. 229.
[7] Jer. XXX:11.

NOTES TO PART II

Chapter 1—DECEIT AND TREACHERY SKULK WITH HATRED

[1] See Verhandlung des Reichstags VIII, Wahlperiod, p. 32, also William L. Shirer, The Rise and Fall of the Third Reich.
[2] James K. Pollack, The Government of Greater Germany, p. 41-2.

Chapter 3—CURS OF LOW DEGREE

[1] See also Leo Stein, I Was in Hell with Niemöller, Chapt. IX p. 117.
[2] "A Journalist Wife" by Lilian A. Mowrer, pp. 290-1.
[3] Louis P. Lochner, The Goebbels Diaries, p. 18.
[4] Ibid., pp. 16-17.
[5] Schwarze Korpse, November 1938.

Chapter 5—MILITARY DEFEAT AND MORAL TURPITUDE

[1] Judy Barton, 'Candy Bar Romance' in "This Is Germany," edited by Arthur Settel, pp. 161-176.
[2] Gen. R. Chapt. XXVI—par. 8.

Chapter 6—THE PLAGUE WAS NOT STAYED

[1] IX par. 15.
[2] Ralph Harwood—'Case History of a German Town'—in "This Is Germany," edited by Arthur Settel, pp. 177-194.

NOTES TO PART III

Chapter 1—DUBIOUS CRITERIA OF GOODNESS

[1] Young Academy Student.
[2] Ps. XXXIV:19.
[3] Ps. LI:19.
[4] Micah IV:5.
[5] Tosefta San. Chapt. III, also repeated in other works.

Chapter 2—PERCEIVING EVIL, THE GREAT AND NOBLE MUST SPEAK UP

[1] Rabbi Israel Lipkin (1810-1883) is better known as Rabbi Israel Salanter, after the City in Russia, Salanty, where he resided until he was called to Vilna to be the head of an Academy. In the curriculum of this Academy the moral teachings of Judaism were given an important place. Rabbi Lipkin died in Konigsberg. In the volume, "Students, Scholars, and Saints," by Louis Ginsberg, one will find a superb account of the life and teachings of this revered and morally-sensitive Rabbi.
[2] J. Taanith IV: par. 60.
[3] J. Pea VIII: par. 212.
[4] Deut. XVII:14 ff.
[5] Matt. XXVI:52.
[6] Matt. X:34.
[7] Luke XXII:36.

[8] H. G. Wells, "The Outline of History," One Volume Edition, p. 1005.

[9] Whether Nietzche's justification and glorification of war are his views or imputation of his Nazi-minded sister has no relevancy to the point which the student of Frescati wished to make.

[10] Politics. Vol. I, p. 74, 76, 482.

[11] Voice of Jerusalem, pp. 6-137.

[12] Matt. XVI:18.

[13] Ex. XV:3.

[14] Ps. CVLIV:1.

[15] Gen. XLIX:5 ff—Deut. XX:10, 19 ff.

[16] Ps. XLVI:10, LXXVI:3, 124.

[17] Isa. II:4 ff, Micah IV:1 ff, Ezek. XXXIX:9, Zech. IX:10.

[18] B. Talmud San. 39 b.

[19] Mishna VI: par. 4.

[20] Ex. XX:25, see Lauterbach, Mechilta, Vol. II, p. 290, J.P.S. Edition.

Chapter 3—THE BANEFUL USE OF CREEDS

[1] Matt. VII:1 ff, John VIII:15.

[2] John XII:47.

[3] John VIII:7.

[4] John XIV:2.

[5] Before Hitler came on the scene the Yeshiva Bochur of Frescati, I learned, had studied Theology and Church History with an eye for the Christian ministry. A detailed account of this young man's life story, the disposition of his Jewish father and Christian mother, the impact of the Nazi's on his sensitive nature and his experience and observations in the concentration camp and the conclusions to which he came, merit a separate and different exposition. The detailed biographic data of the Yeshiva Bochur was meagre and known but to the Rabbi. Since he was reluctant to disclose the information even to the students, not to mention a visitor. the author of the book had to piece the tidbits of information into a coherent narrative.

[6] The former version was articulated by Rabbi Simlai (a Talmudic Sage of the Third Century). Moses, said he, was given 613 positive and negative commandments. David reduced them to eleven, Isaiah to six, Micah to three, and Habakuk summed up all religious belief and behavior in the single phrase, "The righteous shall live by his faith." Makkoth 23 B and 24 B, also San. 81. "On the other hand Maimonides thirteen articles of belief were increased by a like number by David ben Yom Tob ibn Bilia while Judah Penini augmented them to thirty-five cardinal principles. And so the trend went until its climactic conclusion which is identified with the position taken by Isaac Abarbanel and the Cabbalists. They insisted that in each of the 613 commandments there is to be found a fundamental principle of faith. B. Makkoth 23b, see I. Abarbanel's "Rosh Amanah."

[7] Gen. XIII:8-9.

[8] Gen. 27:40.
[9] Isa. II:4, Micah, IV:3.
[10] Ex. XX:3-4.
[11] Ex. III:14, XXXIII:20.
[12] Ex. XXXIII:23, for the Prophets elaboration of this view, see Isa. XL:25, and LV:8-9.

Chapter 4—SELF SCRUTINY AND MORAL IMPROVEMENT

[1] Lev. XIX:17.
[2] B. Talmud Sota 3 a.
[3] Had the colloquy taken place currently he very likely would have included Cuba to the list.
[4] B. Talmud Gittin 58a, Yoma 9a and in Aboth R. Nathan, Chapt. VII and in many Midrashim e.g., Lev R. Chapt. XXII, Koheleth R. Chapt. V.
[5] B. Talmud Ber. 5a.

NOTE TO PART IV

Chapter 1—THE SUMMONS

[1] Ex. XXIII:3, 6, Lev. XIX:35, Deut. XVI:18 ff. The Judaic concept of Justice and the strict adherence to it is not devoid of sympathetic consideration and magnanimity. From the dictum of the Book of Proverbs, "If thine enemy is hungry feed him" (XXV:22) to the declaration of Spinoza, "Minds are conquered not by armies but by love and magnanimity" one sees Justice ever tempered with mercy.

Chapter 2—A NATION'S CHARACTER IS NOT PREDETERMINED

[1] That the practice persisted up to the Middle Ages, if not longer, can be inferred from the part which the feud between the houses of Montague and Capulet plays in the plot of Romeo and Juliet.
[2] Voice of Jerusalem, pp. 6-137.
[3] Vindication of Society, Vol. I, p. 15.
[4] Jonathan Swift, Poetry, A Rhapsody.
[5] Albert Einstein—Sigmund Freud, "Why War?" Brochure by International Institute of Intellectual Cooperation, 1933.

Chapter 3—FAITH AND OBEDIENCE MAY ALSO TURN SOUR

[1] "Faith," in The Catholic Encyclopedia, Vol. V, pp. 752 ff.
[2] James Hasting, Dictionary of the Bible, Vol. I, p. 827.

[3] This is also true of patently later glosses which have found their way into the texts of the early works (Matthew, Mark and Luke). These interpolations, which are either colored narrations of actual or reputed occurrences or doctored restatements of a saying of Jesus, were most likely intended to bestow authority and weight on an added or an amplified doctrine or practice of the new sect and Church.

[4] "Faith," in The Catholic Encyclopedia, Vol. V, pp. 752-6.

[5] Heb. XI:1 ff.

[6] I Cor. II:5.

[7] II Cor. V:7.

[8] Rom. X:8-9, Peter I:21.

[9] Rom. III:25.

[10] Act. X:43.

[11] Eph. IV:5, see also Heb. XI:6, XII:2, I Tim. III:9, John III:16, 35, Mark XVI:16.

[12] Matt. 6:28 ff, Luke 12:27 ff; see also Mark V:34, Luke VIII:48, XVII:19.

[13] John XIV:6.

[14] Heb. XI:1.

[15] B Talmud Ber. 33b and Meg. 25a.

[16] Matt. VII:29 appears to me to be a later gloss purporting to explain the multitude's astonishment at Jesus' teachings, Matt. VII:28.

[17] I Cor. XIV:34, I Tim II:12, Titus II:5.

[18] Eph. VI:5, Titus II:9, Col. III:22.

[19] Heb. XIII:17.

[20] Matt. V:39.

[21] I Tim. II:2.

[22] Heb. XIII:17.

[23] "Obedience," The Catholic Encyclopedia, Vol. XI, p. 182.

[24] Ibid p. 183; Here it can be said we have an illustration of Reason being impressed into service to undermine its own validity.

[25] Prov. VII:22.

[26] Ps. XXXI:6.

[27] Ps. XXXI:6, XXIX:15.

[28] Ps. LI:16, CXVII:2, CXLVI:6.

[29] Mal. II:6.

[30] IK XXII:16, IICH. XVIII:15.

[31] B. Talmud San. 64a.

[32] J. Hag. LXXXI par. 11; B.B.M. 59b; Hul. 44a and also in other places.

[33] When some Rabbis state that Scriptural rites are to be observed even though the reasons for their performance are not evident, it does not contradict the above version. The proper aim and function of such rites may be concealed or recondite. The fulfillment however, does not defy the canons of logic. Nor does it prove a disbelief in the regularized procedure of nature. Gamaliel, the head of the Sanhedrin, was deposed from his high office because of his continuous demand for obedience and submission from Rabbi Joshua ben Chananya, even though the time required unity instead of disunion.

Chapter 4—THE SANCTUARY BECOMES THE CITADEL

[1] Gen. XVIII:25. In Ex. XXXII:33 we have already had an enunciation of the principle of "individual responsibility."

[2] Modification of Ezekiel's prouncement may be detected but not its repudiation. For example, the merits of the fathers, it was believed, could ward off a calamity from or bestow benefits upon progeny; the sins of the fathers are conceived in some Scriptural writing to be visited upon the fourth generation, the goodness, however, it was believed, extended to the thousandth generation.

[3] Even before Hitler tricked and bludgeoned many of the representatives of the non-Nazi Parties in the Reichstag to give him absolute and irrevocable power, the well-trained Nazi henchmen terrorized the population. Once in power the Nazi lost no time in crushing all opposition. They made janitors, house maids, and teachers in elementary schools auxiliaries of the Gestapo. Parents were afraid to utter a word of criticism of the régime lest their very children might wittingly or unwittingly repeat to their teachers or playmates what they had heard in the privacy of their homes, and thus expose them to great danger.

"If a mother told her child she didn't want her to join a youth group" reported Judy Barden, "that child might innocently repeat this at school. Such a confession could result in the arrest of both parents. They would be sent to a concentration camp for three months to learn obedience." Arthur Settel, This Is Germany, p. 166.

Chapter 5—TO THE CHURCH NO MILITARY EXPLOIT MERITS A BLESSING

[1] Life of Reason p. 69.

Chapter 6—THE DELUSIONS OF UNATTAINABLE STRIVINGS

[1] Peter A. Sorokin, The Crisis of Our Age—The Social and Cultural Outlook, p. 213.
[2] Ibid p. 216.
[3] Ecc. VII:16-18.
[4] B. Talmud Horayoth 3b.

Chapter 7—HEROES WITHOUT MEDALS

[1] B. Talmud San. 103b.
[2] B. Talmud Yoma 38b.
[3] B. Talmud Yoma 38b.
[4] Prov. X:25.
[5] Moed Katan 16b "I rule man; who rules Me? [It is] the righteous: for I "the sage makes God to say," make a decree and he [the righteous may] annul it."

Chapter 8—JUDGMENT MUST BE WEIGHED

[1] Even such an acknowledged liberal as the present President of the West German Republic was duped to cast his vote for the Enabling Act.
[2] Amos VII:7-17.
[3] Lev. XIX:17.
[4] B. Talmud Shab. 39a.
[5] B. Talmud Betza. 30a.
[6] Lev. XVIII:5.
[7] B. Talmud Yoma 85b.
[8] Ezek. III:16 ff, also Ezek. XXXIII:1 ff.
[9] II Chr. XIX:8-10.

Chapter 9—THE SHARE OF EACH IN THE GREATNESS OR BASENESS OF ONE'S PEOPLE OR AGE

[1] Mishna Sota I par. 7.
[2] Jonah III:9-10.
[3] Deut. XXI:21:1-9.
[4] Sifri, comment on Deut. 21:7—quoted by Rashi (Rabbi Solomon ben Yitzchak).

Chapter 10—THE LIGHT THAT FAILED

[1] Prov. XXII:7.
[2] To these subconscious dispositions must be added the reactions that are fostered by the newspapers, the sensational headlines which feature kidnappings, hold-ups, divorces, and political scandals, items which are not absent in European life, but are not paraded before the eyes of Europe's or the world's inhabitants.
[3] The practical confiscation of the wealth of Jews provided the Third Reich with much of the means to support the program of rearmament. When this source was drained the momentum necessitated aggression and invasion of neighboring states. With complete control of all avenues of communication and with glittering and appealing slogans such as the German's need for "lebensraum" and security, the German people allowed themselves to become mesmerized. All their thoughts and feelings conformed to the foreordained course of Goebbels, the press agent of Reich's Messiah, Hitler who was to many also the very incarnation of God.
[4] Information Bulletin Magazine of U. S. Military Government in Germany No. 155, February 22, 1949, p. 5.
[5] Ibid., p. 6.
[6] Robert Haeger, 'No More Conquerors' in "This Is Germany," edited by Arthur Settel, p. 20-1.
[7] Robert Lewison, 'Education for What?' in "This Is Germany," edited by Arthur Settel, pp. 89-115.

It is pertinent to note that a fourteen parts TV documentary entitled "The Third Reich" was recently telecast in Germany. For the first time millions of Germans saw the true story of Adolf Hitler's Third Reich.

Chapter 11—EVIDENCE OF INCORRIGIBILITY

[1] Writers and Politics in Post-War Germany, Sat. Rev. of Lit., Aug. 15, 1953.
[2] Juenger's hero, the forest rambler represents "The old freedom, disguised by time; the essential, elementary freedom which awakens in healthy populations when tyrannies of parties or foreign conquerors oppress a country — the forest rambler experiences a new solitude as it is produced above all by a satanic, innate weakness— the walk in the woods bears a closer relationship to freedom than any armament, gives life to the original will to resist, only volunteers will be qualified to perform; they will defend themselves under any circumstances no matter whether they are prepared, armed or called by the state. Thus they give a demonstration of their freedom, in an existential sense. People never lose the hope for a new Doetrich or a new Augustus, for a potentate whose mission is announced by a new constellation in the skies. They know that a myth lies as a golden hoard right under the surface of history."

Chapter 12—EVIDENCE OF CONTRITION

[1] Versammeltenn Synode der Evangelischen Kirche in Deutschland. "The guilt of the German people exists." Martin Niemöller asserted. "There is no doubt about it, even if there would be no other guilt than that of six million clay urns, in which the ashes of burnt Jews from all over Europe have been put to rest." Guilt and Hope, pp. 13-15.
[2] The exact wording is "To err is human but contrition felt for the crime distinguishes the virtuous from the wicked."
[3] An English translation by E. B. Ashton was published by the Dial Press, N. Y.
[4] Ibid., pp. 21, 28.
Dr. Jaspers distinguishes four kinds or degrees of guilt. One is *Criminal Guilt* attributed to the individual who knowingly and overtly committed outrageous acts. The second is termed *Political Guilt* resulting acquiescence in the Nazi regime. Under three is assumed *Moral Guilt*, the self-judgment which the individual forms of himself, based on the role he assumed for himself in the crisis. Lastly comes the *Metaphysical Guilt*, the sense of default which belongs to one who chose to remain alive rather than die in protest against ruthless and powerful perpetrators of evil.
[5] There is a laggardness in the implementation of some aspects of the Indemnification and Restitution Legislation that, however, regretable as it is, does not detract from the intent and wish which have been incorporated in an approved enactment.

Chapter 13—A RENDEZVOUS OF GERMAN YOUTH—A KOSHER RESTAURANT

¹ Ps. XXIV:6.
² B. Talmud—Eruk. 17a.
³ Romans V:19.

Chapter 14—THE TESTS OF GENUINE REPENTANCE

¹ Deut. XXIX:28.

NOTES TO PART V

Chapter 1—MAN, NATURE'S SUPREME BLUNDER OR MASTERPIECE

¹ Gen. XVI:12.
² Gen. II:7 also Gen. I:27.
³ Gen. III:1 ff.
⁴ Phil. IV:7. Gen. III:24. The concluding clause "to keep the way of the tree of life" has latent significance and meaning, calling for homiletical exposition.
⁵ Gen. VIII:21.
⁶ Ethics of the Fathers, Chapt. IV, par. 2.
⁷ Ethics of the Fathers, Chapt. III, par. 9. B. Talmud Yoma 38b San. 104a.
⁸ Hos. II: 21-2.

Chapter 2—MYTHS AND LEGENDS, INDICES OF NATIONAL ASPIRATIONS

¹ In an essay on "Psychoanalysis and the Psychology of Religion," Ernest Jones asserts from the study of comparative mythology "we learn that pure intellectual curiosity concerning the abstract nature of the universe must have played a much less prominent part in the genesis of those conceptions than was at one time thought. It is now known that they have far more to do with the emotional and conative (wish) aspects of man's nature, that they mirror his mundane desires, hopes and fears."⁽¹⁾
² p. 59.
³ Gen. XII:3.
⁴ Gen. R par 6.

Chapter 3—THE SHACKLES OF BYGONE CREEDS AND CUSTOMS

¹ Henry E. Krehbiel, A Book of Operas, p. 207.
² Ibid., pp. 209-10.

³ Song of Songs, I:4, 13, 15, 16; IV:1-5: VII:1-10.
⁴ B. Talmud Ber. 34b San. 99a.

Chapter 4—THE KEY TO MORAL RENEWAL

¹ Catilina VIII.
² Supporting comment by Eugene Hevesi who read the manuscript.
³ Harry E. Fein, Titans od Hebrew Verse pp. 57-9.
⁴ Micah VI:8.
⁵ Amos V:21-4, Isa. I:11-17, Jer. VI:20, VII:21-3, Ezek. XX:30 ff.
⁶ This belief was persistently stated in Talmud, the Prophets, e.g. Ezek. XX:11, Deut. XXVIII:1-68, Lev. XXVI:3-43, XXXIII ff.
⁷ B. Talmud Gittin 55b-56a.
⁸ Ethics of the Fathers, Chapt. V par. 10-11.
⁹ B. Talmud Ber. 5a.
¹⁰ Isa. LIII:3-5.

Chapter 5—VICTIMS OF MISINFORMATION

¹ Anti-Semitic Stereotypes of God Humanist, August 1950.
² "Harriet"—by Florence Ryerson.
³ Here are the remarks of Aldous Huxley (End and Means) "In this remarkable compendium of Bronze Age literature (Old Testament) God is personal to the point of being almost subhuman. Too often the believer has felt justified in giving way to his worst passions by the reflection that, in doing so, he is basing his conduct on that of a God who faces jealousy and hatred, cannot control his rage and behaves in general like a particularly ferocious oriental tyrant. . . ." In a letter entrusted to friends with instructions that it be opened only after his death Irvin S. Cobb prescribed the rites that he desired on that occasion. There we find the following: "All Hitler needed to do was to let his whiskers sprout and sit on a nest of thunderbolts and naked swords, thinking of plague and pestilence and rapine and slaughter, and slavery for the vanquished, to be a fit understudy for the vengeful, murderous Jehovah of the forepart of the Old Testament." See N. Y. World Telegram, March 11, 1944.
For James Truslow Adams denigration see The American, pp. 74-5.
"The God of the Old Testament was a Vengeful God He is the direct contrast to the New Testament God, a merciful, understanding Father, which God do Christians worship," Edmund W. Browne, Life, Jan. 16, 1950.
⁴ Dollard review of Fine Book—N. Y. Times Sunday Book Review Section, June 19, 1955.
⁵ Review of B. Fine's "One Million Delinquents"—N. Y. Times Sunday Book Review Section, May 29, 1955.
⁶ Dollard's reply in N. Y. Times Book Review Section, June 19, 1955.
⁷ Ex. XV:3.
⁸ Isa. II:4, Micah IV:3.
⁹ Ex. XIII:2, Micah VI:8.
¹⁰ Some students of the New Testament, amongst them a Bishop Bir-

mingham, England, extended the period much beyond a century.
[11] In the Varieties of New Testament Thought, Prof. Ernest F. Scott of
the Union Theological Seminary, maintains: "The New Testament
has commonly been regarded as a uniform book, made up of a number of writings which are yet in full agreement . . . This attitude
has now been abandoned. It is freely recognized by all modern
scholars that various types of teachings are represented in the New
Testament . . . The effort to harmonize the New Testament teaching does an injustice to Christianity itself, which is identified with
one form of belief while it embraces many."
[12] Matt. XIII:36-42.
[13] Mark III:28-9.
[14] A few passages will offer ample evidence of the unrelenting vindictiveness of the New Testament God. For instance Luke XVI:19-26
in which a supliant sinner is consigned to unbearable torments in
spite of pleadings for mercy. II Thes. VI:9—"in flaming fire taking vengeance—punished with everlasting destruction." or Heb.
X:13 "it is a fearful thing to fall into the hands of God." (Compare
the latter with II Sam. XXIV:14). Also Rev. XIX:20-1 where men
are deceived and "cast alive into a lake of fire burning with brimstone and the remnant slain with the sword—" What untold cruelties were sanctioned by reference to these passages!
[15] See Apocalypse of Peter, Edition M. R. James, 1892 p. 44.
[16] Ps. LXVIII:5; CIII:13, 14.
[17] Mal. II:10.
[18] Ps. CIII:4.
[19] Neh. IX:17.
[20] Isa. LIV:8-10.
[21] Ibid., I:16-18.
[22] Jer. XXXI:20.
[23] II Sam. XXIV:14.
[24] Ex. XX:5.
[25] Ibid., XXXIV:6.
[26] Ibid., XX:5, 6.
[27] Luke XXIII:34, Matt. VI:12, 14, 15.

Chapter 6—THE MYTH OF JEWISH VENGEFULNESS

[1] Lev. XIX:33-4 see also Ex. XX:22, Lev. XIX:10.
[2] Ex. XXIII:4-5
[3] Ethics of the Fathers Chapt. IV par. 24.
[4] Yiddish Dailies published in New York City.
[5] Gen. XXXIV:30.
[6] Ibid., XXXIV:31.
[7] Ibid., XL:5-7.

Chapter 7—JEW AND GERMAN, ANALOGUE OR OPPOSITE?

[1] Ex. XIV:29, XV:22-5.
[2] Ibid., XXIV:7.

[3] Ibid., XXXII:1-6.
[4] Ibid., XIX:6.
[5] Isa. XLIX:6.
[6] B. Talmud Shek. 2b.
[7] B. Talmud Meg. Shek. 16a.

NOTES TO PART VI

Chapter 1—THE FUTILITY OF UNIMPLEMENTED PROFESSIONS

[1] Maimonides, Guide to the Perplexed, Part I, Chapter LXVI, Parts III Chapter LI.
[2] Gen VIII:21.
[3] Jer. XVII:9.
[4] Col. III:5.
[5] Gen. I:31.
[6] Gen. R., Chapt. X, par. 7.
[7] B. Talmud Ned. 10a.
[8] B. Talmud Kid. 66a.
[9] Ethics of the Fathers, Chapt. I, par. 1.
[10] Mishna, Ber., Chapt. I, par. 1.

Chapter 2—LAW—INSTRUMENT FOR INDIVIDUAL AND SOCIAL BETTERMENT

[1] Prov. XXII:6.
[2] In a volume just published the authors show that the surest, if not the only course, which will lead to universal peace, is through the enactment of laws to that end and to the observance of which individuals and nations will sincerely commit themselves. See "World Peace Through Law," by Grenville Clark and Louis B. Solim, Harvard University Press.
[3] George Foote Moore "Judaism" Vol. II, p. 145-6.
[4] Job. XIII:15.

Chapter 3—THE PENITENT'S CLEANSING TEARS

[1] Eccl. IX:2.
[2] Ethics of the Fathers, Chapt. I, par. 7.
[3] Ibid., Chapt. II, par. 21.
[4] Lev. XXVI:14 ff.
[5] Isa. XLVII:8 ff.
[6] B. Talmud Yoma 86b.
[7] Ex. R. XXXI par. 1 and Scriptutal bases is Ezek. XXXIII:19.
[8] Eccl. R., Chapt. I, par. 6.
[9] Matt. VIII:21-2.
[10] Ethics, Book IV, Prop. LIV.
[11] From King David the composer of heaven-soaring Psalms who

refashioned his character from a passion-pampering Cellini to that of a Tolstoi who spurned the ease and luxury indulged in by nobility and preferred the simple austere and dedicated mode of living of the Nazarene, this vast society of saints is all made up of repentent and self-redeemed individuals.

Chapter 4—THE GLORY OF THE REDEEMED

[1] Isa. Chapt. I:10-18.
[2] Jer. II:12-13; II:18-22.
[3] Ibid., II:3.
[4] Isa. XLIII:2.
[5] Jer. XXXI:34-5.
[6] Isa. XLII:19.
[7] Luke XV:11-24.

Chapter 5—SHOALS AHEAD

[1] Ethics of the Fathers Chapt. IV par. 1.
[2] George Herbert, The Temple.
[3] Childe Harold Canto III St. 2.
[4] B. Talmud Ber. 33b, Nidah 16b.
[5] Vivian Grey Vol. II Bk. VI Ch. 7.
[6] Short Studies on Great Subjects, Education.
[7] Deut. XVII:18-20. See also Ps. CXXXVIII:1, 3; LXXXIX:15 and LXXXV:14. In these passages even God is deemed to abide by the Moral Law.
[8] Col. III:22.
[9] Heb. XIII:17.
[10] Josh. XXIV:24.
[11] Queen Mab., Pt. III.
[12] Cf. Deut. XXIX:28.
[13] Ethics of the Fathers, Chapt. II, par. 5.
[14] Ibid., Chapt. II, par. 6.
[15] Ibid., Chapt. I, par. 14.

NOTES TO A POSTSCRIPT

Note 1. What abiding value can there be in agreements, covenants, reached even at summit levels?

Note 2. This chapter was penned many years ago and Russia's current transfer of her attacks on the West from military and political manouvers to economic action verifies the author's surmise.

Note 3. Before answering this question I should like to digress and record my belief, which is based on more than four decades of study of Americans, and nearly a like period of association and dealing with the owners and controllers of industrial establishments and financial institutions, that they are averse to initiating a war. Their aversion is prompted in no small degree by humanitarian considerations. This disposition I find is true, by and large, even of the elements which the Russians are wont to dub "Wall Street Interests."

There is also a keen realization on their part that the material gains of war are deceptive. A modern nation deeming itself enriched by participation in a war is like a farmer who imagines his wealth to have been multiplied because he acquired cash as a result of obtaining a large bank loan for which he mortgaged his farm and dwelling. No victorious nation can now exact reparations and tribute from the vanquished commensurate with its expenditure. On the contrary, after being forced to waste so much of their manpower and send up in smoke so much of their national wealth, the victors feel obliged in current wars to render succor to the vanquished lest in their hopelessness and with their impoverishment they drag down the conquerors with them.

There is an increasing awareness that if the huge sums that are prodigiously spent for devices and instruments of warfare were devoted to the clearing of slums, the building of roads, schools and hospitals, the erection of dams to produce electricity, the irrigation of arid regions, the standard of living which would be enjoyed by the multitude would then engender a prosperity which would make the profits of war times pale into insignificance.

The men at the head of the American Government, of whatever party they may be, are even more conscious of those facts. The Niagaras of their military expenditures are not directed by aggressive designs. No territorial aggrandizement was demanded by the U. S. after each World War. The Kellogg-Briand Disarmament proposals which the American Government scrupulously observed clearly reveal its hope. The speed with which and the extent to which she disbanded her gigantic war machine after the defeat of the Nazis and her naive faith that such was the wish of Russia to whose defence she came and to whom she gave so unstintingly of her not-unlimited means, attest her eagerness to return to a state of peace.

Note 4. Bernard Heller, A Harvest of Weeds, Penn Pub. Co., pp. 68-70.

Note 5. Deut. XXX:19.

"In every work regard the writer's end
Since none can compass more than they intend."
POPE

Rabbi Nehunia ben Hakanah used to recite a short
prayer when he entered the House of Study and when
he came forth. The colleagues said to him, "What is the
nature of this prayer?" He replied, "When I enter I pray
that no offence shall happen through me, and when I
come forth I give thanks for my lot."
J. TALMUD BER. Chapt. IV: Mishna 2